JEWISH ENCOUNTERS

Jonathan Rosen, General Editor

Jewish Encounters is a collaboration between Schocken and
Nextbook, a project devoted to the promotion of Jewish literature, culture, and ideas.

>nextbook

PUBLISHED

FORTHCOMING

Betraying Spinoza

REBECCA GOLDSTEIN

BETRAYING SPINOZA

The Renegade Jew
Who Gave Us Modernity

NEXTBOOK · SCHOCKEN · NEW YORK

Schocken Books and colophon are registered trademarks of
Random House, Inc.

Originally published in hardcover in the United States by
Schocken Books, a division of Random House, Inc.,
New York, in 2006.

Library of Congress Cataloging-in-Publication Data
Goldstein, Rebecca, [date]
Betraying Spinoza : the renegade Jew who gave us modernity/
Rebecca Goldstein.
        p. cm. — (Jewish encounters)
Includes bibliographical references.
ISBN 978-0-8052-1159-7
1. Spinoza, Benedictus de, 1632–1677. 2. Jewish
philosophers—Netherlands—Biography. 3. Heretics, Jewish—
Netherlands—Biography. I. Title. II. Series.
B3997.G65 2006   199'.492—dc22   2005040175

www.schocken.com
Printed in the United States of America
First Paperback Edition
2   4   6   8   9   7   5   3   1

For Steve

DESPITE SPINOZA

CONTENTS

Betraying Spinoza

I

Prologue: Baruch, Bento, Benedictus

By what right is Benedictus Spinoza included in this series, devoted as it is to Jewish themes and thinkers?

Can the seventeenth-century rationalist, who produced one of the most ambitious philosophical systems in the history of Western philosophy, be considered, by any stretch of interpretation, a Jewish thinker? Can he even be considered a Jew? Benedictus Spinoza is the greatest philosopher that the Jews ever produced, which adds a certain irony to his questionable Jewishness.

He was excommunicated at the age of twenty-three by the Portuguese-Jewish community in which he had been raised and educated. It was a community of refugees from the Spanish-Portuguese Inquisition, a Jewish calamity whose tragic proportions would be exceeded only in the twentieth century. The members of the community were predominantly former Marranos, who had lived on the Iberian Peninsula, mostly in Portugal, as practicing Christians since Judaism had been formally outlawed on the peninsula at the end of the fifteenth century. The word *marrano* is believed to derive from the old Castilian for "swine," a particularly apt slur to insult those believed to be concealing Jewish practice beneath Christian performance. The relatively liberal city of Amsterdam provided the conditions for their reconnecting to a Judaism that most of them barely knew. Brutal forces of history had given this community its distinctive tone: ambitious for the material trappings of middle-class stability and yet skittish, anxious; enviably accomplished and cosmopolitan and yet filled with religious intensity, confusion, disillusion, and messianic yearning.

Before his expulsion from it, the hothouse world of Amsterdam's Sephardim—as Jews who derived from Spain (*Sepharad* in Hebrew) continue to be called to this day—had been Spinoza's world as well. Yet when it closed its doors to him, he made no attempt to reenter it or any other Jewish community.

Excommunication, as it was practiced in his community, was not as severe and final a punishment as the word now suggests. The period of isolation from the community (the terms of excommunication did not extend outside of Amsterdam) typically lasted anywhere from a day to several years. The imposed banishment was a tool of chastisement resorted to with quite common frequency, fundamentally a form of public embarrassment with which to exert control over the volatile mix contained within "the Portuguese Nation," as the Amsterdam Sephardim continued to identify themselves.

Whereas others among the chastised had obediently— and sometimes desperately—sought reconciliation, Spinoza calmly removed himself from any further form of Jewish life. Nor did Spinoza seek out another religion. In particular, he did not convert to Christianity, though it would have been convenient for him to do so. Spinoza opted for secularism at a time when the concept had not yet been formulated.

He supported himself by grinding lenses, which was no lowly menial occupation, as it is often presented to have been in romanticizing versions of the philosopher's life, but was rather a craft that drew extensively from Spinoza's serious interest in the science of optics. The quality of his wares was highly valued by other scientists of his day. The important Dutch astronomer Christiaan Huygens, who discovered Saturn's rings as well as one of its four moons, preferred Spinoza's lenses to all others. "The [lenses] that the Jew of Voorburg has in his microscopes have an admirable polish," Huygens wrote to his brother in 1667.[1] The one part of the romantic lens-grinding legend that is sadly true is that the dust from the optical polishing was unhealthy for Spinoza, whose mother and brother had both died young from tuberculosis. He himself succumbed to the disease at the age of forty-four.

Spinoza's personal life was, as he wished it to be, simple and relatively isolated. There was a small circle of devoted friends, freethinking Christians from various dissenting Protestant circles, who regarded Spinoza as their master and closely studied, and guarded, his thoughts. He combined a Marranoist cautious discretion about revealing his true views to the dangerously narrow-minded with a touching faith in the power of reason to persuade. So he published his

Tractatus Theologico-Politicus (*The Treatise on Theology and Politics*) anonymously, but also hoped that it would convince the powers that be of its main conclusion, which is succinctly stated in the book's subtitle: *Wherein is set forth that freedom of thought and speech not only may, without prejudice to piety and the public peace, be granted; but also may not, without danger to piety and the public peace, be withheld.* The book evolves into one of the most impassioned defenses of a free democratic state in the history of political theory, an eloquent plea for the separation of church and state. Spinoza allowed himself to hope that, should its argument for tolerance find its mark, he might be able to publish the work on which he had been toiling for years. The rain of abuse that poured down on the author of the *Tractatus*, whose true identity was soon an open secret throughout Europe, made him a very dangerous man to even remotely acknowledge, and all but foreclosed the possibility of his publishing his magnum opus in his lifetime. This is *The Ethics*, a work that makes all the claims for reason that have ever been made.

Some favors came his way. The University of Heidelberg, which had fallen from its perch of previous glory through the prolonged tribulations of the Thirty Years' War, had no professor of philosophy on staff and, in the name of Karl Ludwig, Elector Palatine, offered him a chair of philosophy. "You will not find elsewhere a Prince more favorably disposed to men of exceptional genius, among whom he ranks you. You will have the most extensive freedom in philosophizing, which he believes you will not misuse to disturb the publicly established religion." The philosopher delicately declined: "If I had ever had any desire to undertake a professorship in any faculty, I could have wished for none other than that which is offered me through you by the Serene Highness the Elector Palatine, especially on account of the freedom to philosophize that this most gracious Prince is pleased to grant, not to mention my long-felt wish to live under the rule of a Prince whose wisdom is universally admired." But his instinct for caution had been alerted by the ambiguity of the terms of the offered freedom. "I do not know within what limits the freedom to philosophize must be confined if I am to avoid appearing to disturb the publicly established religion. . . . So you see, most Honorable Sir, that my reluctance is not due to the hope of some better fortune, but to my love of peace, which I believe I can enjoy in some measure if I refrain from lecturing in public."

Some important intellectual figures of the day made their way to the modest rooms he rented in the Hague in his last years, including the up-and-coming young go-getter Gottfried Wilhelm Leibniz, who would emerge as one of the most dazzling figures in the seventeenth century's impressive lineup of genius. Leibniz spent a few days with Spinoza, conversing on metaphysics. The only written record of their extensive conversations was a slip of paper on which Leibniz had written down, for Spinoza's approval, a proof for God's existence. Leibniz was profoundly influenced by Spinoza's ideas but sought always to conceal his philosophical debt, and is on record as denouncing the philosopher. When a professor of rhetoric at the University of Utrecht, one Johan Georg Graevius, wrote to Leibniz, castigating the *Tractatus*

Theologico-Politicus as a "most pestilential book," whose author "is said to be a Jew named Spinoza, but who was cast out of the synagogue because of his monstrous opinions,"[2] Leibniz prudently chimed in with his own diplomatic calumny: "I have read the book by Spinoza. I am saddened by the fact that such a learned man has, as it seems, sunk so low."

A letter from Spinoza to Leibniz. Note his watchword, *caute*, in the lower right-hand corner.

Spinoza remained throughout his life, and well into the eighteenth century, a thinker whom one could admire only in secret, hiding one's sympathy just as his Marrano antecedents had concealed their wayward Jewishness. Open admiration could destroy even the most established of reputations, well into the eighteenth century's so-called Age of Reason. In the 1780s, for example, Friedrich Heinrich Jacobi launched a generalized attack on Enlightenment thought by claiming that the late poet Lessing had been a closet Spinozist, a charge sufficient to compromise the entire movement for which Lessing had been a leading spokesman.[3] Jacobi even went after Immanuel Kant and his successors, arguing that "consistent philosophy is Spinozist, hence pantheist, fatalist, and atheist."

The holy furor aroused by the name Spinoza is in contrast to the man's predilection for peace and quiet. He confessed himself to have a horror of controversy. "I absolutely dread quarrels," he wrote an acquaintance, explaining why he had declined to publish a work that contains some of the main themes of *The Ethics*, titled *Short Treatise on God, Man, and His Well-Being*.[4] The signet ring he wore throughout his life was inscribed with the word *caute*, Latin for "cautiously," and it was engraved with the image of a thorny rose, so that he signed his name *sub rosa*. One might argue that the very form of *The Ethics*, written in the highly formalized "geometrical style" inspired by Euclid's *Elements*, is partially designed for the practical purpose of keeping out any but the most gifted of readers, rigorously cerebral and patiently rational.

Spinoza's ambitions on behalf of reason are staggering: he aims to give us a rigorously proved view of reality, which view will yield us, if only we will assimilate it, a life worth living. It will transform our emotional substance, our very selves. The truth shall set us free. His methodology for exposing the nature of reality was inspired by one of the strands that the seventeenth century's men of science were weaving into what we now refer to as the scientific method, that magnificently subtle, supple, and successful blend of mathematical deduction and empirical induction. Spinoza was keenly interested and involved in the intellectual innovations that we now look back on as constituting the birth of modern science. His inspiration came from the mathematical component of modern science, not its empiricism. The methodology he believed could reveal it all was strictly deductive, which is not the way that science ultimately went. (Still, there are contemporary physicists and cosmologists who are inspired by the Spinozist ideal of "a theory of everything," one in which the mathematics alone would determine its truth. String theorists, in particular, pursue physics almost entirely as a deductive endeavor, letting their mathematics prevail over niggling empirical questions. The spirit motivating them is Spinozism, which sometimes makes other scientists question whether what string theorists are up to really qualifies as science at all.)

But if the claims Spinoza makes on behalf of pure reason can strike us as staggering, there are also, staggeringly, a number of propositions that he produced from out of his deductive system that have been, centuries later, scientifically vindicated. A leading neurobiologist, Antonio Damasio, argues in his *Looking for Spinoza: Joy, Sorrow, and the Feeling Brain* that Spinoza's view of the relationship between mind and brain, as well as the complicated theory of the emotions that he deduced from it, are precisely what the latest empirical findings support. Spinoza, despite his non-empiricist methodology, is not scientifically irrelevant.

But there are claims that come out of Spinoza's deductive system that are even more important for our times, more piercingly relevant, than his happening to have produced a stunningly contemporary answer, through pure deductive reason, to the mind-body problem and given us a view of the emotions that science has caught up with, in thinkers like Damasio, after some three hundred years. What Spinoza has to say about the importance of allowing the discovery of nature to proceed unimpeded by religious dogma could not speak more pertinently to some of the raging controversies of our day, including the recurring public debate in America over Darwin's theory of evolution. The sides are drawn up now much as they were in Spinoza's own day.

Just as relevant to current concerns, particularly in America, is his fundamental insistence on the separation of church and state. John Locke, who spent some years in Amsterdam, right after Spinoza's death, associating with thinkers who had known and been influenced by Spinoza, transmitted this insistence to the founding fathers of America. The spirit of Spinoza lives on in the opening words of the First Amendment to the U.S. Constitution, the phrase referred to as the Establishment clause: "Congress shall make no law respecting an establishment of religion."

Spinoza placed all his faith in the powers of reason, his own and ours. He enjoins us to join him in the religion of reason, and promises us some of the same benefits—while firmly denying us others—that traditional religions promise. Rigorous reason will lead us to a state of mind that is the height of what we can achieve not only intellectually but also, in a sense—the only sense compatible with his rationalism—spiritually. The aim of his ethics is to give us the means to arrive at a "contentment of spirit, which arises out of the . . . knowledge of God." This is the state of mind dubbed "blessedness" by the man who had been known in three different languages—Hebrew, Portuguese, and Latin—by a name that translates into "blessed": Baruch, Bento, and Benedictus.

It is hard for us to appreciate the loneliness of Spinoza's secularized spirituality. For an individual of the early seventeenth century to live outside the bounds of a religious identity—to aim to be perceived as neither Jew, nor Christian, nor Moslem—was all but unthinkable; and, in fact, Spinoza did continue to be called, with predictable disdain, a Jew. Huygens, for example, never refers to Spinoza by name in his letters, even though the two often conversed on such fields of mutual interest as mathematics and optics; but rather Spinoza is always "the Jew of Voorburg" or, even more belittlingly, "our Israelite," "our Jew."

The social frame of reference enclosing every individual of the premodern era was inherently religious. Spinoza's choice was an instance of a principle that had yet to be discerned in even the vaguest outline. Part of the horror he invoked throughout Europe derived from the radical stance he assumed simply by pursuing a life with no religious affiliation. Though the Romantic poet Novalis called him, and for good reason, "God-intoxicated," he was also routinely excoriated as an atheist. He seemed to have been genuinely dismayed by the charge, though his conception of God is sufficiently peculiar—and subtle—that one can see how his constant talk of God might strike even us today as disingenuous, yet another old Marranoist trick of hiding one's unacceptable beliefs under formulaic insincerities. We should accept Spinoza's dismay at face value and use it to guide us to understand what he meant by "religion" and "piety," both of which he nonhypocritically endorses.

The terms of his excommunication were the harshest imposed by his community, uncharacteristically including no possibility for reconciliation or redemption. Though the statement of his excommunication is long on curses, it is short—to the point of silence—on the exact nature of his offenses. Only vague and general "evil ways" and "abominable heresies" are referred to. Were his deviations practical, doctrinal, or attitudinal? The fact that he was so young, with the philosophical results for which we celebrate him now still years ahead, confounds the situation.

Scholars still ponder the actions of the Amsterdam Jews, propounding theories to explain the unusual vehemence and finality of the denunciation pronounced against the young philosopher. Others had questioned principles of the faith and been meted out their penance and then returned. Why was Spinoza alone deemed irredeemable? The answer is, I believe, entangled in a set of issues that were especially fraught for this community of first- and second-generation refugees from the Spanish-Portuguese Inquisition, struggling to reclaim their Jewish identities. Having thrown off their enforced Christianity, they were trying, very consciously and deliberately, to shape their new identities as Jews. What other Jews might have taken for granted, they could not. The preoccupations of the community were ordained to clash violently with its most famous son.

It is no accident that this particular community, which

felt the force of the issue of Jewish identity with unusual passion, should have produced a thinker who still, to this day, confounds us on this very issue. Spinoza probes a historical sore spot for Jews, one which throbbed with special intensity within his own community, but remains tender still. What does Jewishness consist in? Is it theological, biological, ethical, cultural? Are there traits of outlook that define or explain what it is to be Jewish? Is Jewishness an essential attribute for a Jew, part of what makes the person the very person that he is, so that once a Jew, always a Jew? Is it inherited, and if so, is it dominant, or recessive? Just what sort of an attribute is Jewishness?

The Jewish calamity of the Spanish-Portuguese Inquisition had forced these questions into the forefront of the consciousness of Spinoza's Jewish community (just as the Jewish calamity of the Holocaust has forced these questions back into an embarrassed silence). The answers Spinoza was to give touched the exposed nerve of communal Jewish passions. They still do.

Even should one decide that Spinoza cannot be considered a Jewish thinker—that he belongs only to the greater world but not particularly to the Jews—the process of drawing this conclusion reveals the tangled difficulties of coming to terms with the meaning of Jewishness. Spinoza certainly struggled with these issues, though one must probe beneath the mathematical austerity of his system to discover the buried signs of his struggle. Perhaps the indication that he wrestled with the question of Jewishness is in itself sufficient claim to Jewishness. And perhaps, too, the sense of an intense, if covert, conflict over the issue of Jewish identity provides at least part of the explanation of why generations of Jews have felt a mysterious kinship with this philosopher whose system would seem, on the surface, to offer no special meaning or message for Jews.

The philosopher is firm in the denial that any true philosophy could offer some special meaning to some particular group of people. The truth makes no such distinctions. From its remote point of view, that is, the point of view of truth itself, the sort of differences around which groups construct their social identities and distinguish between "them" and "us" could not appear more inconsequential. From the point of view of truth itself, the view that Spinoza dubs "the Infinite Intellect of God," those differences that loom so large in human affairs are not represented at all. These differences emerge only in our limited points of view—finite, all too finite. These insistences on difference are all confused, albeit understandable—*all* is understandable—attempts to substantiate that peculiar and necessary significance one confers on one's self by erecting a view of all reality that would do justice to it. So it is that religions distinguish themselves from one another by declaring their own adherents the favored of God. All such confusions are relegated by Spinoza to the status of superstitions, including any and all difference to which Jews may cling.

The name "Spinoza" derives from the word for "thorn" in Portuguese, which was the language of the Amsterdam Jewish community in which he had been reared and out of which he had been cast. It was the language in which Spinoza remained the most comfortable throughout his life, no doubt the language in which he thought out his incomparable philosophy. The language in which the most universal of systems was excogitated—a system designed to bleach out any reference to personal points of view determined by the contingencies of historical narratives—was itself maculate with the extraordinary history of Spinoza's community.

The name Spinoza strangely suits. Spinoza, as a Jew, presents himself to us adorned in a crown of eternally thorny questions.

II

In Search of Baruch

The *Senhores* of the *ma'amad*,[1] having long known of the evil opinions and acts of Baruch de Espinoza, have endeavored by various means and promise, to turn him from his evil ways. But having received more and more serious information about the abominable heresies which he practiced and taught and about his monstrous deeds, and having for this numerous trustworthy witnesses who have deposed and borne witness to this effect in the presence of the said Espinoza, they became convinced of the truth of this matter; and after all of this has been investigated in the presence of the honorable *hakhamim*[2] they have decided, with their consent, that the said Espinoza should be excommunicated and expelled from the people of Israel.

By decree of the angels and by the command of the holy men, we excommunicate, expel, curse and damn Baruch de Espinoza, with the consent of God, Blessed be He, and with the consent of the entire holy congregation, and in front of these holy scrolls with the 613 precepts which are written therein, cursing him with the excommunication with which Joshua banned Jericho and with the curse which Elisha cursed the boys and with all the castigations that are written in the Book of the Law. Cursed be he by day and cursed be he by night; cursed be he when he lies down and cursed be he when he rises up. Cursed be he when he goes out and cursed be he when he comes in. The Lord will not spare him, but then the anger of the Lord and his jealousy shall smote against that man, and all the curses that are written in this book shall lie upon him, and the Lord shall blot out his name from under heaven. And the Lord shall separate him unto evil out of all the tribes of Israel, according to all the curses of the covenant that are written in this book of the Law. But you that cleave unto the Lord your God are alive every one of you this day.

We warn that none may contact him orally or in writing, nor do him any favor, nor stay under the same roof with him, nor read any paper he made or wrote.

—Congregation Talmud Torah, July 27, 1656

Without intelligence there is not rational life, and things are only good in so far as they aid man in his enjoyment of the intellectual life which is defined by intelligence. Contrariwise, whatsoever things hinder

man's perfection of his reason, and capability to
enjoy the rational life, are alone called evil.

—BENEDICTUS SPINOZA
The Ethics, Part IV, Appendix V

I first heard the name Baruch Spinoza uttered as an admonition, a cautionary tale of unbridled human intelligence
blindly seeking its own doom.

This is what happens, the voice of my teacher warned,
when someone thinks that human reason is sufficient unto
itself and that the truth divinely given to us can be ignored.
This is what happens when philosophy takes the place of
Torah.

Baruch Spinoza had come from a good family of God-
fearing Jews, similar to your families, girls—all too similar
in certain ways. Like so many of your parents and grandparents, your aunts and uncles and cousins, Spinoza's family had
suffered *al-Kiddush ha-Shem*, for the sanctification of the Holy
Name. No, not in Germany or Austria or Poland. Not in
Hungary, Rumania, or Russia. The persecution had been in
Spain and Portugal, starting in the fifteenth century and
continuing for hundreds of years.

The Espinozas, the philosopher's family, had been Marranos, those who, even though they had been forced by the
Church to convert to Christianity, still continued to practice Judaism in secret, hiding their observance of the Torah
from the cruel edicts of the Spanish-Portuguese Inquisition.
The slightest suspicion that they still obeyed the Torah—

that they remembered the Shabbos and kept it holy, that they would not eat pig—and they would have been subjected to brutal torture and horrible death. In Spanish, *auto-da-fé* means "act of faith." What it really meant was the mass trial of those accused of being secret Jews, and then the mass burning to death of all those who were condemned.

And still, as you well know, girls, many of you, from the examples of your own families, not even this terror was able to extinguish the spark of *Yiddishkeit* from their souls. Look at what your own families went through under Hitler, and yet one of the first things that concerned them when they got to this country was to make sure that the next generation—your generation, girls—would still learn Torah. They never lost their faith.

And that was how it was for Spinoza's family. After generations of their dangerous secret Jewish allegiance, his family, like many others before them and after, managed to make their way to the Dutch city of Amsterdam, where a community of Portuguese-Jewish exiles was thriving as it could in few other European cities of that day.

Amsterdam was the most tolerant city in all of Europe. But don't think that it was as free as what you girls have come to take for granted here. Don't make the mistake of thinking that it was as tolerant as New York City in 1967.

Baruch Spinoza had reaped the benefits of the long years of danger and suffering that his family had endured. He had been born into blessed circumstances, had been educated at the yeshiva the community of Portuguese refugees had organized almost as soon as they got to their new shores. It was, by all accounts, an excellent school. Rabbis from other parts of Europe who visited the Talmud Torah of Amsterdam marveled at the level of learning attained there. Baruch had studied under worthy rabbis, including the chief rabbi of Amsterdam, Rabbi Morteira, and he had distinguished himself. He was a brilliant student, a boy born with blessings. His very name, of course, means "blessed" in the holy tongue.

Yet this misguided young man, my teacher continued, ascending toward the climax, who might have used his superior mind to increase our knowledge of the Torah, had died with the pagan name of Benedictus, excommunicated and cursed by his own people, condemned and reviled as a dangerous heretic even by believing Christians. Let the history of the philosopher Spinoza serve as a warning to you, girls, against the dangers of asking the wrong questions.

In my teacher's telling, this Baruch Spinoza might have been one of the no-goodnik boys attending one of the several yeshivas in the neighborhood, the Lower East Side of Manhattan, where Mrs. Schoenfeld taught at an all-girls yeshiva high school. There was only one such girls' school in the neighborhood, but there were several boys' schools, anachronistic reminders of the once teeming Jewish immigrant neighborhood that was largely dismantled by then. I had a long commute to it from a suburb out in Westchester, where my father served as the community's cantor.

It was an extremely Orthodox school, the sort that had to be single-sex, since its outlook included the dictum that there be no mixing of girls and boys until it was time to think of marriage, and then the necessary encounters would be carefully supervised. And yet, despite the many *oughts* and *ought-nots* drilled into us, some among us still managed to achieve waywardness. There were girls who were not as pious as they might have been. There was a certain kosher pizza shop on East Broadway that was favored by certain girls from my school, the kind who rolled their skirts of regulation length (down at least to the calf) up above their knees as soon as they were out of the sight of our teachers. These girls would go to the infamous pizza shop for the purpose of flirting with "bumulkes," as my father used to call them, bums with yarmulkes, yeshiva boys who were out on the streets or in pizza shops, up to no good, when they ought to have been in the *beit midrash*, the house of study, bent over their Talmudic tomes from morning until night.

Mrs. Schoenfeld's discussion of Baruch Spinoza suggested that she had seen his type before, and so, she feared, had we. A boy who thinks he knows better than his rabbis and the Torah, who flaunts the Law and flirts with girls. Baruch Spinoza, a bumulke.

Mrs. Schoenfeld was a serious woman of middle age. At least I remember her as middle-aged. I was of an age when middle age might have meant late twenties. She wore matronly suits with calf-length skirts, and her prim head was topped by both an unbecoming wig and an unbecoming felt hat, a double precaution against committing the sin of a married woman's hair being seen in public. (Actually, the double precaution is taken so that nobody fooled by the verisimilitude of her wig, might mistakenly think a married woman's hair is uncovered. From what I remember of Mrs. Schoenfeld's wig, there was little reason for the hat.) Mrs.

Schoenfeld's students were not yet married (though many of us, including me, would become engaged in our senior year of high school), and so our hair, unlike our teacher's, was still exposed in all its maidenly glory. Otherwise, we were dressed not unlike her, in skirts that modestly hid most of our legs and blouses with cuffs that nestled our wrists, even though the scandalous sixties were raging all around us. The psychedelic swirl of Washington Square Park was no more than a twenty-minute walk from the door of our little school world, and sometimes I walked through this foreign land to watch the blissful braless girls and long-haired boys, forever at play.

Mrs. Schoenfeld taught various of the *limudei kodesh*, or sacred subjects, at the school, but this was the first time I'd ever had her as a teacher. The subject she was teaching was *historia*, or Jewish history. I had high expectations for this class, and for this teacher. I was encouraged not only by the seriously unattractive black glasses perched on her nose, but also by her English accent, so different from the nasal singsongese that prevailed in the school. I liked the cool, crisp tones of her voice, admired the way she used the English language, distinguishing between "who" and "whom," using the occasional polysyllabic word that sent me to the dictionary.

And I liked the subject, too, at least that year, which was devoted to the modern European period. This was exciting for me. Not only did I have a teacher who appeared to be smart, but I was finally learning some *historia* that seemed more like "regular" history, less like the other *le-mudai kodesh* subjects that I had already come to doubt counted as genuine knowledge at all, which was a dispiriting thought, given the high percentage of my student life that was taken up by them. I felt the doubt as a sensation in my chest, gnawing away like some sharp-toothed rodent.

I had an urgency in me to become knowledgeable. I had stared into the hideous face of my ignorance and confusion and grown sick at the sight. I wasn't at all certain that the large portion of each school day that was devoted to holy scholarship was redressing my lack of knowledge in the least. Mrs. Schoenfeld's class seemed the one exception offered to me that year.

Ever since I could remember, *historia* had gotten no further than the Roman destruction of the Second Temple in Jerusalem, in 70 C.E. Jewish history that was so remote had felt to me continuous with *khumash* and *navi*, the Five Books of Moses and the books of the prophets. This impression was underscored not only by *historia*'s being taught in the mornings, together with all the other religious subjects, but also taught in Hebrew, while our secular subjects were taught in English, mostly by moonlighting public school teachers.

The public school teachers brought, at least for me, the sweet breath of real knowledge into the classroom, even though I knew they had to censor themselves. I had caught the look of discomfort on my tenth-grade biology teacher's face, listening to our rabbi-principal explain to us that, because of the New York State Regents exam, we were going to have to study an untrue theory fabricated by Charles Darwin, but that we should not forget for a single moment that it was scientifically unproven and, more important, contradicted by Torah.

Studying the Jews of modern Europe seemed to carry the subject of *historia* a thrilling distance away from the religious sphere and closer to the domain of credible secular fact. With relief, I felt that I could put aside my spiky doubts in Mrs. Schoenfeld's class, reassured by her intelligent accent and syntax. And because of the complexity of the material that year, we were being taught *historia* in English, again reassuring me of its proximity to trustworthy temporality.

It would be some while into the school year before I would hear tell of the *apikorus*, or heretic, Spinoza. Spinoza's introduction into our classroom awaited the discussion of the touchy subject of the Haskalah, or Jewish enlightenment. Only, in our classroom it wasn't called by the approbatory term Haskalah. We called it "modernity," pronouncing it with a Hebrew accent.

The pivotal figure in modernity was the late-eighteenth-century thinker Moses Mendelssohn, grandfather of the famous composer, both of whom were also mentioned as part of the extended cautionary tale. Moses Mendelssohn had urged that Jews not keep themselves intellectually and culturally separate. He had argued that adherence to the Torah, to which he held firm—he was not an *apikorus*, girls—did not exclude participation in the arts and sciences. He had urged that Jews educate themselves in the accomplishments of Western civilization. So had argued the grandfather. And the grandson, Felix, was a great musician. His compositions are still played by famous orchestras all over the world. But, girls, he was also a convert to Christianity. The descendents of this illustrious family probably don't even remember that they were once Jewish. They probably don't know the first thing about the *Yiddishkeit* of their ancestors.

Mrs. Schoenfeld's expressions, both on her face and in her voice, made the articulation of the moral of the Mendelssohn story gratuitous: admiration leads to accommodation, which leads to assimilation, which leads to the worst. The so-called Haskalah had wanted to mix the immiscible: the insular Torah Jew into the modern world, the modern world into the Torah Jew. We were in favor of insularity, and Mrs. Schoenfeld was no exception, despite her fancy way around English syntax. I still unconsciously think of the word "modernity" as being a Hebrew word, hearing it pronounced with its *r* rolled and with a tone of stern admonition.

Spinoza predated Moses Mendelssohn by a good century and a half, but Mrs. Schoenfeld spoke of him as a precursor. He was, she very rightly suggested, the first modern Jew. Spinoza headed the long line of yeshiva boys who were not as pious as they might have been. He was one of the so-called enlightened Jews, a so-called *maskil*, long before the term had been introduced. (I remember a student in the class once mistakenly saying *masik*—which means "a little devil," often used affectionately for children—for *maskil*, an error which propelled sober Mrs. Schoenfeld to the very verge of laughter.) This Benedictus-né-Baruch was an early sign of the sickness to come, and his own community had tried to keep the contagion from spreading. That is why they took the drastic step of putting him into *kherem*, girls, excommunicat-

ing him when he was only twenty-three years old. Had
Moses Mendelssohn studied the case of Spinoza a little better, he might have saved himself, his family, and the Jewish
people a lot of *tzurris*.[3]

Mrs. Schoenfeld suggested that a lot could be learned
from understanding the case of Spinoza, as opposed to the
philosophy of Spinoza. About the latter she said very little;
only that he had had two basic beliefs: The first was that the
Torah was not a divine revelation but rather written by
man—written in fact by several men who came much later
than Moshe Rabbenu, Moses Our Teacher. And the second
was that God was identical with nature.

Mrs. Schoenfeld used the English word "God," which was
not a word we normally used. Instead we said *Ha-Shem*,
Hebrew for "The Name," a designation that at once circum-
vents and underscores the prohibition against uttering
God's true and awful name. If His true name were tran-
scribed, then the paper on which it was written would be too
holy to be thrown away. It would have to be buried like a
human corpse. Even the English word radiated sanctity,
which is why we were taught to write "G—d."

As brief as it was, Mrs. Schoenfeld's synopsis of Spinoza's
philosophy intrigued me, by reason of its very incompre-
hensibility, so that I couldn't stop thinking about it. First of
all, if Spinoza thought that God was identical with nature,
then of course he didn't think the Torah was revealed by
God. The denial of divine authorship seemed barely worth
mentioning, once one had made the astounding claim that
God and nature were one.

But what did the man mean by this inscrutable identification?

Did he mean that nature had hidden mystical qualities, that it was imbued with *nefesh*, with spirit, the very spirit of God? Did he think that nature was a great deal more than what we normally think of it as being?

Or was Spinoza saying that nature is only nature—that it was all those things that the Torah taught were created on the first five days (light and dry land and the heavenly bodies and plants and animals)—and was his assertion that God is nature just a sneaky way of denying the existence of God?

I rarely posed questions in class, preferring to try to think things out for myself, but I was intrigued and confused enough to ask Mrs. Schoenfeld to explain more about what Spinoza had meant by saying that *Ha-Shem* was nature. Ironically, given how happy I was that *historia* was being taught in English, I had used, out of habit, the Hebrew designation for the Unutterable.

Mrs. Schoenfeld's response came mainly in the form of rebuking me for saying *Ha-Shem*. She had deliberately said "God" and not "*Ha-Shem*" because whatever Spinoza meant by the word, it certainly wasn't *Ha-Shem*. *Berayshis barah Elokim es ha-shemayim vi'es ha-eretz*—In the beginning the Lord created the heavens and the earth. This is the first sentence of the Torah, and if someone doesn't know this about *Ha-Shem*, he doesn't know the first thing about *Ha-Shem*. *Elokim*—the Lord. *Ha-Shem* is the Lord over all He creates. He chose to create nature. He chose *that* it should be and *what* it should be. If someone says that God is nature—is the heavens and the earth—then he is not talking about *Ha-Shem.*

Then Spinoza was an atheist?

Yes, she answered me, an atheist. Why do you look so baffled by that? Do you still have a question, Rebecca?

I did, and since she was pushing me, I asked it: Why did he take such a roundabout way just to say that God doesn't exist? It sounds like he was trying to say something more by saying that God is nature.

No, Mrs. Schoenfeld answered me, and so assertively that I thought to ask her if she herself had read the works of the heretic. Of course, I didn't pose the question that rose to my lips, since it could have been heard as disrespectful of her, a veiled challenge, and *derekh eretz*—literally, "the way of the land," a phrase meaning "respect for parents and teachers"—was a virtue drilled into us from an early age.

Spinoza, my teacher reiterated, was an atheist, even though when the Amsterdam community excommunicated him he hadn't yet revealed the full extent of his godless immorality. He had left the yeshiva when he was a teenager. We don't know why exactly, since a student of his caliber would have been expected to go on and get *smikha* (the ordination for the rabbinate). His teachers, including Rabbi Morteira, an Ashkenazic scholar who had come from Vienna to lead this Sephardic congregation (*Ashkenaz* means "Germany" in Hebrew), had permitted themselves to indulge the highest expectations for him, a true *talmid khokhem* (a gifted scholar, literally a "disciple of the wise"), emerging out of this community of first- and second-generation former Marranos. But Spinoza left the yeshiva and instead went into his father's business, importing dry fruits. Maybe his father's business was suffering and he had to help him out—his younger brother also went into the family business—or maybe, despite his brilliance in the yeshiva, he had already begun to think like an *apikorus* and that's why he didn't pursue his yeshiva studies.

He hadn't yet published any of his blasphemous works when he was put into *kherem*, but he had spoken to people about some of his ideas. It was a very close community, as you can well imagine, girls, since such hardship as they had suffered, and over generations, make for very strong bonds. They had clung to *Yiddishkeit* under cover of silence and secrecy, risking their lives, but much had been lost, forgotten, sometimes confused with Christian beliefs. Some of the Sunday prayers of the Christians had gotten mixed up into their own liturgy. They would refer to Queen Esther (the heroine behind the Jewish festival of Purim) as St. Esther, just like the Catholics, who have official saints. Now they were relearning what it means to be good Jews, the centerpiece of their efforts being the yeshiva, the Talmud Torah, where Baruch had studied. Because of his brilliance, people were interested in him, in what he thought.

But soon rumors of Spinoza's strange ideas began to emerge, so that his community began to be afraid for him and also afraid of him. Some of his former schoolmates from the yeshiva, knowing how he was straying into alien *goyisha* ideas, asked him whether he thought, as they had heard he did, that God is made out of matter, and that there are no angels, and that the soul isn't immortal. Remember, girls, that Maimonides, the greatest Jewish philosopher of all time, had laid it down in his Thirteen Articles of Faith that we must never think of God in bodily terms and that we must believe in *tekhiyas ha-maysim*, the resurrection of the dead.

Think about it, girls: Of course the soul must be immortal, must survive bodily death; otherwise, how could there be an *olam haba*—a world-to-come? And if there is no *olam haba*, then how can the soul come before the Ultimate Judge and be held accountable for its conduct during its life? How could the good who had suffered during their lives receive their reward, and how could those who were evil and had gotten away with it get their divine punishment? Think of the *tzadikim* (the righteous) who died in Hitler's ovens. Think of the innocent children. And think of the Nazis who escaped, who are enjoying life right now in Europe or South America. Without *olam haba*, we can't make any moral sense out of the world; without *olam haba*, there *is* no moral sense to the world. This is why denying the soul's immortality is tantamount to denying *Ha-Shem*.

Spinoza tried to evade the young men who asked him his views, and when they continued to press him, he used his Torah learning to confuse and mislead, making it seem as if he were still a good Jew, citing the Torah. He said that since the Torah says nothing about noncorporeality we are free to believe that God has a body; and also that the Torah says nothing about the creation of angels, which is why the Sadducees[4] were never declared heretics even though they didn't believe in angels. As for his thoughts on immortality, here Baruch let slip out probably more than he intended. He argued that the Torah uses the Hebrew words for "soul"—*ruakh* or *nefesh* or *neshama*—only to mean life or anything that is living, and that it nowhere commits us to believing that the soul survives the body's death. On the contrary, he said, there are many places in the Torah where the exact opposite of immortality can be shown, and nothing is easier than to prove this.

When word of Spinoza's ideas got back to the rabbis, they were stricken with horror. Here was one of their most brilliant students spouting ideas that not even the non-Jewish *apikorsim* would dare to contemplate. It was terrible to think that a boy who had shown so much promise and who had received such a fine education from the best rabbis in the community—learned rabbis, who had published books of their own—could reject everything. And the community also had to worry about what the *goyim* would think if word got out that such a wild heretic was living among them.

Remember, girls, these were former Marranos who had seen the very worst of what Christian intolerance can mean for the Jews. Amsterdam was a relatively tolerant city, Protestant rather than Catholic. Still, who knew how far their tolerance could be extended? It was true that the seventeenth-century Dutch were a very practical society, concerned at least as much with their economy as with their theology, and this practicality was good for the Jews. At the time of Spinoza's birth, 1632, the Jews had been living in Amsterdam only a few decades, but they were already contributing to the thriving Dutch economy, using their connections to other Marranos scattered around the world, including those still back in Spain and Portugal, to import and export. Still, there were Protestant theologians even in Amsterdam, particularly the Protestants known as "Calvinists," who weren't thrilled about the Jewish newcomers. The Calvinists were not as tolerant as some of the other Protestant sects. And it had been a condition of the Jews being allowed to reside in Amsterdam—because, of course, they had had to get official permission—that they keep order and decorum among their own, in regard not only to behavior but to beliefs as well. Strangely enough, the Dutch authorities wanted the Amsterdam Jews to abide by the Torah. They wanted Amsterdam's Jews to be *frum* (pious).

So the community leaders approached Spinoza and gently tried to change his mind. When he showed his stubborn arrogance, they begged him at the least to keep his ideas to himself, lest the Christian authorities learn of them and bring sanctions against the whole community. But apparently it did no good. The community met together in the synagogue. It was the *parnassim*, the community's lay leaders, who, strictly speaking, had the power of excommunication, rather than the rabbis. The rabbis were also present in the synagogue, except for the chief rabbi, Rabbi Morteira, who had an obligation elsewhere.[5] The community met to give Spinoza an opportunity to answer his accusers.

The two young men who had questioned Spinoza stood before the congregation and told them that they had spoken with Spinoza several times and that his views were full of heresies, and that he didn't deserve to be held in such high esteem as a brilliant scholar by his former teachers. They said that Spinoza had spoken of the Jews as "a superstitious people born and bred in ignorance, who do not know what God is, and who nevertheless have the audacity to speak of themselves as His people, to the disparagement of other nations."[6] Spinoza had said that so far as the authorship of the Torah was concerned, it had been by someone other than Moses. The Five Books of Moses, he was saying, weren't written by Moses, but rather by someone who had come many generations later, and someone who had known more about politics than about religion. It would take only some small good sense to discover the imposture, this *apikorus* said, and whoever continued to believe in it was as naïve as the Jews of Moses' time.

This is how it often is, girls—that the vilest accusations against the Jews come from irreligious Jews themselves. It is as if, betraying the special task of holiness that *Ha-Shem* bestowed on the Jewish people, they must go to the opposite extreme, become leaders of godlessness among men.

I don't have to remind you girls that Karl Marx was Jewish.

Spinoza refused to defend himself against his accusers. He said only that he was sorry for everyone there who had chosen to judge him so hastily and so harshly. Rabbi Morteira, informed of how his former prize student was accounting for himself at the synagogue, now rushed there and confronted the *apikorus* himself. He asked Spinoza whether this was to be the fruit of all the pains that he, his former teacher, had taken with his education, and whether he wasn't afraid of falling into the hands of the living God? The scandal was great, but there was still time to repent. But if there was to be no sign of contrition, then the community would have no choice but to excommunicate him.

And do you know, girls, how this so-called philosopher, whom the world has decided to call great, answered his former rebbe, how he threw off his *derekh eretz* together with all else that he had been taught? He answered his teacher that he understood very well the seriousness of the charges against him and the nature of the threats that were hanging over his head, and in return for the trouble Rabbi Morteira had taken to teach him the Hebrew language, he, Spinoza, was quite willing to show him the proper method of excommunicating someone.

When Rabbi Morteira heard the way this young man spoke to him, with so much chutzpa, he dismissed everyone and left the synagogue. He saw that he had been completely mistaken in who this young man was. Before, he had told people that he was as impressed with Spinoza's character as with his mind,[7] that it was rare that one so brilliant would also be so modest. But now he saw that the situation was exactly the reverse. Baruch Spinoza was a monster of arrogance. There was no way of reasoning with this young man, as brilliant as he no doubt was.

Human intelligence is the greatest gift that *Ha-Shem* gave to human beings, making us closer to the *malakhim*—the angels—than to the beasts of the field. But if we forget from Whom we got this divine gift, if we begin to believe that we are somehow the source of our own intelligence and that we are capable of figuring out everything for ourselves without relying on the Torah, then we fall even below the animals. This is why all philosophy is *apikorsus.* The very word *apikor-*

sus, girls, comes from the name of a Greek philosopher, someone who was called Epicurus, who believed that pleasure is all that people have to live for.

After this confrontation in the synagogue, Spinoza moved away from the community, taking rooms with a non-Jewish friend of his outside of Amsterdam. He had already, for some time now, been mixing with non-Jews, preferring them to his own people. He had been studying Latin with a former priest who had also become a heretic in his own religion, by the name of Franciscus van den Enden.

In fact, there are some who say that Baruch tried to marry van den Enden's daughter but that she rejected him for another student of her father's who wasn't going to become an impoverished philosopher, like Spinoza, but rather a doctor. Some say that this young man gave the young lady in question a pearl necklace and that is what finally decided her. Whether it's true or not that he had tried to marry this non-Jewish girl, Spinoza never did marry, and in fact it seems that he never again tried to.

He lived alone, very simply, supporting himself by grinding lenses for telescopes and other optical instruments, and writing his blasphemous works. He had a small group of friends with whom he discussed his ideas. These were all Christians, although renegades among the Christians. Once he moved away from his old home, he had nothing more to do with Jews, nor with his old yeshiva friends, or even with his family. Because of the *kherem*, which in his case was permanent, no Jews were allowed to speak with him for the rest of his life, so he really had no choice here.

He had been studying Latin, girls, because in those days all the *goyisha* scholars wrote in Latin. If Baruch wanted to reject his *rabbayim* and study *apikorsus*, then he would have to learn Latin. He was particularly interested in studying the works of René Descartes, who was a French-Catholic philosopher whom many of the so-called freethinkers in Europe were excited about.

Descartes believed that there is a God, but he had still made the Catholic Church angry enough to put him onto its list of banned writers, called the Index.[8] The reason he was considered dangerous to the Catholics was that he had written that people should not believe in God unless they can prove His existence according to the strictest rules of logic. If there are errors in the proofs for God's existence, then the believer should no longer believe. In other words, Descartes taught that there is no room for *emunah*, for faith.

Spinoza agreed with this heresy of Descartes, only he, the Jew, went much further. Unlike Descartes, Spinoza would go on and argue for atheism, saying that the God that we can prove is nothing over and above nature, which, of course, girls, isn't God at all, not for the Christians and not for the Jews. For no one. Spinoza wasn't fooling anyone by playing around with words, saying that he believed in God, only making God be nothing more than nature, which of course everybody believes in. Who doesn't believe in nature, since it's what we see all around us? Really, girls, when you think about it, it's ridiculous.

It *was* ridiculous, at least the way that Mrs. Schoenfeld had presented it—which is why I found myself wondering whether she was doing justice to Spinoza's thoughts. Otherwise, why would the *goyim* proclaim him a great philosopher? I knew enough to know that the thinkers whom the world called great weren't stupid.

But none of these ideas of his were yet known at the time of his excommunication, Mrs. Schoenfeld was explaining. All that the Amsterdam community knew was what the young men had reported about Spinoza's views and the way that he had conducted himself in the synagogue when the accusations had been brought before him; they had heard for themselves the terrible way in which he had spoken to his former teacher, Rabbi Morteira.

And so the *parnassim* voted to put Spinoza into *kherem*. Others from the Amsterdam community had also been placed in *kherem*, sometimes for a day or two, sometimes for longer. It depended, of course, on the *khayt* (the transgression). This community of returnees, trying to find their way back to Judaism, relied on the *kherem* as a means of guidance. Sometimes it was a matter of not keeping the law the right way, of buying meat from an unauthorized butcher or cheating in business. Or if someone wrote a letter to a Marrano in Spain or Portugal that put the recipient into danger of being discovered by the Inquisition, then this, too, was grounds for excommunication.

Then, too, even before the famous Spinoza, there had been other heretical thinkers who had been placed in *kherem* because of their so-called philosophical ideas. There had been a very famous case, when Spinoza himself was a child, of a man named Uriel da Costa, who had been excommunicated. This da Costa had been born in Portugal into a family of converts from Judaism. His father was a very religious Catholic, and he himself had become a minor church official. However, from reading the Torah he became convinced that Judaism is the true religion and he went to Amsterdam to live as a Jew. But he wanted his Judaism to be based on the Torah alone; he didn't accept any of the Talmud, any of the laws that derived from the Oral Law and from the rabbinical decisions. The way that he imagined Judaism, as a Christian back in Portugal, that's the way he wanted it to be. You can see some of the difficulties that the rabbis of these former Marranos had to contend with. They had to be *makhmir* (strict) in order to impress on these sadly ignorant Jews the nature of *halakha*.

(*Halakha* means "Jewish law." The term derives from the Hebrew root of the verb "to go," and so connotes the right way to go. The sources of *halakha* are basically three. There are the 613 commandments—or mitzvahs—that are contained in the Torah, the work that is traditionally considered the "Written Law," the author the divinely directed Moses. Then there are the writings in the classical rabbinical sources that are the discussions and debates about the written laws, especially in the Mishnah [referred to as the Oral Law, by tradition taught by Moses and passed down through the ages until it was written down in the third century C.E.] and the Gemorah [which is rabbinical commentary on the Mishnah, the first version authored in Jerusalem in the fifth century; the second, which is the one more commonly studied, authored in Babylonia in the sixth century]. The Mishnah and the Gemorah together comprise the Talmud. And then, third, there is the codified law as it is laid out in the *Shulkhan*

Arukh, a work whose title literally means "The Set Table," composed in the sixteenth century by the Sephardic kabbalist Joseph Karo. The *Shulkhan Arukh* culls from all the Talmudic discussions and controversies and sets forth [as in a set table] the redacted *halakha*. Orthodox Judaism is, for the most part, governed by the *Shulkan Arukh*, which is interesting since mainstream Judaism rejects the kabbalistic approach that was the [suppressed] inspiration for Karo's work. To quote the great secular kabbalist scholar Gershom Scholem, "R. Joseph Karo deliberately ignored kabbalism in his great rabbinic code *Shulkhan Arukh*, yet there is little doubt as to the secret eschatological motives of its composition."⁹)

It's not that the rabbis didn't have *rakhmones* (pity) for these victims of persecution, Mrs. Schoenfeld explained, but it required a stern hand to pull them back into true *Yiddishkeit*.

Da Costa had been put in *kherem* not once, but twice. Both times he had begged the community to allow him back, and they had granted him this, once he had fulfilled the terms of his penance. However, eventually he committed suicide—he seems to have been *meshugga*, a lunatic—and this had been a terrible shock and tragedy for the community, as you can well imagine. And then, at the time of Spinoza's excommunication, there was another man, older than Spinoza but his friend, a Spanish doctor by the name of Daniel de Prado, who also was excommunicated for questioning the basic beliefs of Judaism. He, too, was allowed to make his penance.

For everyone else the ban of excommunication had included ways in which the person in question could repent and have the ban removed when the allotted period was up. Baruch Spinoza's *kherem* was declared permanent, with no possibility of his returning to the Jewish community. His offense was seen as being far deeper than any of the others', perhaps because the young man's arrogant behavior at the synagogue had shown the rabbis and *parnassim* that he was incapable of *t'shuva*, repentance.

When a messenger came to where he was now living with his non-Jewish friend and brought news of his excommunication to him, Spinoza reportedly said to him, "All the better; they do not force me to do anything that I would not have done of my own accord if I did not dread scandal; but, since they want it that way, I enter gladly on the path that is opened to me."[10]

And what was this path, girls? Later he would publish his ideas and he would make the entire world angry—the Christians, too. The worst of his works he couldn't even publish when he was alive. This was called *The Ethics*, and it was in this work that he would say that God is nothing but nature and he would deny that there is any moral truth beyond our own pleasure and he would deny that we have free will to choose what we do, and he would argue that there is no world-to-come when we stand before the Throne of Glory and are judged for the lives we lived here on earth. His false ideas were against every religion, not just Judaism.

Spinoza didn't convert to any other religion. There had been Jewish apostates before him, those who converted to

Christianity or Islam. But a Jew who believed in nothing at all? This was a new phenomenon. This is why he is called the first "modern Jew." This, girls, is what "modernity" means: believing in nothing.

Unfortunately it would be a Jew, at least someone who had been born a Jew, who would take *goyisha* philosophy much further than it had ever gone before into godlessness and immorality. It would be a Jew who would make philosophy into one long argument against the existence of God and against the difference between right and wrong, so that philosophy, girls, has been, ever since modernity, the most dangerous subject that you can possibly study.

Once again I felt reluctantly compelled to ask a question. It seemed so glaringly obvious that I waited for someone else to ask it, but since no one did, I had to: If he didn't believe in ethics, then why did he name his book *The Ethics*?

It was his malicious sense of irony, answered my teacher, with the linguistic facility that so delighted me. Just as he had taken on the name Benedictus after his excommunication, since Benedictus means "blessed" in Latin as Baruch means "blessed" in Hebrew, with that same cynicism he would call this book of his *The Ethics*. But there is nothing ethical about the book. Spinoza goes out of his way to deny that there is anything like the true knowledge of good and evil that the Torah gives us. The ideas in this book were so irreligious and unethical, not only for Jews who wouldn't have read him anyway, but also for Christians, that he never dared to publish it during his lifetime.

Did he ever publish anything? another student asked.

Yes, he did. While he was still working on *The Ethics*, he

broke off for a few years in order to write another book, which he did publish, although anonymously. But it became known who the author was and all those who had a fear of God, Christian people, condemned him. On the title page he listed a fictitious author.[11] But once again nobody was fooled by his sly tricks. Everyone who read it—who of course were only non-Jews, since the *kherem* forbade that any Jew read Spinoza's works—immediately guessed who the real author was. That's how notorious he had already become, how much shame he had already brought on the Jews.

Are Jews still forbidden to read Spinoza?

I remember how strangely she looked at me when I asked her this question (provoked partly out of my wondering whether my teacher had read Spinoza herself). I remember thinking, as she stared at me for several long seconds before answering me, that she liked neither me nor my questions very much. The discovery upset me, since she was by far my favorite teacher.

The *kherem* against Spinoza has never been rescinded, she said, impressing me once again with her mastery of the English language (I'd read words like "rescinded" but never heard anybody use them), even as her tone of voice foreclosed further questions along these lines. I understood her to be saying that yes, Jews were still forbidden to read this philosopher's works, an answer that upset me almost as much as the discovery that my favorite teacher didn't like me.

The roots of this treatise that he published under a false name went back to his *kherem*. Right after he was excommunicated, he had started to write, in Spanish, what is called an apologia, defending his ideas. You should understand, though, girls, that even though such a work is called an apologia, there was going to be nothing apologetic in the work. No *t'shuva*, no remorse. We know this because instead of publishing his so-called apologia, he eventually turned his ideas into this treatise, written not in Spanish, which was the language that the Portuguese Jews often used for scholarly and literary works, but rather in the *goyisha* Latin. This treatise vindicated the two former friends of his who had first brought the charges against Spinoza. His treatise showed that all the rumors and suspicions about him had been justified. The treatise was a twisted perversion of all that his rabbis had tried to teach him. Spinoza denied that there could be any sort of prophecy or revelation. He denied that miracles were possible. He claimed that the Torah didn't come from *Ha-Shem*, that it hadn't been dictated by *Ha-Shem* to Moshe Rabbenu, but rather that it had been written by several men over an extended period of time and that it suffered from internal inconsistencies.

Of course, what seem like inconsistencies are nothing new to you, girls. You know much better than that. You know that sometimes the Torah teaches us through what seem like contradictions. The Torah has endless ways of teaching us, and the appearance of inconsistency itself transmits knowledge. Rashi and the other commentators explicate all this for us, she said, mentioning the famous acronym for Rabbi Solomon ben Isaac (1040–1105), the leading exegete of Torah and Talmud of all times, at least for the Orthodox. We had been learning Rashi's commentaries since elementary school.

But Spinoza had the arrogant love of his own mind, Mrs. Schoenfeld continued, and he seized on these apparent contradictions so that he would not have to recognize the authority of any mind over his, not even *Ha-Shem*'s.

Atheism always comes down to arrogance. Remember that, girls. It might dress itself up as careful thinking, but underneath it is the vanity and arrogance of thinking that human beings are the highest forms of intelligence in the universe.

However, continued Mrs. Schoenfeld, Spinoza did retain one Jewish virtue, and a very important one at that: Respect for his parents. Just think about that for a moment, girls. Even a man like that, completely godless, still honored his parents. He waited until both his parents had passed away before he revealed his *apikorsus*. His mother had died when he was a young boy. He had been brought up by a stepmother. By the year of his excommunication, 1656, she, too, had died, as had his father. In fact, he had only sat *shiva* for his father a year before he was put into *kherem*. He had followed exactly the prescribed mitzvahs for mourning a parent, going every day to the synagogue, saying Kaddish. And while his father lived, he had kept his silence because of *shalom bayis*.

Shalom bayis means peace within the household, within the family. It was an exceedingly familiar phrase to all of us. So important is *shalom bayis*, so constitutive of the Jewish way of life, that sometimes, for its sake, you can do things that otherwise wouldn't be allowed. For example, say a Talmudic scholar, who ought to be devoting his hours to study, has a wife who doesn't see the point of a devotion that keeps him away both from the house and from a good *parnosa*, or living. She doesn't recognize that to "sit and learn," as the expression goes, is the most sanctified activity in which her husband can engage. For *shalom bayis*, the man can forsake his studying, as he himself will know if he is a true scholar, a *talmid khokhem*, which in Judaism entails not only intellectual but moral merit. A *talmid khokhem* will know the fundamental importance of a household free from resentment, rancor, discord: he will sacrifice even learning Torah for the sake of *shalom bayis*.

Mrs. Schoenfeld's choice of this particular phrase suddenly brought the story of Baruch Spinoza home to me in a startlingly immediate way. All along, I had listened with special interest to this tale of a man whose trajectory of philosophical reasoning had brought him into disastrous collision with his close-knit Jewish community, a collision that inaugurated this intriguing thing called "modernity," of which I was uncertain whether to approve or disapprove.

But now, with this phrase, Spinoza burst into vivid life before me. It was as if I suddenly knew him, knew the manner of person he was. I certainly felt that I understood him better than I did those bumulkes lurking around the kosher pizza shop. "That's how it was," I thought, with that familiar phrase peircing me inside, "that's how he was."

He had not wanted to hurt his family by speaking his doubts aloud. Though he was a man who had given himself over entirely to the search after truth—I knew this instinctively—still he would not speak the truth so long as his doing so might hurt those whom he loved.

And from this one fact about Spinoza I knew that Mrs. Schoenfeld was mistaken in thinking that it was his arrogance that explained his departure from Orthodoxy. An arrogant person would not have shown such heightened consideration for others' sensibilities. He would not have waited until his father had died before revealing how deeply he questioned the beliefs of the fathers. The thought occurred to me that he must have been a lovable man.[12] I sat in Mrs. Schoenfeld's class and I felt that I loved him.

My teacher had tried to make us feel Spinoza's betrayal as our own, as if we, too, were part of that close-knit community of former Marranos, which in some sense we were. She had tried her best to put the seventeenth-century philosopher into familiar terms, and she had succeeded, though, at least in my case, not exactly as she had intended. Though I could not fathom what his ideas truly were, had no sense of what he might have meant by saying that God was nature, still, I felt that I knew him. An ignorant little girl in a calf-length skirt, I felt myself astonished with the sudden sense of knowing this philosopher, Benedictus Spinoza, who held such a formidable position in a construct of which I had only the dimmest notion: the Western canon.

I remember one more thing that Mrs. Schoenfeld had to say about Spinoza. It was in her summation of him.

There was nothing at all of *Yiddishkeit* that remained in Spinoza, she said. If you, God forbid, were to read any of his works, you would not find anything that would betray who Spinoza really was, that he had been brought up as a God-fearing Jew, a brilliant student who had once been a favorite of his rabbis, who were themselves great Torah scholars. He had learned to write in the language of *goyisha* philosophy, Latin, and this language pervades all his thinking, so that none of Torah's truth could survive in it.

Think about it, girls: If he were a true Jewish thinker, then would he have found his place among the philosophers? If he hadn't betrayed *Yiddishkeit*, would the world have called him great?

I t would be some years before I would find my way back to Spinoza, even though I did go on to become a professional philosopher. But my studies in philosophy were confined to what is called analytic philosophy, which is generally quite opposed to the very possibility of metaphysics, meaning here by "metaphysics" the attempt to use pure reason (as opposed to experience) to arrive at a description of reality. ("Metaphysics" can be used in a wider, looser sense, referring just to ontological commitments—commitments concerning what sorts of things exist in the world. In the latter sense of "metaphysics," even analytic philosophers have a metaphysics. The sense in which they reject the very possibility of metaphysics is in the sense of a nonempirical deduction of the nature of reality.)

And Spinoza's project is metaphysics on a grand scale—the very grandest, in fact. Never had there been quite so ambitious a metaphysical project as Spinoza's. He is audacious in the claims he makes for pure reason. Logic alone, he argues, is sufficient to reveal the very fabric of reality. In fact, logic alone *is* the very fabric of reality. And into this fabric are woven not only the descriptive facts of what *is*, but the normative facts of what *ought to be*.

In the philosophical tradition toward which I gravitate, such overinflated talk of reality—of, even more preposterously, Reality, and a Reality enriched with ethics, no less—is philosophically absurd. Or, as my old yeshiva mentors would have put it, such talk is *assur*, forbidden.

The new mentors with which I replaced the likes of Mrs. Schoenfeld might well, much like her, have alluded to Spinoza by way of a cautionary tale, and one, too, that bespeaks a certain arrogant overconfidence in the powers of human reason. Of course, my new teachers wouldn't be arguing that reason's powers must be augmented by divine revelation, but rather by observation and scientific explanations. We learn the nature of reality—though that word itself, even uncapitalized, was slightly off-color in the analytic circles I frequented—through the laborious, peer-reviewed, one-step-forward-three-steps-backward collective efforts of science. A project such as that of Benedictus Spinoza's, metaphysical to the heights, was one upon which I was trained to look askance, as exceeding not just the limits of knowability but the very conditions for meaningfulness. Such a system was composed of not just unsubstantiated speculations, but of highfalutin nonsense. It was presumptuous to think that we might be able to use pure reason to deduce, with absolute certainty, not only the nature of Reality but even the nature of our ethical obligations: how we ought to go about living our lives, what we ought to care about. Such claims impute far too much power to the faculty of reason.

Spinoza had made such claims—all of them. In fact, in the panoply of Western philosophers, Spinoza stands out as having made the strongest claims for the powers of pure reason, unassisted by empirical observation and induction. Anything which we can truly know is to be known through purely deductive thought, which begins with axioms and definitions (which capture the very essence of the things defined) and proceeds onward by strict logical deductions. Spinoza took as his model the system of Euclid's geometry, which is what gives the strikingly eccentric form to his philosophy. All the truths arrived at in this way are necessarily true, and we know them with absolute certainty. Though we cannot know all truths, since these are infinite and we are finite, still reason can take us far indeed. It can take us all the way to our salvation.

Reason reveals, according to him, the surprising nature of reality, which is so extraordinarily different from what our senses misleadingly present. And reason, too, shows us where our true salvation lies: the truths we must think about *ourselves* in relation to reality, which truths shall change our very nature in the knowing, setting us free.

Mighty claims indeed for the power of pure thought, and claims that my philosophical training led me to condemn as the height of philosophical delusion. The philosophical tasks we analytic philosophers set ourselves were far more modest. We entertained no metaphysical delusions about bypassing science to arrive at a priori certainty about the nature of Reality; and, too, we believed it to be a fallacy—sometimes referred to as the "naturalist fallacy," or that of ignoring the "is-ought gap"—to think to derive, as Spinoza claimed to have derived, normative statements from descriptive statements. *Conceptual* truths (which trace the logical connections between concepts and can be known a priori) do not entail *descriptive* truths—concerned with what exists; and descriptive truths do not entail *normative* truths—concerned with what ought to exist, what values ought to guide our actions and lives. Spinoza, outrageously, makes claim to all of these entailments.

Not even reason can produce something out of nothing. It can't get more out of the premises than what is already implicitly deposited within them. But this would seem to imply, or so an analytic philosopher is apt to argue, that conceptual truths—stating the logical possibilities—can't entail descriptive or ontological truths—describing the way the world really is, what sorts of things exist, what properties they have; and, in turn, descriptive truths can't entail normative truths—proclaiming what ought to be. The putative divide between the descriptive and the normative is famously referred to as the "is-ought gap." The putative divide between the conceptual and the descriptive might be dubbed, though so far as I know no one ever has, the "if-is gap."

To give some sense of Spinoza's audacity on behalf of reason, let's consider just the first claim for now, his denying that there is what I have just christened the "if-is gap." A cosmologist I once read (I wish I could remember who or where) compared two different sorts of deterministic necessity that might hold in cosmology.

The first sort of necessity involves there being various possible cosmological dial settings, so to speak, corresponding to different possible initial conditions at the beginning of the world, the Big Bang; in addition to these settings, there's also an ON-OFF switch. The laws of nature don't in themselves determine which of the possible dial settings the universe got set to, and, too, the laws of nature don't force the ON-OFF switch to either position. But once the dial is set, and once the switch is turned to ON, the laws of nature determine everything that follows from there on in. That's the first level of deterministic necessity. It says that *if* the dial was set to so-and-so, and *if* the ON-OFF switch was switched to ON, then, given the laws of nature, this is the way the world would be.

The second, and stronger, sort of necessity that the cosmologist distinguished was this: there is only one dial setting, and then there's the ON-OFF switch. Once the switch is turned to ON, everything follows from the laws of nature. But the laws couldn't, of themselves, force the switch to the ON position. So this second sort of determinism says: *if* the switch is turned to ON, then, given the laws of nature, this is the way the world would have to be.

Spinoza's claim of deterministic necessity exceeds even this second alternative. Spinoza claims that the laws of nature are such that not only is there one dial setting, but the switch must, of necessity, have been pointed to ON. It's been pointed to ON for all eternity. Nature, meaning the laws of nature, needs nothing outside of itself to explain itself. There is no "if-is gap" because there's just no *if* about it. This world, exactly as it is, necessarily exists. Its very nature, captured in its laws (in Spinoza's terminology, its "essence"), entails its existence. It is, in his language, *causa sui*, the cause of itself, both in terms of what it is (there's only one dial setting) and that it is (the switch is permanently turned to ON). Nature itself satisfies the opening statement of *The Ethics:* "By that which is self-caused (*causa sui*) I mean that of which the essence involves existence, or that of which the nature is only conceivable as existent."

Nothing outside of the world—no transcendent God, in other words—explains the world. Its explanation is immanent within itself. To conceive of the world in terms of its explanatory immanence is to conceive of God. God, he will therefore say, is immanent in nature, not transcendent.

Of course, denying the "if-is gap" means defusing one of traditional religion's major arguments for God's existence: the need for a Transcendent Something to have, at the very least, turned the cosmological switch to ON. So, too, Spinoza's denial of the "is-ought gap" defuses a second of traditional religion's major arguments, the need for a Transcendent Something to have established the difference between right and wrong. Just as the explanation of the world is immanent within its own nature, so, too, he will argue, the difference between right and wrong is immanent within our human nature.

His denial of both gaps derives from the stringent requirements he places on explanation. An explanation can have no inexplicable danglers protruding from it. Appealing to a Transcendent Something in both cases, the cosmological and the ethical, commits one to inexplicable danglers. What were the *reasons* the Transcendent Something had for His choices, both cosmological and ethical? If He had none, then there is inexplicability. If He did have reasons, then those reasons in themselves provide the explanation, and the appeal to Transcendence is redundant. So it's either, in both cases, immanence or inexplicable danglers. Therefore it is, in both cases, immanence: there is no "if-is gap" and there is no "is-ought gap." A priori reason executes both leaps, and *The Ethics* aims to show us how.

Mrs. Schoenfeld had accused Spinoza of arrogance—the arrogance of thinking that the human mind exceeds all forms of intelligence. She happened to have been wrong about this. Spinoza believes that our finite minds are limited because of their necessary finitude. Reality is infinite and we are finite and so there is a necessary mismatch between our knowledge of the world and the world itself. We know the truth only to the extent that our ideas approach asymptotically closer to congruence with God's infinite mind, which divine mind we should think of as the world's being aware of its own explanation. As this infinite explanation exceeds any that we can arrive at by orders of magnitude, so, too, God's mind exceeds ours by orders of magnitude. Be that as it may, analytic philosophers, too, a bit like Mrs. Schoenfeld, see a system like Spinoza's as hubristically oblivious to the limits of human reason.

And so I can imagine one of my philosophy professors—say, Peter Hempel, at that time one of the last of the original members of the legendary Vienna Circle, which had propounded a radical form of empiricism known as logical positivism—translating Mrs. Schoenfeld into the language of positivism:

"A priori reason can yield only empty tautological truths. 'All bachelors are unmarried.' Yes, that is a priori, but only because it is analytically true. Its truth is a function of its meaning alone, and therefore it says nothing at all about the nature of the world. *All* analytic truths are empty of descriptive content, and *all* a priori truths are analytic. To know the nature of the world we must depend on experience. So yes, 'it is either raining or not raining.' Or 'if there is a God, then there is a God.' Or 'since matter is composed of elementary particles it is not the case that it is not composed of elementary particles.' True, true, and true, but completely devoid of descriptive content! To know whether it is raining, whether there is a God, whether matter reduces to elementary particles, we must look for empirical evidence. A priori reason alone lays out only what is logically true, therefore true in all possible worlds and simply because of what the proposition means. To know what is true in *this* world, we must make contact with it, through experience. To even know what a descriptive proposition is asserting, to grasp its meaning, is to know how we would go about empirically confirming or disconfirming it, the sorts of experiences that would show us whether it was true or false. If no experiences could, in principle, count for or against a proposition, then it is not only unknowable. It is devoid of content! A priori reason is certain, yes, but only because it tells us nothing of what is, much less of what ought to be. And if one thinks otherwise, one is doomed to uttering nonsense!

"Think about it, philosophy graduate students. What are

the experiences that could possibly confirm or disconfirm such propositions as these—and I choose now randomly from the work entitled *The Ethics: The more reality or being a thing has the greater the number of its attributes.* This is from part one, and it is the ninth proposition. *God or substance, consisting of infinite attributes, of which each expresses eternal and infinite essentiality, necessarily exists.* This is part one, proposition eleven. *Individual things are nothing but modifications of the attributes of God, or modes by which the attributes of God are expressed in a fixed and definite manner.* Part one, proposition twenty-five, corollary. Or—and here Spinoza passes from meaningless metaphysics to meaningless ethics: *The mind's highest good is the knowledge of God, and the mind's virtue is to know God.* This is part four, the twenty-eighth proposition. Or—and now I flip toward the end of this deluded exercise to part five, proposition twenty-two: *Nevertheless in God there is necessarily an idea which expresses the essence of this or that human body under the form of eternity.*

"Is any of this in principle verifiable? Does any of this have a precise meaning such that we could know what to look for in the world to determine whether it is true or false?

"Let the name of Benedictus Spinoza serve as a warning to you against the folly of metaphysics, which can only end in systematic semantic nonsense, compounded by the fallacy of ignoring the is-ought gap!"

In other words, none of my education, running the gamut from Mrs. Schoenfeld to Peter Hempel, had prepared me to appreciate the philosophical system of Spinoza.

But my interest in the famous "mind-body problem" got me interested in Descartes, so that when the chairperson of the Barnard philosophy department, in which I was then teaching, suggested that I take over the course titled "Seventeenth-Century Rationalism: Descartes, Spinoza, and Leibniz," I agreed, mostly because I was a young assistant professor who found it pragmatic to agree with most of the suggestions of my chairperson. I read *The Ethics* for the first time the semester I was teaching it, and I want to take this opportunity to apologize to the students who took that course with me that year, as well as for the next couple of years.

But at some point, *The Ethics* began to make sense to me, despite my first-rate analytic education. I'm not saying that I actually believed the system to be true, but only that it all made sense: each of its individual proofs, and how they all hung together into one structure. The insight came when I grasped that the fundamental intuition underlying Spinoza's thinking was simply this: all facts have explanations. For every fact that is true, there is a reason why it is true. There simply cannot be, for Spinoza, the inexplicably given, a fact which is a fact for no other reason than that it is a fact. In other words, no inexplicable dangling threads protrude from the fabric of the world.

This intuition, which we can call the "Presumption of Reason," is the fundamental metaphysical intuition for Spinoza, so fundamental that it is never stated as an axiom, just as the laws of logic are not explicitly stated as axioms[13] but rather only make themselves known in their application. Spinoza treats the Presumption of Reason as on a par with a law of logic, as a rule of inference that he avails himself of in the course of deriving his propositions. It is the invisible piece that closes the lacunae in proof after proof. It is the assumption about the world from which his rationalism follows.

He was wrong in simply treating the Presumption of Reason as a law of logic. The laws of logic are such so that they cannot be logically denied: if you deny them, you end up contradicting yourself. The logical laws therefore stake no claim on the way the world is. Their negation describes no possible world. The Presumption of Reason is not like that. It stakes a claim—a reasonable claim, but a claim neverthe-less—on what our world is like, and that claim may be true or it may not. Spinoza would have liked to have proved—he thought he had—that he had deduced the only logically pos-sible world. This is why he could write with such consum-mate confidence to a young man he had once taught, who had just converted to Catholicism and was now challenging Spinoza's philosophy in an admittedly obnoxious way.[14] "I do not presume that I have found the best philosophy," Spi-noza wrote back. "I know that I understand the true phi-losophy. If you ask in what way I know it, I answer: In the same way as you know that the three angles of a triangle are equal to two right angles." If there are no arbitrary aspects of reality, he argues, and there *can't* be, he asserts, then logic itself *must*—logically *must*—explain the world.

What he will assert, in fact, is that logic itself *is* the world, which can be conceptualized alternatively as God or nature. The world is self-aware logic. The appearance of contingency—of things being the way they are for no other reason than that's the way they are—is merely that: appear-ance, a product of our finite mind's inability to assimilate the infinite sweep of the logical implications that comprise reality. The infinite intellect of God is aware of the whole infinite sweep. Its awareness and its being are one and the same.

What his system amounts to, in effect, is a working out of the Presumption of Reason. The world as it is described in *The Ethics* is one of the two ways that the world would have to be were the Presumption of Reason true. (The other possible way is the one that Leibniz pursues in his *Monadology*.) The fact that it is a strange world (as is Leibniz's), not much at all like the world of our experiences, demonstrates that this intuition, in itself quite reasonable—after all, it is simply the assertion that the world is, thoroughly, reasonable— is not so easy to uphold. It leads us far afield of common sense.

In a sense, here are our choices. If we want to retain the intuition that the world is thoroughly rational, with an explanation for *all* facts, we can go either the Spinoza way or the Leibniz way, which will lead us to maintain that the real world—Reality, God help us—corresponds nary at all to our experience of it. We will be inclined, like Spinoza, to file away experience, our seeming contact with the world, as just a species of imagination, the lowest step on the cognitive ladder. Or we can give up the Presumption of Reason; but that move, too, leads to some unpalatable conclusions, as the Scottish empiricist David Hume conclusively demonstrated. It leads to a conclusion that makes it deucedly difficult to distinguish at all between justified and unjustified beliefs about the world, at least insofar as those beliefs extend beyond the immediate content of our present experiences. What we are left with is—this is the conclusion of Hume, the most rigorous working out of the consequences of the *rejection* of the Presumption of Reason—a sort of hollowed-out solipsism, with not even an ongoing subject of experience to console us, but only the experience itself, and only while it is happening. I can't know about anything outside my own mind, and that mind itself reduces to a series of mental events. All that I can really know to exist is the mental event I happen to be having at the time. Just try confining yourself to that parsimonious ontology when you are doing anything but philosophy.

So the rigorous consequences of accepting the Presumption of Reason and the rigorous consequences of rejecting the Presumption of Reason both lead us to counterintuitive points of view. Perhaps rigor is just not in our cards. But that's a pretty unpalatable conclusion, too.

One could perhaps be inclined to counter Spinoza's Presumption of Reason by enumerating all the ways in which our contemporary knowledge seems to belie it. Our most powerful scientific theories—evolution in the biological sciences, quantum mechanics in the physical sciences—enshrine chance and contingency at their most fundamental explanatory levels. And when it comes to our accounts of human behavior—history, psychology, economics—then there is even less appearance of deterministic necessity. A Spinozist response would be to say that these explanations—whether in physics, biology, or the human sciences—appear fundamental only from the human point of view, which by its nature must be limited. From the point of view of God, of logic itself, there is neither chance nor contingency.

As mentioned in the last chapter, there are contemporary

physicists and cosmologists who have Spinozistic aspirations to banish chance and contingency in "the theory of everything." String theorists, in particular, are Spinozistic in their goal of having their physics emerge fully formed from their mathematics. Recall, too, the famous final sentences in Stephen Hawking's *A Brief History of Time:* "If we do discover a complete theory, it should in time be understandable in broad principle by everyone, not just a few scientists. Then we shall all, philosophers, scientists, and just ordinary people, be able to take part in the discussion of the question of why it is that we and the universe exist. If we find the answer to that, it would be the ultimate triumph of human reason—for then we would know the mind of God." Hawking's statement eloquently attests to the fact that Spinoza's understanding of what the laws of nature could tell us, if only we were capable of assimilating them in their entirety, is not foreign to modern scientific sensibilities.

Signature of Albert Einstein in the visitors' book in Spinoza's house in Rijnsburg. It is dated 2 November 1920.

But of all great modern scientific minds, Albert Einstein's stands out as having been the most self-consciously influenced by Spinoza. (The guestbook at the little house in Rijnsburg where Spinoza had lived, now a museum, has Einstein's signature, signed 2 November 1920.) He often described himself as a "disciple of Spinoza," and speaks of him often, either explicitly or implicitly, as when he refers to "the grandeur of reason incarnate." His views on nature and our knowledge of it were clearly informed by a deep study of the philosopher. "The religious feeling engendered by experiencing the logical comprehensibility of profound interrelations is of a somewhat different sort from the feeling that one usually calls religious. It is more a feeling of awe at the scheme that is manifested in the material universe. It does not lead us to take the step of fashioning a god-like being in our own image—a personage who makes demands of us and who takes an interest in us as individuals. There is in this neither a will nor a goal, nor a must, but only sheer being."[15] Almost every answer that Einstein ever gave when asked to expound on his philosophy of science and his views on religion echoes with strains of Spinoza.

Despite Spinoza's extreme rationalism, the most extreme in the history of thought, he remains of scientific relevance, from brain science to string theory, from Damasio to Einstein and Hawking.

With time, "Seventeenth-Century Rationalism: Descartes, Spinoza, and Leibniz" became my favorite class to teach, and Spinoza my favorite among the mighty triumvirate. We would work our way through the whole of *The Ethics*. My students would always begin as I had begun, with unmitigated bafflement before the eccentricity—both in form and content—of this seemingly impenetrable work. I would witness, year after year, the transformation that would come over the class as they slowly made their way into Spinoza's way of seeing things, watching the entire world reconfigure itself in the vision, no matter how unsustainable over the long run that vision proves to be for most of us—no matter how unsustainable we would even want it to be, since, in its ruthless high-mindedness, it asks us to renounce so many passions. (Among the passions we must renounce is romantic love, which, Spinoza deduces, will almost always end badly: "Emotional distress and unhappiness have their origin especially in excessive love towards a thing subject to considerable instability, a thing which we can never possess. For nobody is disturbed or anxious about anything unless he loves it, nor do wrongs, suspicions, enmities, etc. arise except from love towards things which nobody can truly possess." Paramount among "things which nobody can truly possess," of course, are people.)

And no matter how unsustainable that final vision is, no matter how taxing the leap of faith in the Presumption of Reason one must make in order to get there—still the rigorously intellectual process of beholding Spinoza's vision of the world is also, always, an emotional one, just as Spinoza promises. One feels oneself change, however impermanently, as one beholds Spinoza's final point of view—the point of view that approaches, though it can never match, "the Infinite Intellect of God." One's whole sense of oneself, and what it is one cares about, tilts—in a direction that certainly feels like up. Year after year, I've watched what happens with my students when Spinoza begins to take hold, and it's always moving beyond measure.

Still, no matter how intimate with Spinoza's formal and formidable system I've come to feel over the years, Spinoza himself, the man behind the system, has remained remote.

This is just as he would have wanted it to be, since "Spinoza himself" is of no account within that system, just as each of us, in our singular individuality, is of no account. The ultimate insignificance of the personal self emerges, as we will see, in the immanence of ethics. (As one of my friends quipped, when I was explaining this aspect of Spinoza to him, Spinoza was the original Bu-Jew.)

I certainly never thought to connect the philosopher I taught in my course on seventeenth-century rationalism with the Baruch Spinoza I had first encountered in Mrs. Schoenfeld's *historia* class. I taught Spinoza in the context of Western philosophy, in particular in the context of that fascinating movement represented by Descartes, Spinoza, and Leibniz. I never connected the middle philosopher of the lineup, not in my class and not even in my head, with that "bumulke" I'd first heard tell of in Mrs. Schoenfeld's class. Spinoza was the philosopher who came after René Descartes and before Gottfried Wilhelm Leibniz. I traced the development of his ideas from the Frenchman who had influenced him, most especially with the inspiration to look to mathematics as the model for all knowledge, to his slightly younger German contemporary, whom he had strongly influenced, most especially with the intuition that all facts have explanations, the assumption that I am calling the Presumption of Reason, and which Leibniz formalized as "The Principle of Sufficient Reason."

The personal sense of the philosopher that had come upon me in the moment of hearing the phrase *shalom bayis* inserted into his tale had long ago disappeared. That phrase had carried all the heavy intimacy of the life that was then closest to me. In the moment of hearing it I had thought that I grasped something immediate and essential about a great philosopher, something that brought him home to me, making him a figure of piercing sympathy. Now, too, strangely enough, given my antimetaphysical tendencies and training, I believed I had come to have an intuitive understanding of him, could study each of the proofs of *The Ethics* and shadow his thought processes. But the two understandings of him—the first in terms that were both personal and Jewish, the second in terms that were strictly philosophical—didn't intersect with each other. If anything, they were at odds.

The philosophical understanding of Spinoza seems to forbid understanding him in terms that are personal and Jewish. To have indulged in a sense of a special bond with Spinoza, forged by reason of our shared Jewish experience, would have been to forsake the rational project as Spinoza understood it, and as he deeply influenced me to understand it as well. To have intimated an extraphilosophical intimacy with Spinoza, come to me by way of the sheer accidents of my and his precedents, would have amounted to a betrayal of his vision.

I spoke of his vision to my students as "radical objectivity," and from its vantage point all the accidents of one's existence, the circumstances into which one was born—including one's own family and history, one's racial, religious, cultural, sexual, or national identity—appear as naught, and the lingering emotional attachments to such accidents are only evidence of impartial rationality and obstacles in the way of achieving a life worth living.

To the extent that we are rational, merely personal matters matter not at all. To the extent that we are rational, personal identity itself shrivels away into insignificance. The fact of who I happen to be in the infinite scheme of things disappears altogether in the apprehension of the scheme itself.

I was being true to Spinoza in leaving behind the personal sense of him that had opened up to me within the space of one small Hebrew phrase; and yet it is back to that personal sense of him that I am trying now to return, even knowing what I know about his philosophy. I would like to recapture the sense of the man behind the formidable system, locate the pounding pulse of subjectivity within the crystalline structure of radical objectivity.

There was a moment long ago when I knew next to nothing about the magnificent reconfiguration of reality laid out in the system of Spinoza, and yet when I felt I knew something about what it was like to have been him, the former yeshiva student, Baruch Spinoza.

I would like to know that feeling again, even though I know that the desire amounts to betraying Spinoza.

III

The Project of Escape

The most characteristic literary genre of our day is the memoir. Unlike an autobiography, the author of a memoir needn't have distinguished herself in her life in order to have earned the right to tell her life's story. Many contemporary memoirs are written by people who are famous for having done nothing but write a memoir, often to much acclaim.

The appeal of the memoir says something about the temperament of our times. *What*, precisely, it says, I'm not prepared to say, though I suspect it's nothing good. I suspect that what it says is mixed up with the nondecorous celebration of celebrity that is also such a salient feature of our days.

And who, after all, am I to condemn the memoirist turn in contemporary letters when I myself have seized upon it in approaching this very discussion of Spinoza? I have insisted on speaking in personal terms of the philosopher who insisted most on impersonality. To bring in the personal and the temporal—references to one's self and one's times— is to place oneself outside of Spinoza's reason-sanctioned scheme of things, the view, as one contemporary philosopher has wonderfully put it, "from nowhere."[1] Spinoza himself puts it this way in *The Ethics*: "It is in the nature of reason to perceive things sub quâdam aeternitatis specie," that is, under the guise of a certain form of eternity.[2]

Still, the personal and the temporal is where we all begin. Even Spinoza began by being only himself. The question is whether that is where one ought to end. Spinoza tells us no. He urges one to forsake, in a sense, one's own temporal identity as it has passively come down to one through the contingencies of what he calls "external causality," contingencies that have nothing to do with one's own true essence. He asks one to construct—through the *active* reflective work of philosophy, seeking the true explanations of all things— a new identity.

To become rational, believing only what we have good grounds for believing, is to transform the self so substantially as to change its very identity. His astounding conclusion: to the extent that we are rational, we, all of us, partake in the same identity. (The rationally reconstructed cannot fail to get along: this provides the key to his political theory. Philosophy is good for the polity.)

To arrive at an identity that is not uniquely one's own? Isn't that, in a certain sense, to simply forsake personal identity altogether? Yes, it is, in a certain sense, and in that sense it is what he asks of us. To disinhabit our selves, and thereby save ourselves. It is in that sense that he will even offer us, at the end of *The Ethics*, a certain form of immortality, the immortality that comes from abandoning one's own personal identity, giving it up for the infinite web of necessary connections that he identifies as the *causa sui*, the self-explained, the thing that can be conceived alternatively as God or nature and which he dubs *Deus sive natura*. It is that vast and infinite scheme of things that pure reason can get us to precisely because it is constituted of the very stuff of reason: logic. It consists of all logical implications spun out in their entirety.

We can survive our death to the extent that we have already let go of being our singular solitary selves. (But do we particularly care about that universalized self surviving? An *aperçu* of Woody Allen's seems peculiarly pertinent at this point: "I don't want to achieve immortality through my work. I want to achieve it through not dying.")

Immortality, for Spinoza, is impersonal; I survive my necessary death to the extent that I have ceased identifying with that mere thing that I am, and identify with the whole intricate web I have assimilated in the knowing. The first-person point of view that I *am* is relinquished for the View from Nowhere, which is the same for all of us.

All of this is to say that we, whose distinctive literary voice is the memoir, are perhaps peculiarly ill placed to grasp the vision of Spinoza. Where we are endlessly captivated by the drama of the self in all its distinctive singularity, Spinoza sought only to escape it. The priority of that fascinating singularity, that problematic and precious "I," is, for Spinoza, a symptom of a passivity, the acceptance of the contingently given, that weakens our capacities, drains and stunts us, impedes our driving force to persist in our own being, to flourish in the world. Paradoxically, the only way to flourish in one's being is to cease being only that being. That singular self, that localized "I," that "me" which is "me" and no other, that tantalizingly elusive but inescapably ubiquitous reality that is my substance, my identity, my very being, yes, *that* thing is, for Spinoza, a thing to be cast off into the mists of unreality, outgrown as one stretches outward into reality. Escape from it in order to save it. (But then, if we truly escape from it, why care about it enough to want to save it? Is the way to his salvation barred by paradox? Are we in Woody Allen Land again?) The distinctive singular self is not what we ought to think about. It is not even what we ought to *be*.

Spinoza wrote the only story of himself of which he would have approved, and it is called *The Ethics*.

This is the way his self-approved memoir begins: "Definition 1: By that which is self-caused I mean that of which the essence involves existence, or that of which the nature is only conceivable as existent."

That is as personal as he wanted his story to get (see the next two pages to see how his story continues). It doesn't sound, on the face of it, as if it is about Spinoza at all, and it isn't, on the face of it. It is of the whole world that he is speaking in that definition of the *causa sui*, the vast system of logical implications that is the necessary expression of necessary existence itself. Spinoza is, as each of us is, but one of the implications in the implicative order that is the world. So, in a sense, Spinoza is implicitly speaking of himself in that first definition. To the extent that he—that any of us—becomes rational, he will cease to identify with that one implication and identify instead with the vast implicative order itself.

So the *causa sui* is where he begins *The Ethics*. But the *causa sui* is not where *he* begins, Baruch Spinoza, who sought to

THE ETHICS.

PART I. CONCERNING GOD.

DEFINITIONS.

I. By THAT which is SELF-CAUSED, I mean that of which the essence involves existence, or that of which the nature is only conceivable as existent.

II. A thing is called FINITE AFTER ITS KIND, when it can be limited by another thing of the same nature; for instance, a body is called finite because we always conceive another greater body. So, also, a thought is limited by another thought, but a body is not limited by thought, nor a thought by body.

III. By SUBSTANCE, I mean that which is in itself, and is conceived through itself; in other words, that of which a conception can be formed independently of any other conception.

IV. By ATTRIBUTE, I mean that which the intellect perceives as constituting the essence of substance.

V. By MODE, I mean the modifications * of substance, or that which exists in, and is conceived through, something other than itself.

VI. By GOD, I mean a being absolutely infinite — that is, a substance consisting in infinite attributes, of which each expresses eternal and infinite essentiality.

Explanation.—I say absolutely infinite, not infinite after its kind: for, of a thing infinite only after its kind, infinite attributes may be denied; but that which is absolutely infinite, contains in its essence whatever expresses reality, and involves no negation.

VII. That thing is called free, which exists solely by the necessity of its own nature, and of which the action

* *«Affectiones.»*

Spinoza's "memoir": the opening pages of *The Ethics*, stating definitions, axioms, and the first two propositions.

is determined by itself alone. On the other hand, that thing is necessary, or rather constrained, which is determined by something external to itself to a fixed and definite method of existence or action.

VIII. By ETERNITY, I mean existence itself, in so far as it is conceived necessarily to follow solely from the definition of that which is eternal.

Explanation.—Existence of this kind is conceived as an eternal truth, like the essence of a thing, and, therefore, cannot be explained by means of continuance or time, though continuance may be conceived without a beginning or end.

AXIOMS.

I. Everything which exists, exists either in itself or in something else.

II. That which cannot be conceived through anything else must be conceived through itself.

III. From a given definite cause an effect necessarily follows; and, on the other hand, if no definite cause be granted, it is impossible that an effect can follow.

IV. The knowledge of an effect depends on and involves the knowledge of a cause.

V. Things which have nothing in common cannot be understood, the one by means of the other; the conception of one does not involve the conception of the other.

VI. A true idea must correspond with its ideate or object.

VII. If a thing can be conceived as non-existing, its essence does not involve existence.

PROPOSITIONS.

PROP. I. Substance is by nature prior to its modifications.
Proof.—This is clear from Def. iii. and v.

PROP. II. Two substances, whose attributes are different, have nothing in common.
Proof.—Also evident from Def. iii. For each must exist in itself, and be conceived through itself; in other words, the conception of one does not imply the conception of the other.

purge his point of view of the personal, to become one with the radical objectivity that he dubs *Deus sive natura*. But that passive identity, the one he aimed to discard? That is the one I'm searching for now, the identity come to him by way of the contingencies of external causality. What were those contingencies that passively shaped him, a passivity he sought to wrest back and dissolve in the pure activity of philosophy? How far back must we go to get a sense of the man who did *not* identify himself with *Deus sive natura*—the purely personal part that was left over, dangling outside of the rational enterprise, the finite modification, the isolated implication, the son and brother and teacher and friend? The Jew.

The community into which he was born was also, as he would be, obsessed with issues of identity. They, too, were in the process of trying to construct a new identity, to save themselves by realigning their identities with what they took to be their essential selves. The confluence of preoccupations with identity and salvation can't be irrelevant. It can't be irrelevant to the way that Spinoza would react to his community, to the way that they would react to him, to the ferocity of their mutual disavowal.

For the Sephardic Jews of Amsterdam, too, questions of identity were meshed into the project of escape, of bringing out into the open the secret but true identity that they had been forced for a century to conceal, the Jewishness they took to be essential to themselves. The contingencies of external causality had shaped their passive identity as well, and they, too, sought to wrest that passivity back and reshape it, to actively and freely redefine themselves.

They lived in Amsterdam, mainly concentrated into two districts, the Vlooienburg and the Breestraat (later called the "Jodenbreestraat"—"Jews' Broad Street"), but not because they were required to live in a ghetto, as in the Jewish community of Venice, which was also predominantly Sephardic, but simply because their communal life necessitated it. There were synagogues, kosher butcher shops, and of course the Talmud Torah, that model school that Mrs. Schoenfeld had praised to us, even though it had failed to inculcate its Jewish values into its most famous graduate. A Polish scholar named Shabbethai Bass visited Amsterdam and came away even more impressed with it than Mrs. Schoenfeld had been:

> [In the schools] of the Sephardim . . . I saw "giants [in scholarship]: tender children as small as grasshoppers," "kids who have become he-goats." In my eyes they were like prodigies because of their unusual familiarity with the entire Bible and with the science of grammar. They possessed the ability to compose verses and poems in meter and to speak a pure Hebrew. Happy the eye that has seen all these things.[3]

The area of Amsterdam where the Jews mostly lived was a business and mercantile area, as well as being residential, surrounded by canals on which barges and boats were anchored right beside the streets. Engravings of the time portray tidy, tree-lined streets, lined with tall and narrow wooden houses, the distinctive stepped roofs rising like the prosperity of the merchant owners who inhabited them. Gentiles lived in the Jewish quarter, including for a time Rembrandt, who often chose his Jewish neighbors as subjects, the richer ones sitting for their portraits, while others served the artist as models for his works on biblical themes. One of the rabbis of the community, Manasseh ben Israel, said to have been the most famous Jew of Amsterdam and certainly the most worldly of the Sephardic rabbis, counting many Gentiles as his friends, was painted by Rembrandt.

Etchings and portraits from Rembrandt and other artists show the Portuguese Jews affecting the dress and style of the Amsterdam mercantile class, from the sweeping feathers in their capacious caps down to the silver buckles on their blackened boots. Within a few short decades, a high degree of affluence and a certain degree of acclimation had been achieved, and whatever security can be gained from donning rich brocades and other signs of bourgeois respectability had been gained. The treasures of Dutch art were also of interest to the prospering Sephardim. They were acquiring Rembrandts as well as sitting for him. One family was said to have paintings worth "a ton in gold."

Insofar as the Portuguese Jews' outward presentation, little marked them as being foreigners rather than just swarthier-complexioned Dutch. They appeared to be adapting to the lifestyle of the prospering city with flair and exuberance, contributing to the economic rise of the middle class. Their successful and rapid acclimation was in contrast to their Ashkenazic brethren. The latter were arriving in ever bigger numbers, especially as the Thirty Years' War and pogroms created catastrophic conditions in Germany and Poland. The Ashkenazim of Amsterdam did not catch on as dexterously as did the Sephardim to life in Amsterdam.

They remained impoverished and presented something of a burden for, and an embarrassment to, the Portuguese Jews. In 1632, the very year of Spinoza's birth, a bylaw was passed by the Sephardic community setting up two charity boxes meant for the Ashkenazim, "to prevent the nuisance and uproar caused by the Ashkenazim who put their hands out to beg at the gates."

But though the look of the Portuguese Jews was, at least to the extent that they could affect it, Dutch, the language in the streets and in the homes, in the shops and in the synagogues (including the magnificent one that they would build at the end of Jews' Broad Street, still standing today), was Portuguese. Since they were primarily merchants (even the rabbis often engaged in some trade), and dealt with Dutch Gentiles, they knew Dutch as well, but Portuguese remained the native language.

For Spinoza, too, Portuguese was his native tongue. He might write, as Mrs. Schoenfeld had put it, in the *goyisha* language of Latin, but he thought in the language of his community, Portuguese, as emerges at times in his letters, when he apologizes for the clumsiness of his Dutch:

> I do indeed wish that I might write in the language in which I was brought up. I might possibly express my thoughts better. But please take it in good part, and yourself correct the mistakes, and consider me
>
> Your devoted Friend and Servant
> B. de Spinoza
> The Long Orchard
> 5 January 1665

Another language, too, speaks of the community's long history and the way it continued to live on inside the Portuguese Jews of Amsterdam: Spanish. This was the language reserved for high literature and scholarly works, just as it had been for them in Portugal, preserving in the linguistic practice memories of the culture the Jews brought with them to Portugal after they had been exiled from Spain in the Great Expulsion of 1492.

When they arrived in Amsterdam, they often replaced their Portuguese names with Hebrew ones, though also often retaining the Portuguese name for business purposes outside the community. They also often took on Dutch names, in order to hide their Portuguese, and therefore Jewish, identities, so that they could do business with Iberian New Christians—as the converts from Judaism were known, even generations after the family's conversion—without placing these New Christians in danger. Josef de los Rios became "Michael van der Riviere," and Luis de Mercado became "Louis van der Markt."[4] Collectively, they referred to themselves, even, in Amsterdam, as the "Portuguese Nation," or La Nação, clearly setting down invisible borders between themselves and their neighbors. As they were assiduously assimilating the outward style of the Dutch burghers, participating in the burgeoning mercantile economy, within them there was a very different reality, carrying traces of times long preceding their arrival on the banks of the Amstel River.

The weight of many centuries of history bore down on the collective memory of La Nação. How far back do we have to go to gather a sense of that collective memory and understand how it presented itself in the ongoing life of the community? That life, animated by long memory, must have made itself felt in Baruch Spinoza. He was, after all, a child of that community, born to parents who were first-generation immigrants to Amsterdam. His father, Michael, had fled as a child, most likely sometime in the 1590s, together with his extended family, perhaps because someone in the clan had been denounced to the Inquisition. Once that happened, entire families would decamp in haste, since the Inquisition was never content with investigating just a single individual. Once a person fell under suspicion, so did everyone intimately connected with him.

But the collective memory of the Jewish community of Amsterdam reached further back than the immediate history that had brought each of the Sephardic families there. A memory stretching back over the centuries, even the millennia, is a vital part of the Jewish sensibility. The Jews are a people who are enjoined to recite the Passover narrative each year as if they themselves had personally experienced the exodus from Egypt. Amsterdam Jews had special reasons for recalling centuries of Jewish history as if they had personally experienced the events for themselves.

How far back must we go to get a sense of the communal inner life that had informed the passive identity of Baruch Spinoza, shaping that singular self that his ethics demanded he resist, and that I am seeking?

Long before the official European "Renaissance," the Jews of Spain had experienced, under the relatively tolerant rule of the conquering Moslems, an extraordinary cultural renaissance, still referred to as the Golden Age of Spanish Jewry.

In the eighth century, the Moslem Moors, expanding from Morocco, had captured large chunks of Spain from the Christian Visigoths, and the Jews, who had largely been forced into conversion under the Visigoths, welcomed the Arabs as liberators and allies. Victorious Islam was then barely one hundred years old. Under the new Moslem rule, many former converts, who had secretly clung to their faith, not only returned to Judaism but entered into concourse with Moslem high culture to produce their own heady concoction of science and poetry, mathematics and art, rationalistic philosophy and the esoteric mysticism known as kaballah.

The intellectual Sephardic tradition as it emerged out of those golden days of inspired intermingling of cultures was more slanted toward philosophical reflection and mystical speculation than was the mainstream Ashkenazic intellectual tradition, which to this day remains focused almost exclusively on Talmudic legalistic disputations. This last comparison should not be understood as a slight to Talmudic study, despite the fact that "legalistic disputations" might seem to have a pejorative tone to it. But the legalistic logic of Talmudic analysis encloses a unique form of spiritual activity. Here, too, we encounter, as we do in Spinoza, the sacramentalizing of logic, reason as the means of unifying with God.

Isaac Bashevis Singer has a lovely, if gently mocking, description of Talmudic scholarship in the opening paragraphs of his novel *Shosha:*

I was brought up on three dead languages—Hebrew, Aramaic, and Yiddish—and in a culture that developed in Babylon: the Talmud. The cheder where I studied was a room in which the teacher ate and slept, and his wife cooked. There I studied not arithmetic, geography, physics, chemistry, or history, but the laws governing an egg laid on a holiday and sacrifices in a temple destroyed two thousand years ago.

The applications of the Law to quotidian life is of some concern, of course—what *is* one to do with the egg laid on a holiday?—but the analytic reasoning itself is the real focus. Talmudic logic is understood as a spiritual activity, a meshing with the Divine Presence. The Law is the way God is seen as interacting with His people, and to study it is to approach Him in the most direct way that we can. What might seem from the outside to be dry anachronistic hairsplitting is, from the inside, experienced as shot through with the radiance of Divine Intentionality. In this tradition, the dialectics of *pilpul*—Talmudic argumentation—is spiritual activity at its very highest, and it became mainstream Jewish scholarship. Philosophical ruminations about the nature of God are decidedly not part of this mainstream.

But the Sephardic thinkers of the Golden Age were much more drawn to such philosophical ruminations. The towering figure of Sephardic rationalistic philosophy was the philosopher Maimonides (1138–1204), also known as the Rambam, derived from the initials of his name, Rabbi Moses ben Maimon. "Maimonides" is actually his Greek appellation, meaning "son of Maimon." He was born in Córdoba, Spain, though when the city fell to Muslim Berbers, the Almohades, the family fled to Morocco. After spending some time in Jerusalem he settled in Fustat, Egypt, where he was doctor of the Grand Vizier Alfadhil and to the Sultan Saladin of Egypt.

Maimonides is generally acknowledged as the greatest of Jewish philosophers (excluding Spinoza, of course, who belongs to the Western canon rather than to the Jewish one). He was controversial in his day, and in my high school we weren't altogether certain of him still. He was a bit too *modern* for us (pronounced with a long *o*, a rolling *r*, accent on the second syllable). His main project was to reconcile Judaism with what he considered the best scientific thinking of his day, which was the Aristotelian system. Aristotle's was an impressively inclusive system that set forth the proper place of each and every thing in the universe, working outward from us, the inhabitants of the earth, around whom the entire universe, laid out in concentric spheres, literally revolved. Aristotle also offered a rich strategy for explaining events by explaining the end that would be accomplished by means of the event. In other words, his model for explaining the physical world was the way that we explain intentional actions, namely by citing the intention. This is what is meant by saying his explanations were *teleological* (*telos* means "end" or "goal" in ancient Greek). Alternatively, one says his explanations relied heavily on *final causes*; a final cause is the end for which the event or process took place. So, for example, Tom's going to the all-night convenience store at 11 p.m. could be explained by his having just discovered that there is no beer in his fridge and his wanting a beer. The final cause is

Tom's procurement of his bevarage of choice. So, too, in the Aristotelian system a dropped stone's falling to the earth is explained by the stone's being composed primarily out of earth and therefore belonging on the earth, from which it had been displaced and to which it is now returning. In other words, the stone is moving toward the earth, as Tom is moving toward the convenience store, because those are the places toward which each wants to go, each wanting to correct a condition which is a privation given their particular natures. Aristotle's was a system in which physical space was not the same in all directions; rather, different parts of space were the province of the four different elements: earth, water, air, and fire. These spatial differences provided the orientations that explained motions, the end of the motion identical with its final cause..

Aristotle's system *was* the best scientific thinking of Maimonides' day, though the great thinkers of the seventeenth century—Galileo, Descartes, Newton—would have to declare themselves its enemy and dismantle its teleological explanatory apparatus in order to lay the foundations of modern science. Spinoza, as we will see, could not have been more irreconcilably opposed to all teleological thinking. He was thoroughly conversant with, and hostile to, the general thrust of Maimonides' thinking, not only in its Aristotelianism, but in its reconciliatory theism. Maimonides' method in interpreting Scripture derived from his reconciliatory theism, which could be simplified into a principle something like this: Since scientific truths are true and the Torah, too, is true, there is always a way to interpret the Torah so that it is consistent with science. The method of biblical interpretation Spinoza pursued in his *Tractatus Theologico-Politicus* avoided any such external principles. Railing against traditional rabbinical interpreters of Scripture, clearly having Maimonides very much in mind, he wrote in his *Tractatus:*

> It is not enough for them to share the delusions of the Greeks: they have sought to represent the prophets as sharing in these same delusions. . . . And this is further evident from the fact that most of these assume as a basic principle for the understanding of Scripture and for extracting its true meaning that it is throughout truthful and divine—a conclusion which ought to be the end result of study and strict examination, and which they lay down at the outset as a principle of interpretation. . . .

Thomas Aquinas (1225–74) would do some years later for Christianity what Maimonides had done for Judaism, namely "Aristotelize" it. The Dominican friar, author of *Summa Theologica* and one of the most important of Catholic theologians, was highly influenced by "Rabbi Moyses," though Christian apologists would often try to conceal the Jewish influence. Scholasticism was the enterprise of translating Christian theology into Aristotelian terms, and it dominated post-Thomistic Catholic thinking. In the early years of the Middle Ages, when Maimonides was alive, Plato rather than Aristotle had been the more influential ancient thinker among those Christian thinkers who tried to reconcile Christian thought with ancient philosophy. St. Augustine, one of the early Church fathers, had been a Platonist, and his influence dominated. Maimonides, a religious thinker with a distaste for the mystical, was far more drawn to Aristotle than to Plato's brand of rationalism. Aquinas's influence would mean that Christian thinking of the later Middle Ages was dominated by Aristotelian rather than Platonic thinking, which is why the seventeenth century's great scientific innovators would have to defeat the hegemonic grip that Aristotle had come to have on Church dogma.

Maimonides' Aristotelianism was perhaps quite intellectually compatible with his profession as a physician. The body, after all, would appear to be a teleological system, its various processes acting in order to accomplish some end. So, for example, if the body becomes too hot, it perspires in order to cool itself down. If it becomes too cold, it shivers, the muscular contractions causing it to warm up.

Though Maimonidean philosophy, just because it *is* philosophy, has been controversial ever since the Rambam's own day, raising generations of Jewish eyebrows (the position in my high school was to keep a respectful distance), there was one aspect of his work that became ensconced firmly in the mainstream, perhaps precisely because it eschews philosophical grounding for straightforward faith. This is the Thirteen Articles of Faith, which have become such an accepted aspect of Judaism that they are recited on Yom Kippur, the holiest day of the year. It is as if Maimonides vindicated his dalliance with the dangerous seductions of Hellenistic rationalism with his straightforward assertion of belief:

1. I believe with perfect faith in the existence of God which is perfect and sufficient unto himself and which is the cause of the existence of all other beings.

2. I believe with perfect faith in God's unity, which is unlike all other kinds of unity.

3. I believe with perfect faith that God must not be perceived in bodily terms, and the anthropomorphic expressions applied to God in Scripture have to be understood in a metaphorical sense.

4. I believe with perfect faith that God is eternal.

5. I believe with perfect faith that God alone is to be worshiped and obeyed. There are no mediating powers able freely to grant man's petitions, and intermediaries must not be invoked.

6. I believe with perfect faith in prophecy.

7. I believe with perfect faith that Moses is unsurpassed by any prophet.

8. I believe with perfect faith that the entire Torah was given to Moses.

9. I believe with perfect faith that Moses' Torah will not be abrogated or superceded by another divine law nor will anything be added to or taken away from it.

10. I believe with perfect faith that God knows the actions of man.

11. I believe with perfect faith that God rewards those who fulfill the commandments of the Torah, and punishes those who transgress them.

12. I believe with perfect faith in the coming of the Messiah.
13. I believe with perfect faith in the resurrection of the dead.

Of these Thirteen Articles, Spinoza will aver 1, 2, 4, 5, and 10, though their meanings shift radically in alignment with his system. One might say that the second principle, in particular, is adamantly assented to in his system; the unity of *Deus sive natura* is certainly unlike all other unity. Spinoza denies—though again according to the special meaning he gives the relevant terms—principles 3, 6, 7, 8, 9, 11, 12, and 13. But far more ardent and fundamental than the rejection of some eight of the requisite articles of faith is the philosopher's rejection of the Maimonidean ethics of belief. For Spinoza, far more thoroughgoing in his rationalism than Maimonides, there is *no* virtue whatsoever in believing with perfect faith. The virtue is in believing because you *know*, which requires proof.

Another strain of Jewish thinking also emerged from the Iberian soil, though later in the Sephardic experience than Maimonidean rationalism: the mystical tradition known as kabbalah. Here, too, the soil was seeded by ancient Greek thinking—not Aristotelianism this time, but rather Platonism, or rather Neoplatonism, particularly Plotinus and Proclus. It was the Arab scholars who transmitted knowledge of the Greeks, translating their works, and this is how Spanish-Jewish scholars came to know them.

The *Zohar*, which is traditionally translated into English as *The Book of Splendor*, is considered the most important of the kabbalistic writings. It is written as if it were an ancient text, with commentary added to it by the Spanish kabbalists, but modern scholarship has revealed it to be almost incontrovertibly composed in Spain, in the southern city of Gerona, in the late thirteenth century. The author of the *Zohar* was most probably Moses de Leon, though he claims it to be the work of a scholar named Simeon bar Yohai, a second-century sage, who was himself a student of the legendary Rabbi Akiva.

I had heard tales of Rabbi Akiva from youngest childhood. One of the greatest of Jewish scholars, he had not even learned to read until he was a grown and married man. He had married above himself, a rich man's daughter, and she had agreed to marry him only if he became a scholar. He and his son learned to read at the same time. (I remember learning this in kindergarten, when it had a special enchantment.) He died as a martyr at the hands of the Romans, by legend being flayed to death at the age of ninety. The traditional tale is that Simeon bar Yohai hid from the Romans in a cave near the Dead Sea, fed for years on a spring of freshwater and the fruit of a carob tree that sprang up in his hiding place, and it was there, in the miraculous hiding place, that the mystical form of Midrash, or Torah interpretation, is said to have been inspired, though Rabbi Akiva, too, had possessed esoteric knowledge.

The Spanish kabbalists traced their ideas back to this ancient tradition, but some new spring was flowing into their thoughts as well, and this new spring, too, was very ancient, only it wasn't Jewish. It was Greek. It was the thinking of Plato, most especially as it had found expression in the Neoplatonists.

The Jewish poet and philosopher Ibn Gabirol (c. 1020–

c. 1057) was a Neoplatonist living in Gerona. He presented his metaphysics in his major work *Mekor Hayyim* (The Source of Life), which was written in Arabic. (The Arabic version is no longer extant, but a medieval Latin translation, *Fons vitae*, exists.) It is written in dialogue form, as Plato had written, and the only authority who is ever mentioned by him is Plato. Although Ibn Gabirol was an undeniably Jewish thinker whose religious poetry found its way into the liturgy, *Mekor Hayyim* is rigorously nonsectarian. As the *Encyclopedia Judaica* puts it succinctly, "*Mekor Hayyim* is unique in the body of Jewish philosophical-religious literature of the Middle Ages, because it expounds a complete philosophical-religious system wholly lacking in specifically Jewish content and terminology. The author does not mention biblical persons or events and does not quote the Bible, Talmud, or Midrash. To some extent this feature of the work determined its unusual destiny."[5] Part of its unusual destiny is that its ideas and even its terminology found their way into Spanish kabbalah.

Kabbalah, in contrast to mainstream Jewish thinking, which concentrates almost exclusively on Talmudic legalistic disputation, speculates heavily on metaphysical questions, especially those concerning the beginning of all things. Why, as philosophers are wont to put it, is there something rather than nothing? Why did God—referred to in kabbalistic terminology as the *Ein Sof*, That Without End—have to create the world? What is the relationship between the *Ein Sof*, existing outside of time, and the created temporal world? How does, how *can*, eternity interact with temporality?

According to kabbalistic thinking, the *Ein Sof* is beyond our understanding, beyond all our words and concepts. But there are what the kabbalists referred to as the *Sefirot*, the emanations of His infinite power, in which the divine attributes are turned into acts of creation, and *Sefirot* can be grasped by the human understanding; they can be gleaned from the structure of being. The *Ein Sof* is unrevealed, non-manifest, and unknowable. Only the emanations of his power (the *Sefirot*) transform the *Ein Sof* into the Creator-God and a personal God.

As the kabbalistic tradition meditates on the beginning of all things, so, too, it ponders the awful mystery of suffering, most poignantly, most bafflingly, represented by the example of children who suffer, children who die. The *Zohar* says of children "who still as sucklings are taken from their mother's breast" that "the whole world weeps; the tears that come from these babes have no equal, their tears issue from the innermost and farthest places of the hearts, and the entire world is perplexed: . . . [I]s it needful that these unhappy infants should die, who are without sin and without blame?" Clearly, an answer has to be offered, and here is the one that the *Zohar* offers: "But . . . the tears shed by these 'oppressed ones' act as a petition and protection for the living . . . and by dint of their innocence, in time a place is prepared for them . . . for the Holy One, blessed be He, does in reality love these little ones with a unique and outstanding love. He unites them with himself and gets ready for them a place on high close to him."[6]

There is a path to be traced from Athens to Gerona, and then from Gerona to Amsterdam, for kabbalism was a distinct aspect of the inner life of the Portuguese Nation. The Sephardic community of Amsterdam, for a host of reasons, was deeply susceptible to the mystical tradition that was part of their Sephardic heritage, especially as that tradition was transformed by the pain of the Spanish exodus and its aftermath, as we shall see, so that it transformed itself into a historical narrative obsessed with the theme of national— and cosmic—redemption. One of the most influential rabbis in the community, Isaac Aboab, was a kabbalist. Manasseh ben Israel, another Amsterdam rabbi who has been briefly mentioned (as having posed for Rembrandt), was also deeply influenced by its redemptive narrative. Spinoza gives ample evidence of being conversant with the esoteric Jewish texts—both Aboab and Manasseh were most likely his teachers in the yeshiva—though he was plainly irked by the kabbalist habit of seeing each word of Torah surrounded by an aura of mystical secret meanings:

> [T]hey say that the various readings are the symbols of profoundest mysteries and that mighty secrets lay hid in the twenty-eight hiatus which occur, nay, even in the very form of the letters. Whether they are actuated by folly and infantile devotion, or whether by arrogance and malice so that they alone may be held to possess the secrets of God, I know not; this much I do know, that I find in their writings nothing which has the air of a Divine secret, but only childish lucubration. I have read and known kabbalistic triflers, whose insanity provokes my unceasing astonishment.[7]

Nonetheless, despite Spinoza's impatience with the kabbalistic methodology, despite his emphatic rejection of the specific answers that kabbalah offers for the profound questions it poses; still many have claimed that the spirit of kabbalah was not altogether foreign to Spinoza. I have long thought that the distinctly Platonic tone of Spinoza's philosophy, which consists not so much in his actual picture of reality but in the ecstatic impulse that irradiates it, and that sharply distinguishes his rationalism from both Descartes' and Leibniz's, came to him by way of the kabbalistic influences which were vividly alive in his Portuguese community. And Spinoza's system will offer us, as we shall see, its own solutions to the two mysteries that are most central to kabbalistic speculations: the ontological mystery of why the world exists at all, and the ethical mystery of suffering: why does suffering—and of such mind-numbing magnitude—exist in this world, if God is both all-good and all-powerful?

As the fortunes of Spanish Jewry declined, the kabbalists' meditations on suffering deepened and darkened. The meaning of Jewish suffering, in particular, occupied more and more of their mystical speculations, and the theme of national redemption made its appearance. As the travails of Spanish Jewry increased, so increased the redemptive preoccupations of the Spanish kabbalists. In the time of exile, they speculated, the truth, too, had been exiled. The redemption of the world is intimately intertwined with the destiny of the Jews, and they believed themselves to be living in the messianic era. There were esoteric signs that the Messiah's arrival was imminent, that he would reveal himself in the Jewish year 5250, or, in the world's way of reckoning time, the year 1490.

The Amsterdam Jewish community would be heavily influenced by these kabbalistic preoccupations, and the influence fell, though in subtle ways, on Spinoza, too. It is not that Spinoza has any sympathy at all for Jewish mysticism, or for mysticism of any sort for that matter. Spinoza's rationalism is not mysticism. It is, rather, Cartesianism, though with some major tinkering. But the ultimate mysteries he seeks to solve with his revamped Cartesianism are nowhere to be found in Descartes—nor in Galileo, nor in any of the "scientist rationalists" who precede him. Instead, Spinoza turns the Cartesian methodology, meant to focus in the "natural light of reason," to illuminate the mysteries of the kabbalists, no matter their dubious methods of enlightenment: the beginning of all things, the *Ein Sof*'s relationship to creation and to our knowledge, the mysteries of evil and of suffering.

These three strains in Jewish scholarship—the legalistic analysis of the Talmud; the rationalist semiphilosophical approach represented by Maimonides (semiphilosophical in the sense that not all questions are open to philosophy: religion has the final say); the mystical confabulations of the kabbalah—are, quite obviously, in tension with one another. The Talmud famously warns against the other two approaches, but the kabbalistic one in particular: "Whoever ponders on four things, it were better for him if he had not come into the world: what is above, what is below, what was before time, and what will be hereafter."

The story is told of four who went into the garden or orchard (it is the Persian word *pardes*) of mystical study. One went mad, one became an apostate, and one took his life. Only one came out whole, and this was Rabbi Akiva. Again the Talmud cautions that no one should study kabbalah who has not yet attained the age of forty, marriage, and a full belly—a degree of mundane ballast to safeguard against being "blasted by ecstasy" (as in Ophelia's speech).

Though the influence of ancient Greece made itself felt in both the Maimonidean philosophical and kabbalist ecstatic strains in Sephardic culture, still some of the most prominent participants in the Golden Age voiced wariness of the Hellenist legacy. For example, Judah Halevy (before 1075–1141), who was perhaps the greatest of all the Hebraic-Spanish poets, and whose religious poetry found its way into the liturgy, acknowledges the heavy influence of Greek philosophy on his Judeo-Spanish culture in his poetic admonition:

> *Turn aside from mines and pitfalls.*
> *Let not Greek wisdom tempt you,*
> *For it bears the flowers only and not the fruits.*

To balance the impression of stern rectitude on the part of Judah Halevy, it is only fair to share other stanzas that show him in a softer, more sensual mood. (Iberian sensuality also contributed its flushed warmth to the heady concoction of the Golden Age of Spanish Jewry):

> *Pity me, you of the hard heart and soft hips,*
> *Pity me, let me bend the knee before you!*
> *My heart is pure, but my eyes are not!*

There were other exoticisms, in addition to philosophy, mysticism, and poetry, that bloomed in the garden of Sephardic Judaism. Science, too, and particularly medicine, attracted many Spanish Jews. Rulers often had their own

Jewish physicians, and often these physicians were themselves philosophers or poets or both. Both Maimonides and Judah Halevy had been doctors. And Jews contributed to Spanish science in other ways as well. For example, King Alphonso X commissioned Isaac ibn Said, the cantor of Toledo, to compile correct astronomical tables. The Alphonsine Tables were completed in 1256, the most complete heavenly topography ever assembled.

It had not only been in intellectual, spiritual, and cultural inroads that the Spanish Jews had broken new ground, but also in more worldly-minded ways as well. They were not only poets and philosophers, scholars and mystics, but treasurers and advisers and landowners. Court Jews, who helped rulers in administrative and financial capacities, came to have real political clout. They were sent on diplomatic missions. They established family dynasties, so that they constituted their own "nobility." According to some estimates, the Jews of the eleventh and twelfth centuries owned more than a third of all the estates in the county of Barcelona. A culture at once distinctively Jewish was yet contributing to the culture at large, and both cultures were incalculably the better for it.

While the Spanish Jews were reaping the benefits of relative Moslem tolerance, rising to lustrous preeminence in the arts and sciences, the Jews of Christian northern Europe, the Ashkenazim, were pressed into squalid marginality or worse. The worse was truly terrible. Jews had been accused of causing the Black Plague by poisoning the wells, and mobs burned masses of them alive.

In the towns of northern Europe—in Rouen, and Cologne, and Prague, and Mainz, and Worms—the Jews were on the brink of a wild terror that came down on them in the form of the Holy Crusades. "The Unholy Crusades" is what the Jews called them. In 1095, Pope Urban II had called for a Crusade to liberate the Holy Land from Moslem rule, and the knights and feudal lords, with the masses that they mobilized, wreaked their fury on the Jews they encountered on their way east, reasoning, "Why wait until we get to the Holy Land to punish the nonbelievers?" The French exegestist Rashi, whose commentaries on all the sacred Jewish works are still the first commentaries that an Orthodox child studies and will continue to consult throughout his life of scholarship, had witnessed the ravaging of the communities of the Rhine, the destruction of the centers of learning in which he himself had studied and taught. He composed a heart-wrenching prayer addressed not to God but to the Torah, beseeching that it intercede on High, so that its words, and not the Crusaders' swords, would prove victorious in Jerusalem. "Explain thy lovely words for men to understand," Rashi wrote, a poignant plea from a scholar devoted to explaining each and every word of all of Holy Scripture, sometimes spinning out an elaborate interpretation from nothing more than an extra squiggle over a Hebrew letter.

In England the accession of the Crusader Richard had spelled disaster for the Jews, who were set upon by mobs in many towns. The most dramatic atrocity had taken place in York, during the Third Crusade. Jews had sought refuge in a castle. Surrounded by their enemies, with no hope of escape, they committed mass suicide. The first of the blood libels, accusing Jews of murder for ritualistic purposes, took place at Norwich in the twelfth century. And even when English rulers had offered protection to their Jewish communities, they had levied such exorbitant taxes on them, enriching the royal coffers, that finally the Jews were too impoverished to be of any use. The culmination came in 1290. Edward I banished the now useless Jews from England, decreeing that every one of them must leave by All Saints' Day.

One of Chaucer's *Canterbury Tales*, "The Prioress's Tale," tells of a widow's child murdered by the Jews because he was singing the hymn to the Virgin "Alma redemptoris mater" while walking on the "Jewes Street" in some unspecified Asian city. The Jews cut his throat and then threw him into a pit, in Chaucer's telling, where he miraculously continued to sing, so that the ritual murder was discovered and the Jews of the town were triumphantly tortured and massacred. Chaucer himself refers to the twelfth-century story of Hugh of Lincoln, one of the early blood libels. The poet could not himself have known any English Jews, since they had been banished from England a century before, but the tales of the libels lived on as poetic inspiration.

France, too, had banished its Jews in the thirteenth century, King Louis IX (canonized in 1297 by Pope Boniface VIII) canceling all Christian debts to them and confiscating their property. They were eventually invited back, again for the economic advantages they could offer, but their position always teetered precariously toward disaster, and they were subject to ongoing systematic attempts to get them to see the "Jewish error" of their ways and convert.

It was under the expansive tolerance of sophisticated Moslem life that the perfumed essence of Sephardic culture had been distilled, a culture poetic, philosophical, scientific, mystical, and also worldly. At certain times, among certain more fundamentalist Moslem groups, the tolerance abated. Maimonides, for example, had been forced to flee, as a boy, with his family, from his birthplace in Cordoba when it was conquered by the Almohades, a Moslem sect that demanded the conversion of all Jews. But, for the most part, Moslem rule proved conducive to Sephardic flourishing.

The Christian attempt to regain control over Spain had begun almost coterminously with the Moslem conquest in 711; the mountainous northwest region had always remained Christian. Over the centuries there was a steady erosion of Moslem dominion, especially as Moslem rule had been destabilized by invasions from the Moslem Berbers, whose outlook was far less enlightened than the Moors. By the end of the fifteenth century, the Moslems ruled over only Granada. But Sephardic culture continued on, and the Moslem and Jewish blend was at times and places enhanced, too, by Christian intermingling, achieving a state that was called *convivencia*, literally "living together."

As the Christians unified their hold on Spain, the sorts of intolerance that had dominated in other European lands began to creep into Sephardic existence as well. The first blood libel came to Spain in 1250. Soon after, the most famous Sephardic rabbi of the day, Nachmanides, provoked by an apostate Jew, engaged in a formal disputation on the relative merits of Christianity and Judaism. Nachmanides also known as the Ramban, came from the city of Gerona, the center of mystical Judaism, and he himself was an important kabbalistic thinker. The famous disputation, however, was held in Barcelona in 1263 over a span of four days, before the king and gathered bishops. Nachmanides had secured permission to speak frankly, and so he did, arguing that the evidence that Jesus had ushered in messianic times was scant, for had not the prophet Isaiah foretold of the perfect peace that would follow upon the Messiah's coming?

> Yet from the days of Jesus until now that whole world has been filled with violence and pillage. The Christians, moreover, shed more blood than other nations; and how hard it would be for you, your Majesty . . . and for these knights of yours if they were not to learn war any more?

There were to be many more such formal disputations, not only in Spain but throughout Christian Europe, often with the set purpose of determining the fate of the Jewish communities in which they were held. Riots, torture, forced conversions, and murder increasingly concluded these staged debates. Nachmanides would be the last Jewish representative who would speak with what he had thought was impunity; in fact, he was brought to trial for publishing his own account of the debate and, though acquitted, was forced to leave Spain, resettling in Jerusalem.

Now once again, with the turning of the tide against the Jews, the ranks of the New Christians swelled in Spain. The upper Jewish classes, in particular, converted to Christianity in increasing numbers. And Nachmanides' uncensored words, charging Christianity with shedding more blood than other nations, took on prophetic tones.

The practice of burning heretics at the stake was introduced in the last years of the twelfth century. The Holy Inquisition was a procedure devised and named by Pope Innocent III (1198–1216) for exposing Christian heretics, though it was another pope, Gregory IX, who established it as an institution. It was to last for 350 years. Its stated targets were Christian heretics; the Church claimed no official authority over non-Christians. But since the mere presence of Jews was seen as conducive of heresy, they were to suffer severely at the hands of the Inquisition, most especially when the Inquisition took on a new ferocity as it entered Spain and then Portugal. And of course all New Christians were ipso facto Christians, and thus fell under the jurisdiction of the Inquisition.

The first mass burning of Jews at the stake took place in 1288, following a blood libel. This was in Troyes, France (where Rashi himself had lived a century before). But the Inquisition had already infiltrated Spanish life by this time, quietly at first. Right around the time of Nachmanides' public disputation, Pope Clement IV granted the Inquisition freedom to interfere in Jewish affairs by allowing the inquisitors to pursue converted Jews who had relapsed into their former faith. *Conversos,* some of whose families had become Christians centuries before, at the time of the Visigoths, were considered true Christians by the Church, and the lapse of any Christian back into Judaism was punishable by death. Therefore, the Inquisition had jurisdiction over their souls and went after them in elaborate ceremonies of intrigue and torture.

The attitude toward Jews had changed in Spain well before the Inquisition took on its full formidable power. By the mid-1300s, the mobs, incited by the anti-Semitic tirades of priests, were attacking Jews, the authorities intervening only when Christian lives and property were threatened. In 1391, a year which is a blood-soaked marker for the changing fortunes of the Jews of Spain, marauders went from town to town throughout Castile and Aragon, massacring men, women, and children. Sometimes women and children were sold as slaves to the Moslems. All the synagogues of Barcelona were destroyed, and the community that had existed for eight hundred years came to an end. The mounting numbers of *conversos* after 1391 reflected the markedly different situation that now confronted the Jews.

The new century brought new violence against the Sephardim. The notorious friar Vicente Ferrer preached in the towns of Castile, his Sunday-morning sermons often followed by long nights of violence against Jews. He instigated new anti-Jewish regulations in Castile, proclaimed on January 2, 1412. Jews now had to wear their hair and beards long so that they could be recognized by all. They could no longer be addressed with the honorific "Don." They could no longer be tax collectors, nor perform any other public services, nor collect interest, nor engage in commerce. Almost all professions were to be closed to them, and Jewish physicians could no longer treat Christian patients. These edicts, however, were difficult to enforce and were largely ignored. Still, they tolled doom.

In June of that same year Ferdinand I became king of Aragon, through the assistance of the very same rabble-rousing friar. Now Ferrer could extend his anti-Jewish edicts in Aragon as well. At this same moment Pope Benedict XII ordered a new staged disputation to be held in Aragon, the designated topics to include the veracity of the Talmud. The rabbis who had been sent to represent the Aragonese community were given no opportunity to express themselves, and a new wave of forced conversions followed their preordained defeat, with Ferdinand ordering that all copies of the Talmud be submitted for inspection so that remarks deemed anti-Christian could be excised.

The final end of Spanish Jewry was determined by a marriage. In 1469, Ferdinand II of Aragon, son of John II of Aragon and grandson of Ferdinand I, married Isabella of Castile, the unification of their kingdoms effected by 1479. The royal couple were not only in the debt of various zealot churchmen whom they repaid by imposing restrictions against Jews and *conversos;* they were also sincerely committed to a religious and ethnic solidification of their country. Their statesmanship was, in many ways, so admirable and enlightened that the question of their acquiescence to the formidable beast that the Inquisition would become forcefully presents itself. Interestingly, there is evidence that both monarchs had *converso* ancestors, Ferdinand several generations back and Isabel even further back. The Jews of the time secretly believed that Ferdinand had Sephardic ancestry, which might explain why court Jews—the highly influential Abraham Seneor and Isaac Abrabanel in particular—pushed so hard for the match, even providing the betrothal gifts that Ferdinand required to seal the deal, according to contemporary Hebrew sources.[8]

The first problem, at least as it was explicitly stated, was not with the Jews but with the New Christians. The very designation "New Christian" was itself an indication of the suspicion with which "Old Christians" regarded the *conversos*. "New Christian" simply meant that the family had once been Jewish, even though the conversion might have taken place generations, even centuries, before.

Some *conversos* had ardently embraced the new faith. In fact, many who had stirred up anti-Jewish sentiments had been enthusiastic apostates bent on demonstrating the Jewish fallacy. There were important Christian thinkers and reformers who were New Christians. Other *conversos* did not take their new religion as seriously. There were many, especially among the upper classes, who had pragmatically converted in order to further their social, political, and economic advance. But others had only converted under duress; the Jews called such converts *annusim*, or "forced ones" (as opposed to *meshumadim*, voluntary converts), and Christianity perhaps had reason to doubt the forced ones' sincerity, though not as much reason as the diabolical machinery of the Inquisition could warrant. The historian Benzion Netanyahu argued in *The Marranos of Spain*, partly on the basis of the response of rabbis outside of Spain and Portugal, that the great majority of New Christians, even when their original conversions were forced, were not secret Judaizers and that this was well known in the Church. Netanyahu's conclusion leads him to search for covert motives of a political nature behind the relentless persecution of New Christians under the Inquisition.

Still, there is the sinister presence of racist ideology that lurks in the notion of a New Christian, the suggestion that Christian conversion, both in faith and in practice, no matter how sincere, cannot succeed in removing the stain of Jewishness. In fact, this suggestion is more than borne out by the statutes that were enacted as early as 1449 demanding *limpieza de sangre*, or purity of blood, for those who would perform all but the lowliest tasks in churches, for admittance to guilds, colleges, religious and military orders, and even for residence in certain towns. There were those in the Church who protested that the conversion of the Jews to Christianity had been taking place over so long a period of time, stretching back to the time of the Visigoths, that it was impossible for any Spaniard to establish *limpieza de sangre*. Perhaps this very impossibility fed the racist anxiety. (In varying degrees the Spanish obsession with blood purity would last into the nineteenth century. Blood purity was finally abolished as a requirement for admission to the military academy in 1860.) The persecution of the New Christians, a designation that neither religious belief nor practice could eradicate, was the first European experiment with racist ideology. It was, more specifically, the Marranos who were the designated target of Old Christian wrath, those who had converted to Christianity and whose souls therefore belonged to the Church, but who continued to practice Judaism secretly. But racist animus tended to blur the line between New Christian and Marrano.

The two communities of Jews and New Christians were still deeply intertwined, living side by side with each other, related, at the very least, by blood and history. The royal couple took steps to segregate the Jews, so that they could not exert any pernicious influence on the New Christians. Though previous rulers had been wary of allowing the formidable power of the Inquisition to compete with their own rule, in 1478 Ferdinand and Isabella invited the Inquisition into their land. It was in Spain that the full fury of the Inquisition would develop, becoming a powerful political institution that answered to no one, not even the pope. It would terrorize Jews for hundreds of years to come, pursuing its prey all the way to the New World. Late in the twentieth century, Catholic Mexican-Americans in Arizona and other western states would reveal secrets to university researchers, telling of their families' practice of not eating bread during Holy Week, and of closing all the shutters and lighting candles in secret cupboards on Saturday nights. The tone in which they imparted these family secrets was still one of hushed nervousness, yielding us, over five centuries later, some small sense of what the terror must have been like in its most hellishly active period.

The Dominicans were chosen to manage the Inquisition in Spain, and Tomás de Torquemada, the head of a Dominican monastery in Segovia and confessor to the queen, was appointed inquisitor-general in the autumn of 1483. Torquemada, too, is said to have had *converso* ancestors, perhaps stoking his hatred. With his ascension, inquisitional reach was extended across the whole of the kingdom. Torquemada was insatiable. There are recorded instances of people being cleared of all charges and Torquemada demanding retrial after retrial, until either the verdict he wanted was reached or he burned the victims anyway. It was he who set up the formidable machinery of the Inquisition, its secret mechanism so perfectly calibrated to do what it was designed to do that it would keep running well after his death (though the greatest concentration of activity was during his lifetime).

Over the course of the next twelve years, the inquisitors, with their irresistible methods of forcing confessions, claimed to have found over thirteen thousand secretly Judaizing New Christians, men and women, many of whom were burned at the stake.[9] Everything—accusations, imprisonment, torture, forced confessions, sentencing—took place in the greatest secrecy, contributing to the terror. The verdicts were announced at great public spectacles, the infamous autos-da-fé, where masses of the condemned heard their sentences announced, one by one, the proceedings often stretching into the night, and sometimes protracted over two or three days. The last to hear their sentence pronounced were those condemned to death, the method of execution specified as being "without an effusion of blood," which meant, of course, being burned alive. This seeming mercy, a bloodless murder, amounted to a death of maximum cruelty and was based on an old legal fiction of the Church dating back to the eleventh or twelfth century and justified by a passage in John 15:6: "If a man abide not in me, he is cast forth as a branch, and is withered; and men gather them, and cast them into the fire, and they are burned." Penitent heretics were granted the mercy of being strangled before their bodies were burned. Those who had died under torture were burned as well, and condemned heretics who had escaped were burned in effigy, their goods confiscated, as were all goods confiscated, by the increasingly wealthy Inquisition, though those who had originally brought the

accusation of crypto-Judaism—a neighbor, a business partner, even a family member—were entitled to some of the
goods, a diabolical plan if ever there was one.

The flimsiest grounds could serve as an accusation. For
example, extreme personal hygiene could be interpreted as
crypto-Judaism. An old habit from the days before conversion, absentmindedly reverted to, could cost a person his or
her life and bring catastrophic attention to his or her
extended clan as well. The guidelines the Church issued for
detecting a crypto-Jew included such behavior as wearing
clean clothes on Saturdays and draining away the blood of
meat and cutting away its fat and gristle. An accused person
never got the opportunity to face his accusers, so personal
vendettas, as well as envy, malice, and greed, could serve as
motives.

In 1492, Granada, the last Moslem holdout, fell to the
Christians. Now it was only the Jews and the backsliding
conversos who spoiled the royal vision of a unified Christian
Spain. The autos-da-fé ceased, as plans for the final solution
were being put into place. There was one more effort at mass
conversion, and then came the announcement. Judaism was
to be officially terminated in Spain. There were attempts to
bribe the monarchs. Various Jews were members of the royal
court or in other ways close to the two rulers, including most
prominently Abraham Seneor and Isaac Abrabanel, and a
large sum was handed over by way of these intermediaries.
Legend has it that Ferdinand and Isabella wavered at the
eleventh hour and Torquemada came rushing in to them,
with a crucifix held aloft, fulminating, "Judas Iscariot sold
his master for thirty pieces of silver. Your Highnesses would

sell him anew for thirty thousand. Here he is. Take him and barter him away." Spain's Jews had two choices: convert or emigrate. The official justification again was put in terms not of punishing Jews for being Jews, but for corrupting Christians:

> We have been informed that within our kingdom there are evil Christians who have converted to Judaism and who have thereby betrayed our holy Catholic faith. This most unfortunate development has been brought about as a result of the contact between Jews and Christians. . . . We have decided that no further opportunities should be given for additional damage to our holy faith. . . . Thus, we hereby order the expulsion of all Jews, both male and female, and of all ages, who live in our kingdom and in all the areas in our possession, whether such Jews have been born here or not. . . . These Jews are to depart from our kingdom and from all the areas in our possession by the end of July, together with their Jewish sons and daughters, their Jewish servants and their Jewish relatives.

Those who converted would of course be allowed to remain in Spain, where the inquisitional torments continued with mounting fury. Considerable numbers of Spain's Jews, including the chief rabbi, Abraham Seneor (who had been appointed to his post by the royal pair following his help with their nuptials), and most of the members of the most influential families, chose baptism over exile, adding their numbers to the *conversos.* But between 100,000 and 150,000 Jews packed up their belongings and left, the exodus beginning in May. By the end of the summer there were officially no Jews left in Spain. As the rabbis remarked, the final expulsion occurred just about the time of the Jewish fast day of Tisha Ba-Av, the ninth of Av, which marks the two destructions of Jerusalem, the first by the Babylonians and the second by the Romans in 70 C.E.

An eyewitness to the exodus, an observer generally unsympathetic to the Jews, Andrés Bernáldez, who had enthusiastically endorsed the work of the Inquisition, gives a glimpse of the pathos as the Jews left Castile and Aragon that hot summer:

> Confiding in their vain blind hopes, [they] left the lands of their birth, children and adults, old and young, on foot and in wagons, and the *caballeros* on asses and other beasts, and each journeyed to a port of embarkation. They went through roads and fields with many travails and [mixed] fortunes, some falling, others rising, others dying, others being born, others falling sick, so that there was no Christian who did not feel sorry for them and always invite them to be baptized. And some sorrowfully converted and stayed, but very few. And on the way the rabbis heartened them, and had the women and youths sing and play tambourines to cheer the people, and so they went through Castile and arrived at the ports. . . . When those who went to embark through Puerto de Santa María and Cádiz saw the sea, they shouted loudly and cried out, men and women, great and small, in their prayers demanding mercy of God, and they expected to see some marvel of

God and that he would open a path through the sea for them.

Among the masses leaving the land of Sepharad in those anguished summer months were the kabbalists, the visionaries who had seen signs of the Messiah's imminent arrival, and in this way explained how it was given to them to have so many divine secrets revealed, and how it was that the people with whom God had made his covenant were being subjected to such unholy torment. They had predicted that the year of 5250, or 1490, would bring the final redemption. What kind of effect did the expulsion and the other horrors that had both preceded and would follow this calamity have on these mystical visionaries? They would take the kabbalist tradition with them, many of them eventually finding their way to the ancient city of Safed, in the northern hills of Galilee. According to tradition, the Messiah, from the House of David, would arise in the Galilee and make his way from there to Jerusalem. Presumably, this is why the Spanish kabbalists, forced from their homes in Gerona, chose this destination, making it the new center of kabbalistic mysticism.

Kabbalah would undergo, in the wake of the Sephardic tragedy, a profound transformation. How could it not have affected their mystical apprehension of the universe? How could men who read the world—its natural laws and its history—as a divine code not have interpreted the great calamity in symbolic terms? "I think that the afflictions visited on the Jews in all the Christian kingdoms between the years 5250–55 (1490–95) . . . are the messianic birth pangs," wrote Joseph She'altiel b. Moses ha-Kohen on the island of Rhodes in 1495, in the margin of a manuscript he was composing.[10]

The catastrophe of the Spanish expulsion changed the nature of kabbalah. The kabbalists of pre-1492 had not been particularly messianic. They had conceived of spiritual salvation as compatible with life in *galut*, in exile. Their spiritual efforts were bent on uncovering the esoteric meaning of the universe in order to effect a personal union with the Godhead, individual salvation. It was in the wake of the Sephardic disaster that kabbalah would become increasingly apocalyptic and messianic.[11]

In the sixteenth century, the kabbalistic giant Isaac Luria, known as Ha-Ari, or the Lion, would come to Safed, and Lurianic kabbalah, still the essence of modern kabbalah, would emanate from out of the narrow medieval alleyways and synagogues of that golden-lit city to sweep across the lands of the Diaspora, infiltrating all levels of Jewish life. It transformed not only practice, with new rituals of meditation and purification, but the very way Jews constructed and understood the narrative of their own religion.

Originally a recluse who would see his wife and children only on the Sabbath, Luria believed himself to see visions of the prophet Elijah, who initiated him into the esoteric system. Luria's mother was Sephardic, though his father was Ashkenazic, and among his small circle of disciples, many of whom believed him to be the Messiah, were Sephardic refugees from the Inquisition. Among the inner circle were Joseph Karo, whom you will recall was the author of the *Shulkhan Arukh* (The Set Table), which Orthodox Jews, Ashkenazic and Sephardic, regard as the official compendium of Jewish Law. Karo, who was born in Toledo, had messianic motivations for his codification of *halakha*, since the right observance of the Law would hasten the coming of the Messiah. Also in Luria's inner circle was Hayyim Vital, originally of Calabria, who was responsible for writing down the lectures of Luria in the form in which they were disseminated throughout Jewry.

Lurianic kabbalah, transmitted from his visions of Elijah, offered a new narrative to explain the moral history of the suffering world, and the role that the Jews were chosen to play in that moral history. It is a tale of a shattering—a *shevirah*—at the very beginning of the creation of the world, when the *Ein Sof*, or That Without End, contracted itself so that the world could be created. The divine light entered into the ten vessels that were waiting to receive it, and some were shattered, the shards falling into the abyss from which the world arose, carrying sparks of the light that were trapped within. From the moment of its first being, then, the world was not as it ought to have been. The exile of the Jews is the historical symbol for the disruption and displacement brought about by the *shevirah*. As Gershom Scholem writes: "This situation of not being where one ought to be, viz. of being removed from one's rightful place, is what is meant by the term 'exile.' In fact, since the breaking of the vessels, exile is the fundamental and exclusive—albeit hidden—mode of all existence. In Lurianism the historical notion of exile had become a cosmic symbol."[12] So, too, spiritual advance must be seen on a cosmic scale. It is *tikkun ha-olam*—healing the world—which in mystical terms is described as the gathering up of the shards of the broken vessels, the divine light caught within them. The rituals and prayers of purification that Ha-Ari devised—what is often called "practical kabbalah"—were means of effecting the *tikkun*. When all is restored to its rightful place, the Messiah will come; his arrival will not deliver our redemption to us, but rather signal that redemption has, through man's spiritual efforts, been achieved.

The majority of the Sephardic exiles were not kabbalists, and they headed not toward Galilee but to the far closer land of Portugal, where history would not wait long to deliver them another of its cruel twists. For though the Inquisition had not yet arrived in this part of the Iberian Peninsula, it soon would, and with equal if not greater ferocity. Manuel I declared, in 1497, a mere five years after the Spanish expulsion, that all his Jewish subjects must be forcibly converted. Not wishing to make the same economically ruinous mistake as the Spanish rulers (whose daughter, Isabella, was his fiancée), Manuel had not given his Jews the opportunity for emigrating. He wanted to extirpate Judaism while retaining the highly lucrative skills and resources of the formerly Jewish. He also decreed, after entreaties from the Sephardim, that he would give the New Christians a period of grace in which to adjust to their new faith; backsliding into Judaism would not be punished until 1527, a period which was then extended to 1534. Practically, this meant that Portuguese crypto-Judaism had some time to evolve its secret practices, and it proved far more tenacious there than in Spain. Also the Portuguese *conversos* were, by definition *annusim*, choosing the traumas of exile from the beloved Sepharad over conversion. Such stalwarts were predisposed toward Marranism.

In fact, a highly complicated culture of fraught subterfuge evolved in Spain and even more intricately in Portugal, an elaborate congeries of masked identities and coded phrases, to be understood only by those who shared the mortal secret. Outward Christian behavior was not what it appeared to be—there are still Spanish Catholics who, before entering a church, mumble a meaningless "incantation" that they were taught to recite by their equally uncomprehending elders, and which linguists have unraveled into a degenerated Hebrew, disavowing the rituals in which the worshipper is about to engage.

The externalities may sometimes have been bogus, but the veiled internality was tenuous as well, its precise content blurring with the years. The crypto-Jews may have disassociated themselves from their assumed identity, but, inevitably, the outward forms seeped inward. The Jewishness they were guarding became unconsciously Christianized, absorbing the symbolism and themes of the Church. As the philosopher Yirmiyahu Yovel describes it: "Religious duality penetrated the consciousness and the subconsciousness of the most ardent Judaizers. Even the Marrano martyrs and heroes were rarely Jews in the conventional sense. The clandestine character of worship, the Catholic education, the lack of Jewish instruction, the mental mixture of faiths, and the isolation from Jewish communities outside Iberia created a special phenomenon in the history and sociology of religion: a form of faith that is neither Christian nor Jewish."[13]

Of course, not all of the *conversos* were stricken by religious duality, at least not consciously. Many, perhaps the majority, were genuine in their conversion, indoctrinating their children in the new faith. Even if the original *conversos* were not motivated by Christian zeal, their offspring, brought up as Catholics, often were. Some became important figures in the history of Christianity itself, important in both conventional and, perhaps even more interestingly, unconventional ways, their torn identity playing a role in the development of Christianity.

St. Teresa of Ávila, for example, the brilliant mystical writer and Carmelite reformer, belonged to a New Christian family, even though many of the Catholic Web sites I've visited list her simply as deriving of Spanish noble stock. It's true that her grandfather, a Toledan merchant named Juan Sánchez de Toledo, transferred his business to Ávila, where he succeeded in having his children marry into families of the nobility, which was a path to which many *conversos* aspired as a way of securing some degree (by no means absolute) of security against the charges of secret Judaizing. The future Catholic saint was born in 1515, twenty-three years after the Great Expulsion. She became one of the *alumbrados*, or illuminated ones, as the Spanish Christian mystics were known. (She was also the teacher of St. John of the Cross, another *alumbrado* and author of *Dark Night of the Soul*.) Her extraordinary personality, as well as the Christian sincerity of her upbringing, can be inferred from this tale of the saint I got from a Catholic Web site: "Her courage and enthusiasm were readily kindled, an early example of which trait occurred when at the age of 7 she left home with her brother Rodrigo with the intention of going to Moorish territory to be beheaded for Christ, but they were frustrated by their uncle, who met the children as they were leaving the city and brought them home (Ephrem de la Madre de Dios, *Tiempo y Vida de Sta. Teresa*)."

St. Teresa's *Interior Castle*, written reluctantly as a guide for her Carmelite Sisters, is one of the classic Christian texts, a masterpiece of mystical literature. The castle, or mansion, as its known in Spanish, is the soul, which has, in her metaphorical vision, seven rooms. Spiritual advance, made through the medium of prayer, is a progressive movement through these rooms, drawing ever nearer to the center of the mansion, which is where one finds unity with God. Teresa makes of spiritual activity an entirely inward private process, the self's communing with itself alone, with all external influences, other than God Himself, rendered irrelevant; and the case can be made that her approach to spirituality has much to do with her *converso* background.[14]

Spinoza, too, will emphasize the entirely inward and self-reliant process of spiritual advancement—though in his case the medium is not prayer but mathematically rigorous reason. It is intriguing to speculate how the Marrano psyche, necessarily oriented inward, found such different expressions in these two spiritual geniuses.

By the 1550s the full force of the Inquisition fell on all *conversos* suspected of Judaizing; and they were *all* suspected. Life was so unendurable, even for those who were faithfully Christian, that some in Portugal returned to Spain, where at least less attention was paid to each and every New Christian. In 1580 the two kingdoms were united, making travel between them easier. And although emigration had been outlawed for them, many *conversos*, whether secret Judaizers or not, tried to escape the Iberian Peninsula. Some left clandestinely, others secured permission to go on business trips from which they never returned, though there was always the fear as to what repercussions would befall relatives left behind. There are even reported cases of *conversos* obtaining permission to make a pilgrimage to the Vatican, and in this way effecting their escape.

By the sixteenth century the term "Portuguese" was simply understood through much of Europe, Asia, and Latin America as meaning Jewish, as more and more New Christians tried to circumvent the laws against immigration. A chosen destination was the city of Amsterdam, whose burghers may not have welcomed the refugees with open arms, but were not inclined to pry into personal religious beliefs, as long as they were praticed with decorum and discretion.

Sephardim began arriving in Amsterdam as early as 1590, some eleven years after the Union of Utrecht (1579) and the birth of the United Provinces of the Netherlands as a Protestant state now independent from Catholic Spain. They didn't openly reveal themselves as Jews for several years. One of the legends is that foreign chanting was heard one night, coming from a darkened house. The Calvinists suspected papists and brought the authorities to investigate. The chanting, however, turned out to be Hebrew, which, though curious, wasn't as threatening to the Protestants as a cadre of Catholics would have been.

In 1614 the Jews were able to purchase some land right outside Amsterdam, in Ouderkerk, as a burial ground. They had to wait until 1615 before Jewish settlement was officially recognized, though outward worship was still forbidden, and the conservative Calvinist clergy were always a hostile force with which to contend. The esteemed legal scholar Hugo Grotius, who had been one of those consulted when the legal status of the newly arrived Jews was being considered, opined that "plainly, God desires them to live somewhere. Why then not here rather than elsewhere? . . . Besides, the scholars among them may be of some service to us by teaching us the Hebrew language." But knowing that the Jews had their share of "atheists and impious people," he demanded the condition that all Jews over the age of fourteen state their faith in God, Moses, the prophets, and the afterlife.

In 1619 the Amsterdam city council officially granted its resident Jews the right to practice their religion, though imposing some restrictions on their economic and political rights and enacting various laws concerning intermarriage and social activities with Christians. They also demanded that the Amsterdam Jews observe Orthodoxy, not deviating from the Mosaic Code, nor from the belief that there is "an omnipotent God the creator, [and] that Moses and the prophets revealed the truth under divine inspiration, and that there is another life after death in which good people will receive their recompense and wicked people their punishment." In other words, the Amsterdam authorities were demanding that their Jews believe at least three of the Thirteen Articles of Faith that Maimonides had articulated. Unlike under the Catholic rulers of the lands they were fleeing, the Dutch Jews now had neighbors who would tolerate their presence just so long as they remained good believing Jews. It had to have been a welcome change, all things considered. Still, such conditions for tolerance aren't entirely reassuring, prodding wounds that hadn't begun to close, reminding people who hardly needed reminding that security is a rare and fragile thing. The Jews of the Netherlands remained a "foreign group" until 1657 (the year following Spinoza's excommunication), when they were finally recognized as subjects of the republic.

But even before recognition of citizenship, they had set about organizing themselves—intensely organizing themselves—into a Jewish community. The Amsterdam Portuguese-Jewish community was the only community of former Marranos that didn't continue for years to hide their religion but practiced openly as soon as they felt they safely could, a testament to the relative tolerance of their Dutch neighbors. Still, as my old teacher Mrs. Schoenfeld had put it in her inimitable way: "Amsterdam was the most tolerant city in all of Europe. But don't think that it was as free as what you girls have come to take for granted here. Don't make the mistake of thinking that it was as tolerant as New York City in 1967."

By 1614, a year before they had any official legal status, the Sephardic community already had two congregations, Beth Jacob (The House of Jacob) and Neve Shalom (Dwelling of Peace). Beth Jacob was meeting in an old warehouse and Neve Shalom, which had raised money to build a synagogue but had been denied its use through the influence of the city's Calvinist clergy, was meeting in a private home. Before long, a controversy within Beth Jacob split the synagogue into two, and a breakaway synagogue, Beth Israel, was the result. The controversy might have revolved around the hiring of a *shokhet*, or ritual slaughterer. The three Amsterdam synagogues would eventually recoalesce into one congregation and build a magnificent edifice, still a showplace today.

It was to be a highly structured community, with head rabbis and rabbinical assistants, *khakhamim*—literally, "wise men"—themselves arranged in hierarchical ordering. Each congregation had its own board of lay governors, the *parnassim*, who had jurisdiction over a great number of issues—business, social, political, judicial, and, trumping the rabbis, even religious. The *parnassim*, for example, set the standards for charitable donations and the koshering of meat. They also made the decisions concerning bans and—their ultimate means of control—writs of excommunication. *Kherem*, which most often was temporary, entailed isolation from the community, and it was employed surprisingly often by Amsterdam's Sephardim, certainly surprising to our contemporary antiauthoritarian sensibilities.

In 1622 a more centralized communal board of governors, the Senhores Deputados, was established, consisting of two *parnassim* from each of the three synagogues, though for the most important decisions all fifteen *parnassim*—the Senhores Quinze—would convene. This highly organized, hierarchical structure might strike one as aspiring toward an approximation of the Catholic Church itself, a Vatican wanna be. That is, I think, how it struck Spinoza, who was to write in the preface of his *Tractatus*:

I have often wondered that men who make a boast of professing the Christian religion, which is a religion of love, joy, peace, temperance, and honest dealing with all men, should quarrel so fiercely and display the bitterest hatred towards one another day by day, so that these latter characteristics make known a man's creed more readily than the former. Matters have long reached such a pass that a Christian, Turk, or Jew or heathen can generally be recognized as such only by his physical appearance or dress, or by his attendance at a particular place of worship, or by his profession of a particular belief and his allegiance to some leader. But as for their way of life, it is the same for all. In seeking the causes of this unhappy state of affairs, I am quite certain that it stems from a wide-spread popular attitude of mind which looks on the ministries of the Church as dignities, its offices as posts of emolument and its pastors as eminent personages.

But however grandiose their ecclesiastical arrangement, the returning Marranos of Amsterdam felt the need to turn to older Sephardic communities, particularly Venice, for guidance. They sought the opinions of the Venetian rabbis when there were interpretations of Law to be decided, controversies to be resolved.

There were to be many controversies. The psychological atmosphere of the community was fraught, to put it mildly. The dark history that the returning Jews brought with them saw to that. The perilous hopes for the religion that had been clung to in secrecy turned, in some, to fierce religiosity, messianic and mystical. In others, it turned to disappointment, disillusion, attempts to argue with the rabbis as to what true Judaism ought to be, sometimes ultimate rejection and a return to Christianity.

Mrs. Schoenfeld had mentioned the sad case of Uriel da Costa, a returning New Jew whose dramatically played-out difficulties in assimilating himself to *halakhic* Judaism sparked a crisis for the community. Though he was, by all accounts, a particularly unstable man—as Mrs. Schoenfeld had put it, *meshugga*—there was something in his constitutional marginality, fated always to be an outside no matter where he turned, that captures the inner turmoil of the community, struggling so hard to lay down a system of double roots, in the soil of the Low Lands and, even deeper, in the body of historical Judaism.

And then of course there was to be the case of Baruch Spinoza, who turned neither to the Christianity his Portuguese ancestors had outwardly practiced, nor to the rabbinical Judaism of *halakha*. Nor was he interested in trying to reform the existing religions, as da Costa had dreamed of doing first with Christianity and then with Judaism, or as St. Teresa of Ávila, yet another *converso*, had managed to accomplish with the Carmelite order of nuns, reforming it so that it answered better to Jesus' vow of poverty and humility.

Instead, Spinoza was to offer something rather new under the seventeenth century's European skies: a religion of reason. His religion asks us to do something that is far more difficult for us than the most severe practices of asceticism. It asks us to be reasonable. It asks us to look at ourselves with unblinking objectivity. It asks us to subdue our natural inclinations toward self-aggrandizement, our attempts to shore up our dreadful fragility by fictions of a God who favors us because we were born—thank God!—into the right group, or have gone through the nuisance of converting to it. And it asks us, as well, to face squarely the terror of our own mortality.

It is the self-deceptive fabrications that emanate out of these two weaknesses in our human nature—self-aggrandizement and death terror, both of them aspects of our own frightening and incurable finitude—that account for the fearsome force of the superstitious forms of religion. "It is fear, then, that engenders, preserves and fosters super-stition," observes Spinoza in the preface of his *Tractatus Theologico-Politicus.* Spinoza distinguishes between religion, which he endorses, and superstitions, which he condemns. Superstitions, as opposed to religion, offer us false cures for our finitude. They make us believe that we are more cosmi-cally important than we are, that we have had bestowed on us—whether Jew, or Christian, or Moslem—a privileged position in the narrative of the world's unfolding. And they make us believe that we can, if we have jumped through the right hoops, live on after our bodily deaths.

There is no privileged access to the truth: this follows from the nature of truth itself. Any viewpoint that denies that we are all, by reason of our very own faculties of reason, in precisely the same position to attain the truth, as well as any of the rewards of consolation that knowing the truth brings, is and must be false.

All things being equal, it is better to believe truly than falsely. But the variety of *superstitious* false beliefs, denying the universal accessibility of truth—the same truth—to all who exercise their faculty of reason, is particularly pernicious. It has delivered unspeakable harm to our species. Superstitions increase rather than diminish the awful suffering to which we are prone by reason of our incurable finitude. These misguided attempts to expand ourselves in the world only succeed in the most violent and painful contractions.

So it was in Spinoza's day, and so it continues into ours. Spinoza could have predicted it. In fact, he did, deducing the weaknesses of our minds from our sorely tried finitude with mathematical rigor.

Yet, even though he deduced our weaknesses, he also tried to save us from them. There is no contradiction. It is the deduction itself that reveals the weaknesses *as* weaknesses. If we follow his reasoning, we will outgrow our tendencies toward skewed points of view.

Strict determinist that he was, Spinoza was no fatalist.

IV

Identity Crisis

Personal identity: What is it that makes a person the very person that she is, herself alone and not another, an integrity of identity that persists over time, undergoing changes and yet still continuing to be—until she does not continue any longer, at least not unproblematically?

I stare at the picture of a small child at a summer's picnic, clutching her big sister's hand with one tiny hand while in the other she has a precarious hold on a big slice of watermelon that she appears to be struggling to have intersect with the small *o* of her mouth. That child is me. But why is she me? I have no memory at all of that summer's day, no privileged knowledge of whether that child succeeded in getting the watermelon into her mouth. It's true that a smooth series of contiguous physical events can be traced from her body to mine, so that we would want to say that her body *is* mine; and perhaps bodily identity is all that our personal identity consists in. But bodily persistence over time, too, presents philosophical dilemmas. The series of contiguous physical events has rendered the child's body so different from the one I glance down on at this moment; the very atoms that composed her body no longer compose mine. And if our bodies are dissimilar, our points of view are even more so. Mine would be as inaccessible to her—just let *her* try to figure out *The Ethics*—as hers is now to me. Her thought processes, prelinguistic, would largely elude me.

Yet she is me, that tiny determined thing in the frilly white pinafore. She has continued to exist, survived her childhood illnesses, the near-drowning in a rip current on Rockaway Beach at the age of twelve, other dramas. There are presumably adventures that she—that is that I—can't undergo and still continue to be herself. Would I then be someone else, or would I just no longer be? Were I to lose all sense of myself—were schizophrenia or demonic possession, a coma or progressive dementia to remove me from myself—would it be I who would be undergoing those trials, or would I have quit the premises? Would there then be someone else, or would there be no one?

Is death one of those adventures from which I can't emerge as myself? The sister whose hand I am clutching in the picture is dead. I wonder every day whether she still exists. A person whom one has loved seems altogether too significant a thing to simply vanish altogether from the world. A person whom one loves *is* a world, just as one knows oneself to be a world. How can worlds like these simply cease altogether? But if my sister does exist, then *what* is she, and what makes that thing that she now is identical with the beautiful girl laughing at her little sister on that forgotten day? Can she remember that summer's day while I cannot?

Personal identity poses a host of questions that are, in addition to being philosophical and abstract, deeply personal. It is, after all, one's very own *person* that is revealed as problematic. How much more personal can it get?

The continued inquisitorial persecution of *conversos* had added yet a new dimension to the mystery of personal identity, merging it with the mystery of Jewish identity. What is it to be Jewish? Is it a matter of creed, of culture, of family or blood—or, as we would now put it, of genes? Having once been Jewish, can one then cease to be Jewish? Or is a Jew essentially a Jew, no matter what religion he might practice or even think himself to be a member of? Was the rejection of Jesus as Christ fated to be repeated, a reversion to type that was embedded in the inherited point of view? Just what sort of an attribute is being Jewish, and how significant is it in constituting the personal identity of those who are Jews?

Jews were not allowed on the Iberian Peninsula. Those who had remained had converted. Were they nevertheless still Jews? Were those who practiced their ever more deformed and Christianized secret Judaism—who spoke of their matzahs as "holy bread," similar to the sacramental host of Mass, and of "St. Esther" as their patron saint—still Jews?[1]

Were those who genuinely gave up their ancestral religion, those who no longer even really knew of it, perhaps weren't even aware of their family history, even so still Jews? Were such ardent believers as St. Teresa of Ávila, who not only gave themselves wholeheartedly to Christianity, but were accepted, even canonized, still incorrigibly Jewish?

Implicit in the constancy of inquisitorial attention is an assumption of ineradicable Jewish essentialism. No matter how sincere the conversion, no matter how devoutly Christian the life, Jewish ancestry branded one as forever suspect.

It was as if certain propositional attitudes—most notably the rejection of Jesus of Galilee as the Messiah—were transmitted in the blood, making true Christian sincerity all but impossible, and for all the generations to come. Recidivism was biologically determined, and the formidable office of the Inquisition was necessary to pry open the outer Christian carapace to reveal the Jewish substance within. A Jew is a Jew is a Jew.

The Marranos were enmeshed in some of the same identity-metaphysics as were their persecutors. For them, too, there was an inviolable fact of the matter concerning true Jewish identity that remained untouched by all outer performance. They may have gone through formal Christian conversions, taken the sacrament, and gone every week to confession, but within the confessional of their inner being they, too, continued to insist on their essential Jewishness.

A Sephardic friend tells me his grandfather used to tell him a joke that perhaps goes back to Marrano times. A Jew has undergone a conversion process, in the course of which the priest has put his hands on the Jew's head and repeated several times, "You were a Jew, now you're Christian, you were a Jew, now you're Christian." A few weeks pass and the priest comes on a Friday to see how his *converso* is getting on. The priest finds, to his shock and dismay, that the New Christian is not eating fish for his Friday night dinner, as he ought to as a good Catholic, but rather a roasted chicken. The Jew, ordered to account for himself, explains that he had simply put his hand on the chicken's head and repeated several times, "You were a chicken, now you're fish, you were a chicken, now you're fish."

Despite the joke, one should not equate the Marrano's notion of private Jewish identity with the Inquisition's essentialist—essentially racist—presupposition. The Marrano's Jewish identity was not so much passively received but actively acquired, even if the activity dare not show itself, requiring precisely the same unobservable inwardness as the fact of Jewishness itself. For the Marrano, the inner avowal of a secret covenant with the nation of Israel, enacted in the inviolable interiority of their own minds, was the very act that made them Jewish. Being Jewish consisted in the private performative act—one was Jewish because one avowed oneself to be.

And, too, the performative act of acknowledging oneself as Jewish also, for the Marrano, effected salvation. Accepting a historical concept of "the chosen people," interpreted in terms of the reception of the Mosaic Code of Law, to acknowledge oneself as Jewish, and thus the recipient of these laws—even if they could not be followed—entailed salvation. Thus their redemption, too, was enacted within the silence of their Judeo-actualizing avowals.

Ironically, the emphasis that they placed on this dichotomous concept of personal "salvation"—one is either saved or one is not—is itself Christian, and an indication of how far from historical Judaism their understanding had strayed. Jews do not traditionally possess such an all-or-nothing concept of personal salvation as is prominent in Christianity. The dichotomous concept of personal salvation is connected, too, with a certain view of personal identity. The very person who one is is changed with the passing from being unsaved to saved. There is a radical discontinuity between the person one was and the person one has become (the born-again). Applying the Christian concept of salvation to their Jewish predicament, the Marranos located their salvation in the acceptance of the Laws of Moses. As the Christian is saved by accepting Jesus as his Savior, so the Marrano was saved by accepting the hegemony over him of the Laws of Moses, as transmitted to his ancestors.

But of course those Laws could not be outwardly followed, though many went to dangerous lengths to perform some small ritual of Jewish significance. So there was, for example, the Marrano "trick" of hanging a statue of the Madonna on the doorpost of one's house and placing within her foot the prayer of the *Shema*—*Hear, O Israel, the Lord is our God, the Lord is One!*—so that the Marrano could transform the Madonna into a *mezuzah*, to be kissed upon entering and leaving their homes, as religious Jews will kiss the *mezuzah*.

But the freedom to fulfill the Mosaic Laws was, to say the least, subject to severe limitations—male circumcision, for example, was obviously out of the question—and over the years the content of the Laws dimmed. Salvation consisted, more and more, in the inner acknowledgment of these outwardly unperformable Laws. What was performed was one's acknowledgment of "them," whatever they were. It was the line of historical causal continuity between the event at Sinai and the personal acknowledgment now that meant that the Laws one acknowledged—even if they could not be performed, even if one did not retain the knowledge of how they ought to be performed—were still the Laws of Moses holding sway over one's will.

The Marrano insisted on an essential Jewish adherence preserved within a Christian life, and this created a dilemma for the rabbis of the time. The rabbinical responsa of the time from outside Iberia are filled with painful discussions of particular Marrano cases. Does the inward avowal of distorted "Mosaic Law" make a *converso*, who goes to church and prays outwardly to the Father, the Son, and the Holy Ghost, a Jew? The Trinity seem to be, on the face of it, a negation of the holy words of the *Shema: the Lord is One!* Insofar as it is a deviation from monotheism, it is *avodah zorah*, idol worship. The Talmud teaches that in general, life being holy, *halakha* can be sacrificed in order to save one's life. However, there are three sins so serious that a Jew must die rather than transgress them. These are forbidden sex, murder, and idol worship. Many rabbis deemed the Trinity a form of idolatry and therefore saw Marranism as an unjustifiable alternative to martyrdom. And if, as many rabbis believed, it is the *practice* of the Law that make a Jew a Jew, then in what sense could the Marranos be Jews? Their predicament was tragic, but compassion could not, at least for some of the rabbis in the debate, override *halakha*.

The Inquisition gave prominence to the question of Jewish identity. In its cruelest interpretation, the Inquisition insisted that Jewishness is part of the personal identity of the Jew, and one that is passed on through the blood. There was no outward act that would transform the substantive essence. Wafers and wine could be transformed into the flesh and the blood of Christ, but no rite or ritual could turn a Jew into a Christian.

In the 1630s there were again a rash of accusations in Portugal that the *conversos* were crypto-Judaizers, and that they were trying to convert Old Christians, particularly their Christian servants. The inquisitor of Llerena wrote in 1628 or soon thereafter, "From the moment of its conception, every fetus permanently carries with it the moral attributes—in the case of the Marranos, the moral depravity—of its parents."[2] This was not a new idea in Portugal. The sermons preached on the occasion of autos-da-fé throughout the fifteenth century often stressed the immutability of the Jews, a moral trait passed on from generation to generation.

The former *conversos* who came to Amsterdam brought with them the interwoven preoccupations with Jewish identity and personal identity that the Inquisition had forced on them. While the rash of accusations were going on in Portugal, *conversos* kept arriving, leaving relatives and friends behind.

In the relative freedom of Protestant Amsterdam, the former Marranos set about organizing themselves into the kind of community required for the full performance of the *halakha* from which they had been severed. At first, rabbis had to be imported to instruct them, though they soon started producing their own; a model school was organized; an elaborate hierarchical system was erected for guidance as well as for chastisement.

But the old painful dilemmas would not so easily be laid to rest; how could they possibly be when the trauma had gone so deep and those who walked the streets of the Vlooienburg and the Breestraat had New Christian friends and relatives in Portugal still kept under the ever watchful eye of the Inquisition? The Jews of Amsterdam—especially those whose unorthodoxy brought them into conflict with the rabbis—were themselves still objects of pointed interest to the Church, and inquisitorial spies walked among the Dutch Sephardim.

In fact, we owe what scant knowledge we have of Spinoza himself during the period that had been known as his "lost years"—the four years between his excommunication and his known fraternization with various dissenting Christians, known collectively as the Collegiants—to investigative diggings in the records of the Inquisition by the historian Israel Révah. Révah discovered reports on the young Spinoza from two different sources. One was a Latin-American Augustinian monk, Friar Tomás Solanao y Robles, who had visited Amsterdam in late 1658 and voluntarily reported to the Madrid Inquisition upon his return. He volunteered the information to clear himself of any suspicion he may have attracted by traveling in non-Catholic lands. And then on the following day, a report was filed, this time upon request, by a Spanish soldier, Captain Miguel Pérez de Maltranilla.[3] Spinoza's surfacing to light from out of the medieval murk of the inquisitorial files of the Church—which still, apparently, considered his soul of their concern, since he was the offspring of *conversos*, and so, in its eyes, still Christian—underscores the anachronistic audacity of Spinoza's choice: to define his life on his terms, not as a heterodox Jew or Christian. But it underscores, as well, how vividly present the powerful and hidden forces of the Inquisition remained in the lives of the community—even in the life of the banished of the community, in a heretic Jew like Spinoza.

The obsession with the questions of who is a Jew, what is

a Jew, can a person be un-Judaized, re-Judaized—all of these questions intertwined with the Marrano preoccupation with redemptive possibilities—would have been, one imagines, like an incessant nervous murmur registering just below audibility, a constant discordant accompaniment to conversations in homes and streets and synagogues, as well as in the inner recesses of unquiet minds. Sometimes the murmur would break out into painfully articulated communal conflicts and contretemps, ripping apart whatever façade of placid Dutch burghers they might have been trying to assume.

The case of Uriel da Costa, in the 1620s when Spinoza was a child, had been one such crisis that had lain uneasily on the collective conscience. His is a tragic, if also controversial, example of the confusions and disillusions that accompanied the attempt to be reintegrated into historical Judaism. The internal aspects of Spinoza's story, so to speak—a sense of the experiences and reflections that led up to his break with his close-knit community and of how he felt about the treatment he received—are hard to come by, Spinoza himself maintaining the perfect high-minded disregard for the merely personal that is consistent with the impersonal point of view that he champions. In contrast, da Costa left behind an achingly personal testament, which he entitled *Exemplar humanae vitae*, documenting—though in a biased and not altogether reliable manner—his troubled relationship with the Amsterdam community, which would twice excommunicate him. The *Examplar* was, in a sense, his suicide note.

Uriel da Costa had been baptized Gabriel, born in Oporto, Portugal. His father was a devout Catholic, but his mother came from a *converso* family and, as the work of recent historians has unearthed, most likely observed some of the secret rites of Marranism. Gabriel studied canon law at the University of Coimbra and was a church treasurer. Da Costa described himself as having become disillusioned with Christianity. In studying and comparing the New Testament with the Five Books of Moses, he found contradictions and reached the conclusion that Judaism, from which Christianity had sprung, presented the authentic experience, with Christianity a corruption of it. He also confessed that Christianity's emphasis on hell's damnation terrified him. Soon both he and his five brothers were inwardly identifying themselves as Jewish. After the death of their Catholic father, the six boys, together with their mother, Banca, determined to leave Portugal.

He presents himself as having voluntarily left Portugal for the freedom to practice Judaism openly, but the historian Israel Révah, researching the records of the Oporto Inquisition, found that, unsurprisingly, the *converso* had attracted the attention of the office of the Inquisition, which was preparing a devastating case against him, so his emigration was most likely not simply a spiritual journey but an attempt to escape with his life.

Once in Amsterdam, da Costa found that the Judaism being practiced there did not live up to his expectations. The departures from the pristine ancient religion of Moses were, in his eyes, unjustifiable extensions of God's direct revelations. The accretions of rabbinical ordinances and Talmudic rulings, the codification of the so-called Oral Law, offended da Costa's construction of what Judaism ought to be. The organized hierarchical religion of the rabbis was as much a corruption of the original Mosaic Code as was Catholicism, and da Costa set about single-handedly to reform it, to purify it of all its post-Mosaic content. As the historian Yirmiyahu Yovel points out, we must read *Examplar* with several grains of salt. It is highly dubious that da Costa believed that "the religion of Moses had been petrified for over two millennia, waiting for Uriel da Costa to perform an unhistorical leap into it. However vaguely and unwillingly, da Costa was aware that post-biblical Judaism was different from the original model. But he hoped and believed that the fluid New Jewish situation offered a historical opportunity to remedy this. . . . Da Costa expected that (unlike the Catholicism of which he had despaired) Judaism *could* lend itself to a purifying reform in the original direction of the Bible, especially within the New Jewish communities where, out of a minimal and shattered basis, former Marranos were trying to reconstruct a Jewish life for themselves. Since these New Jews were already engaged in an effort to recapture their lost essence, they may as well have regressed further back to their origins and restored the purer biblical Judaism that elsewhere had been obliterated."[4]

Needless to say, his efforts did not find favor with the rabbis of Amsterdam, who were charged with the task of transporting the former Marranos back to the *halakhic* Judaism from which history had separated them.

Da Costa reacted with fury to the intransigence of the religious authorities of the community, and in search of a more authentic Judaism left Amsterdam for the Sephardic community of Hamburg, which did not respond any more favorably to his reforming ideas than Amsterdam had. In 1616 he composed a set of eleven theses attacking what he called "the vanity and invalidity of the traditions and ordinances of the Pharisees." He claimed that the rabbis, in equating Talmudic interpretations with the Torah, "make the word of man equal to that of God."

On August 14, 1618, da Costa was put in *kherem* by the chief rabbi of Venice, Rabbi Leon de Medina, who was the teacher of the chief rabbi of Amsterdam, Rabbi Morteira. He was also put under a ban in Hamburg, and returned to Amsterdam, still fighting. He committed his protest to writing, publishing in 1624 his feisty *Exame das tradições phariseas* (Examination of the Pharisaic Traditions), which objects to such laws as male circumcision, the laying on of tefillin, or phylacteries, and also vehemently protests the extrabiblical inclusion of the doctrine of immortality and divine retribution. This doctrine, he confesses, was precisely what had driven him from Catholicism. "In truth, the most distressful and wretched time in my life was when I believed that eternal bliss or misery awaited man and that according to his works he would earn that bliss or that misery." He was terrified by the eschatological metaphysics and found peace only when he realized the absurdity of the claim that the soul might survive the death of the body, since the soul is only an aspect of the body, the vital source that animates it and also accounts for rationality. It thus has as little possibility of surviving the death of the body as has any other corporeal part, da Costa argued, and any religion that claims otherwise is founded on error. Biblical Judaism makes no such claim: "The first proof is an *argumentum ex silentio*: the Law nowhere indicates that the human soul is immortal or that another life, whether of punishment or glory, awaits it." In fact, he claims that the whole thrust of the Bible's message points to the mortality of the soul: "Once he is dead, nothing remains of a man, neither does he ever return to life." Those who pursue virtue with an eye to the afterlife delude themselves with superstition. "It is in this life that the righteous and the wicked receive their just deserts. . . . Let no one be so stupid and mad as to believe otherwise."

The rabbis of Amsterdam responded by placing the would-be reformer under their own ban of excommunication: "Seeing that through pure obduracy and arrogance he persists in his wickedness and wrong opinions, the delegates from the three boards of elders, together with the boards of warders and the consent of the *khakhamim*, ordained he be excluded as a person already excommunicated [i.e., in Venice and Hamburg] and accursed of God, and that . . . no communication with him is henceforth permitted to anyone except his brothers, who are granted eight days to wind up their affairs with him." Nor was this all. Da Costa reports that the "senators and rulers of the Jews" lodged a complaint against him with the public magistrate, charging him with the heresy of publishing a book purporting to disprove the mortality of the soul, and he was arrested and thrown in prison for ten days, until his brothers bailed him out. His book was publicly burned. Once he was excommunicated, no Jews were allowed to have anything more to do with him, even his brothers, on pain of being placed in *kherem* themselves. Only his old mother, who had changed her name to Sarah upon arriving in Amsterdam, stood by him, so that she, too, was placed in *kherem*. In fact, the Amsterdam rabbis wrote for *halakhic* advice to the Venetian rabbis as to whether she should be allowed to be buried in the Jewish cemetery. "Therefore we desire from you in case she dies in this time of resistance if we could let her lay on the soil without burying her at all or should we bury her in consideration of her honorable sons [Uriel's brothers]." On October 4, 1628, a "Sara de Costa" was buried in the Beth-Chaim cemetery at Ouderkerk, indicating what the Venetian *pasak*, or ruling, had been.

But the community was under rabbinical orders to regard the religious renegade as a pariah. Da Costa writes in the *Examplar* that even children mocked him on the streets and threw stones at his windows. Nevertheless, da Costa did not absent himself from the community. Of course, he was already under *kherem* in Venice and Hamburg, and he must have reasoned that wherever he went Jewish communities would find him intolerable. But interestingly, even though he had reached the intellectual conclusion that Judaism, like Christianity, was but a man-made system arising out of man's needs, and that the true religion was deism—the belief, based solely on reason and not revelation, in a God who created the universe and then left it to its own devices, assuming no control over life and never intervening in the course of history or of natural phenomena—still, on an emotional level, da Costa seemed incapable of taking leave of Judaism, or at least of the Jewish community. He lived among the Amsterdam Sephardim as a despised individual, clinging to the margins of a world that had become for him an open narcissistic wound. Yet he did not simply pick himself up and quit Jewish life decisively. Though the Jews had excommunicated him he was not prepared to excommunicate the Jews. His disinclination to think of himself as outside the religious community is telling and casts a dramatic contrast with Spinoza.

In 1633, da Costa sought reconciliation with the Jewish rabbis, using a cousin as an intermediary, and succeeded in having his *kherem* lifted by outwardly recanting his views. Since his inward beliefs remained at variance with the community's, his recantation amounted to a reenactment of the Marrano experience, only now within the community of former Marranos. He writes in the *Examplar* that he resolved to live "like an ape among apes." But sometimes, apparently, his mimicry fell short. A nephew who lived with him found his preparation of meat to be not in accord with Jewish ritual and told other family members, including the formerly helpful cousin, who, feeling betrayed, became, at least according to da Costa's account, da Costa's sworn enemy, interceding wherever he could, in business and personal affairs, to ruin Uriel's life, including stepping in to prevent a marriage.

A short time later, still under suspicion, Uriel was asked for advice by two Christians who claimed that they were interested in converting to Judaism. One of the conditions on which the Sephardim had been granted permission to live in Amsterdam was that they not proselytize among the Christians in an attempt to convert them. Da Costa, as we can well imagine, certainly had little reason to encourage outsiders to enter the community in which he himself felt like an outsider, and apparently he dissuaded the Christians, but perhaps in terms that were too vehement. He made them promise not to report his words to the rabbis, but they did, and once again he was excommunicated; this time his ostracism lasted for seven years.

In 1640, unable to endure the situation any longer, he reapproached the rabbis for readmittance. The rabbis wanted to make sure that this time he really meant it and tested his resolve by putting him through a ceremony of public humiliation. Within the synagogue, before the whole assembled congregation, his stripped back was given thirty-nine lashes, and then he was made to lie down across the threshold so that every member of the congregation could tread on his prone figure as they exited the synagogue. The ceremony seemed to have taken a terrible toll, depriving this proud man (his extreme pride echoes throughout his last testament) of his remaining dignity: the dignity before himself. He writes that it was no longer possible to live with himself, a phrase that has particular resonance for the Marrano—which da Costa still essentially was, even though he lived in Jewish Amsterdam—whose only refuge was the inner sanctum of his own self. He wrote his autobiography, from which I have largely been quoting, and then set out to kill both his cousin and himself. The pistol he aimed at his cousin in the street misfired, so that he didn't succeed in becoming a murderer, but the gun worked when he fired it into his own skull. Onlookers report that his death was terrible.

Uriel da Costa, not surprisingly, has inspired several works of fiction, including a play by the German writer Karl Gutzkow, penned in 1846, in the midst of the liberal upsurge that led to the revolutions of 1848. He is presented there in the terms in which he wrote about his own life, a casualty of religious intolerance. The play *Uriel Acosta* (Acosta was the family name in Portugal) was, significantly, the first classic play translated into Yiddish, first produced in Odessa in 1881, shortly after the assassination of Tsar Alexander II, and it became a standard in the Yiddish theater's repertoire, both in Europe and on New York's Second Avenue.

In 1640, when the da Costa scandal reached its violent climax, Baruch Spinoza was a child of eight, already exposed to personal loss; his mother had died of tuberculosis when he was six. Obviously, the children of the community were well aware of the opprobrium in which the unorthodox man was held, the authorized disapprobation licensing their own childish games of cruelty. An eight-year-old boy, studious and quiet, given to reflecting on things for himself, to pondering the words of the grown-ups, not taking them on authority necessarily; a solemn child, I would imagine, always trying to puzzle out the truth for himself, caring ardently about the truth—and not only the truth about God and the Torah, and the Jewish people, but about people as well. Spinoza's *Ethics* reveals a mind that is not only an abstract systematizer on the grandest of scales, but also one that is fascinated by human nature in all its variety, directing its unblinking gaze into the subtleties of motivations. Yes, he was only eight, but habits of mind, orientations of attention, start early. What, one wonders, did Spinoza make of the excommunicated da Costa? Did his memory of the man's ruin, the crazed rage and loathing that ended his life, guide him toward his very different reaction when, some mere fifteen years later, the rabbis would turn their disapproval on him?

Da Costa's public drama of torn identity helps one to draw a little closer to the private Spinoza. The memory of this man's torment of marginality must have made an impression on the boy. Still, there was another communal crisis that might take us even further toward understanding Spinoza. This one involved a theological controversy that grew into a major rabbinical dispute, once again requiring the intercession of the rabbis of Venice. Two of the rabbis of the community, Rabbi Morteira and Rabbi Aboab, clashed with each other over an issue that reached down into the community's distinctive preoccupations with issues of identity and salvation.

Spinoza was only four years old when the theological controversy reached its denouement, so it is not so much a matter of his having taken in, and remembering, the specifics of that situation. Rather, it is that the rabbinical controversy yields a glimpse into the soul of the community in which Spinoza was raised, a sort of rich group portrait, as revealing as one of the celebrated psychological canvases painted by Rembrandt. Perhaps the group portrait will afford a glimpse of the elusive figure, who stands off to the side, barely visible in the shadows.

Somehow he managed to break away from the intense life of that community, to stand aloof, rendering himself utterly indifferent to its judgment of him, an attitude that the unfortunate da Costa could never achieve. But his aloofness extended much further than toward his own community.

Spinoza's aloofness is absolute. In all of Western philosophy, he is the most singular and solitary.

In 1635–36 there were three different synagogues in Amsterdam's Sephardic community, the triangulation the result of disputes and factionalizing familiar to anyone who has ever been involved in Jewish communal life. Rabbi Morteira was the chief rabbi of Beth Jacob. He had been brought to Amsterdam from Venice when he was only twenty to serve the community and educate them in *halakhic* Judaism. Though Rabbi Morteira had become fluent in Portuguese, he was not of the same background as his congregants. He was Ashkenazic; contemporary sources speak of his Germanic origin. Though he must, of necessity, have attained some insight into the complex inner world of the former Marrano, he was emotionally not of that world. He saw his obligation as that of educating these former Marranos, often applying a somewhat stern hand in ridding them of the Christianized customs and concepts that had become encrusted onto their understanding of Judaism. Some might call him authoritarian. He was a learned man, a Talmudic scholar, who founded the yeshiva Keter Torah and taught the advanced course in Talmud there. His orientation was rationalistic and philosophical, in the Maimonidean mode. In fact, he refers to Maimonides as "the leading spokesman."[5]

Morteira's rationalistic approach to Judaism is noteworthy. There were certainly other currents in Amsterdam. In particular, the messianic mysticism of Lurianic kabbalah had stirred up some of the deepest yearnings across the lands of the Diaspora, and Amsterdam was no exception. The Mar-

Rabbi Saul Levi Morteira

rano experience had perhaps disposed these returning Jews toward a particular susceptibility to the Lurianic narrative of redemptive history. One can understand how the kabbalistic message, especially as transformed through Lurianism into a tale woven around the theme of exile, of the light that had been lost in the great shattering and was slowly being returned to its rightful place, would resonate for the Sephardic Jews of Amsterdam. They had a terrifyingly intimate experience of exile's cruelty and were now in the process of restoring what had been smashed in their national and family histories. Their gathering together, to reidentify as Jews among the tolerant Dutch, must have seemed like a sort of pale reflection of the final *tikkun ha-olam* to which they seemed to be drawing nearer. It was true that the Inquisition's horrors still continued in the lands they had fled, and that family members and friends that they had left there were still caught within the maws of the exile's violence. Still, the narrative of Lurianism provided the means for a hopeful interpretation of even these dark circumstances. Then, too, the mystical tradition was entwined in their history. It had flowered in Gerona and then been exiled, to take root again in the hills of Safed. Luria himself was of both Ashkenazic and Sephardic lineage, and most of those in his inner circle were Spanish Jews. The kabbalah's evolution had been shaped by the history of Spain's Jews.

Rabbi Morteira, by both inculcation (his teacher in Venice was the antimystical Leon de Medina) and inclination, was of a nonmystical cast. Though he was not oblivious, of course, to the mystical leanings of many in the community, including some of his rabbinical colleagues, in his opinion the classical rabbinic sources were "the only trustworthy Kabbala." The other two prominent rabbis in the Amsterdam community were far more touched by the spirit that had emanated out from Safed. Perhaps not coincidentally, both these rabbis were Sephardic, and had in fact been born in the lands of the Inquisition.

Manasseh ben Israel (1604–57), who has already been mentioned several times, was born in Madeira, a Portuguese colony off the coast of Africa, where he had been baptized Manuel Diaz Soeiro. His father, Gaspar Rodrigues Nuñez, had been a penitent at an auto-da-fé, and the family had fled Lisbon when they got word that he was about to be re-arrested as a Judaizer. Upon arriving in Amsterdam, Gaspar renamed himself Joseph ben Israel. He renamed his two sons Ephraim and Manasseh. Ephraim and Manasseh were the sons of the biblical Joseph, and a traditional blessing for parents and teachers to bestow on their children is "May God make you like Ephraim and Manasseh."

Manassah ben Israel's Judaism was strongly messianic. When he became convinced that the Lost Ten Tribes of Israel had been discovered among the natives in South America, he saw this supposed event in terms of the narrative of redemption. According to kabbalistic tradition, the Jews had to be dispersed to the four corners of the world before the Messiah could come. Now that the lost tribes had been located in the Americas, there remained only one country that was devoid of the Jewish presence: England, since the exile of Jews was still in effect there. (Apparently, he considered the New Christians who resided in the inquisitorial lands to be Jews.) It was on this messianic theory that he entered into negotiations with Oliver Cromwell to allow Jews back into England, so that the dispersal could be completed, the path paved for the Messiah. He made a trip to England in 1655, submitting his petition to Cromwell, who was impressed with the rabbi, although formal permission for a return wasn't granted. (As a consequence of this trip, Manasseh ben Israel was not present when Spinoza was excommunicated.)

Manasseh ben Israel was the most worldly among the three rabbis, though his place in the rabbinical hierarchy of

Amsterdam was not the highest. His sphere of interests brought him into contact with many Christians. He was well-published, and one work in particular, *El Conciliador*, which attempts to reconcile seeming contradictions within the Bible, gained him a substantial reputation among Christian scholars.

Another rabbi of the community was Isaac Aboab da Fonseca (1605–93), and it was he who had been most directly and deeply imbued with the spirit of Lurianic kabbalah, which he transmitted to the young men who studied with him, so that a significant number of them also claimed themselves as disciples of the esoteric tradition. The rabbi had been baptized Simão da Fonseca in Castro Daire, Portugal, and the family had fled when he was a child, first to France and then to Amsterdam. He was a disciple of the only kabbalist to have written in Spanish, Abraham Herrera (c. 1570–1635), who was also of a Marrano family and born in Portugal. Herrera's studies of Neoplatonism, as it was taught in the Florentine Academy, together with his studies of Lurianic kabbalah (which also, as was pointed out above, has a strong Neoplatonic cast, inherited from the original kabbalists of Gerona), resulted in his own synthesis. Aboab translated into Hebrew such works of Herrera's as his *Puerta del cielo* (Gates of Heaven), and these translations were in Spinoza's library at his death, presenting once again the tantalizing suggestion that Spinoza's own strongly Platonic orientation, most especially the focus on salvation, which sets him apart from his rationalist confreres Descartes and Leibniz, might have been transmitted to him by way of the kabbalist influence. Interestingly, Herrera also wrote a treatise on logic,

Epítome y compendio de la lógica o dialéctica, which was his only published work.

Aboab's absorption of Lurianic kabbalah, as refiltered through Herrera, left him with a conception of Judaism sharply in contrast with Morteira's, for where Morteira cites the traditional rabbinical authorities as the final word on all matters *halakhic* and theological, Aboab maintains the hegemony of the esoteric tradition. Kabbalah, he asserted, yields the only definitive authority for interpretation of rabbinical dicta. The philosophical approach of Maimonides, whom

Rabbi Isaac Aboab (*Courtesy of The Jewish Museum, London*)

Morteira cites as the final word on the more philosophical aspects of Judaism, did not impress Aboab: "We have no dealings with Maimonides as far as this subject is concerned, for he discussed it from the aspect of philosophical inquiry, and not from the aspect of Kabbalah." Furthermore, he claimed that no one was in a position to interpret kabbalah unless he had been initiated into the esoteric tradition by a qualified teacher who was himself a link in that tradition. Aboab claimed his place here since his teacher Abraham Herrera had received Luria's teachings from Israel Sarug, who was a disciple of Luria's disciple Hayyim Vital.

The rabbinical controversy that broke out in Spinoza's boyhood involved the two rabbis Morteira and Aboab. It was a controversy that had wide implications, pitting the mystical approach to Judaism against the rationalistic, and also revealing the painfully deep and divergent responses to the situation in Iberia, the Jewish tragedy of the New Christians that constantly plagued the mind of the Portuguese Nation of Amsterdam.

In its narrow specifics the argument revolved around the interpretation of a saying in the Mishnah (Sanhedrin 2:1): "All Israelites have a share in the world-to-come." Rabbi Morteira had become distressed by a new doctrine that had caught fire among some of the impressionable young. Citing this statement in the Talmud as their slogan, and claiming the kabbalah as their source of its interpretation, they proclaimed that all Jews, no matter how grave their sins, would partake in the bliss of the afterlife. They dismissed or altogether ignored the Mishnah's own qualifications to the statement, as well as those of classical rabbinic sources, insisting instead that the kabbalah superceded all other interpretations, and the kabbalah proclaims the thesis of universal Jewish salvation.

This cavalier attitude toward rabbinical authority—an attitude that had no doubt often tried Rabbi Morteira's Orthodox patience—proved too much this time. After all, if all Jews, no matter their behavior, were ipso facto guaranteed eternal bliss, what would be the motivation for becoming better Jews? The chief rabbi of Beth Jacob regarded the revisionist eschatology as "a rock of offense and stone of stumbling dressed up as Kabbalah." He took his stand, preaching a sermon in which he quoted a passage from the Talmud (*Rosh Ha-Shana* 17a) that affirms the eternality of punishment in hell for such grave offenders as *minim*, or informers, and *apikorsim*, or heretics. He embellished with copious quotations from other sources supporting the damnation of Israel's sinners. The Mishnah did not mean by "Israelite" anyone who had been born into the nation of Israel; rather, it had meant righteous person. It is not the case that someone born of Jewish origins is saved no matter how his life is lived.

Rabbi Morteira's sermon on the eternality of punishment provoked "cries of indignation" from a contingent of Aboab's students who were in the synagogue and whom Rabbi Morteira described, in his complaints to the Venetian rabbis from whom he was seeking advice in dealing with the incendiary situation, as "young rebels," and "immature disciples," who had been "corrupted by Kabbalists." Their "cries of indignation," in Morteira's words, were such that he had been forced "in my anguish . . . to admit as controversial a perfect doctrine of our faith which we received from our Fathers, the Prophets, the *Tanna'im* [those who wrote the Mishnah] and the *Amora'im* [those who wrote the Gemarah, the commentary on the Mishnah] and which, permitting no doubt, was upheld by the more recent authorities."

For their part, the "young rebels" professed themselves scandalized by a doctrine that, they claimed, was reminiscent of Christianity. "By believing in the eternality of sin and punishment we support the religion of the Christians who say that Adam's sin was eternal and that, on this account, only God, who is eternal, could make atonement for it by incarnation and death." They requested from the community's lay authorities, the *parnassim*, that an injunction be placed against the rabbi's preaching of eternal punishment.

The subtext of this debate was, unsurprisingly, the Marrano situation. The young kabbalists' interpretation of "Israelite" was sufficiently wide to extend to the Marranos still living on the Iberian Peninsula, whose identity as Jews consisted in nothing more than the internal performative act of declaring themselves Jews. The opponents of eternal punishment clearly had the New Christians in mind, arguing that God's compassion must extend to them, and also arguing that the New Christians would have no reason for becoming observant Jews if Judaism, too, offered no remedy for Catholicism's harsh eschatology. And Rabbi Morteira also had the Marranos in mind in making his case for the opposite thesis. What reason would the Marranos have for leaving behind all their goods and their often comfortable positions in society, to seek out circumstances in which they could become fully integrated halakhic observers, if they were guaranteed eternal bliss in any case? In addition, Morteira contended that one should teach in public only what the classical rabbinic sources had pronounced. It was a "criminal offence" to contradict their "splendid tradition-ally received words." The mishnaic statement "All Israelites have a share in the world to come" could not be regarded as an unconditional "absolute verdict."

Then, too, the unfortunate Uriel da Costa, still clinging pitifully to the margins of the community, presented a vivid exhibit for both sides of the debate. He had stressed that it was precisely the terror provoked by Catholicism's vision of eternal damnation that had turned him away from Chris-tianity, so that those who argued for Judaism's promise of salvation might point to him as support. But, too, da Costa had demonstrated the tendency of the returning Marrano to bend the complicated structure of redacted Judaism to his own personal desiderata.

It was after the "immature disciples" had appealed to the *parnassim*, and apparently staged a few more protests in Rabbi Morteira's synagogue, that the tried rabbi wrote to the older community of Venice, seeking their counsel.

So far, Rabbi Aboab had kept a low profile, but it soon became clear on behalf of whom the young rebels were protesting, and to whom Rabbi Morteira had been referring when he described them as corrupted by "Kabbalists." Rabbi Aboab was himself a young man then, barely thirty, and his rapport with his young students, as well as the always intriguing promise of initiation into esoteric secrets, no doubt made for a heady experience. One young disciple declared that he himself wished to have the soul of Jeroboam, son of Nebat, having perhaps heard from Aboab the kabbalistic belief that Jeroboam was to be reincarnated as the Messiah. Jeroboam, the first king of the ten tribes of Israel, after the split from the kingdom of Judah, became the prototype of the wicked king, having introduced golden calf idols into his kingdom, so that the expression "evil like Jeroboam" was not uncommon. The traditional version of this chapter in ancient Jewish history is that Jeroboam's sins were realized in the utter desolation of the kingdom of Israel, with the result that the ten tribes that had composed it were carried away as slaves and disappeared from the world as Israelites. The restoration of Jeroboam—as the Messiah no less!—was an ardent symbol of the ingathering toward salvation that was at the heart of Lurianic kabbalism, and one which one might expect reverberated for the newly Judaized former *conversos*, who had been in danger, too, of entirely disappearing from the world as Jews. Then, too, the moral transfiguration involved in iconic evil becoming iconic goodness reinforced the redemptive promise held out in the kabbalah's reading of history.

The Beth Din (Rabbinical Court) of Venice did not want to get involved in this particular controversy, preferring that the Amsterdam community work things out for itself both as a sign of its growing independence and because they did not want to confuse the congregants by making it appear that a Beth Din needed to issue a ruling on an issue that they, too, along with Rabbi Morteira, considered to be part of the codified theology of Judaism. And so, instead of taking on the issue, they wrote to Rabbi Aboab with finessed diplomacy. They launched their appeal by first extolling him for the impressive scholarship of which they'd heard tell, which had long prompted them to desire his friendship. God had willed that he now be presented with the opportunity to demonstrate his leadership by suppressing the revisionist views that had been disseminating among the impressionable youth. "We were hoping for the day that would bring the message of peace . . . but our expectation has been frustrated. For we were again informed that the conflict persists and that the spokesman of those denying the belief in the eternality of punishment is none other than you." They took solace, they continued, pursuing the vein of ecclesiastical tact, in the fact that the person who led the recalcitrant group was a God-fearing Jew, and thus could be counted on to heed the wisdom of Proverbs 12:15: "He that is wise hearkeneth unto counsel." They advised him to convene a public forum in which he could announce his change of mind, saying that he would best know how to phrase his recantation and how to warn the group against venturing rash opinions on subjects of this kind. And they made explicit reference to the Marrano situation that lurked, for all of them, behind the Talmudic altercation, stating that the warning was particularly appropriate to "those of our people who came from those places," that is, Marranos, who "should seek only one thing, namely the way how to serve God in sincerity and how to fulfill the *mitzvoth* according to *Halakha* in all their minutiae."

The young rabbi's response to the delicately worded appeal of the Venetian rabbis was his defiantly fiery tract *Nishmat Hayyim* (literally, "Souls of Life"). (Rabbi Manasseh ben Israel would in 1651 publish a book of that name as well, having brought out, in 1631, a tripartite treatise on the Resurrection of the Dead in both Latin and Spanish.) That he had written such an unpublished Hebrew manuscript had long been known, but it is only recently that it has been brought to light, and published, together with commentary, by Alexander Altmann, from whose fascinating article "Eternality of Punishment: A Theological Controversy Within the Amsterdam Rabbinate in the Thirties of the Seventeenth Century" I have largely been drawing.

Aboab's manuscript opens on a note of brazen defiance, before those rabbinical authorities who had pulled rank on him in an effort to muzzle him: "Truly speaking, matters of this kind have been entrusted only to the Kabbalists, illumined as they are by the light of truth." The tone of defiance continues throughout. There follows an ardent attack on the sterilities of rationalistic philosophy, of the Maimonidean sort, those who "lean upon a broken reed" and are unqualified to interpret the profound utterances of the rabbis. Aboab asserts that though he was young in years (thirty in 1636, which was when, Altmann argues, the manuscript must have been written), the true "elder" was the one who had acquired wisdom, and in this respect he was older than his opponents, who became more foolish as they advanced in years. Most importantly, as a kabbalist, he claimed to know certain truths of an esoteric nature that put an entirely new and different complexion on things. If those truths had been withheld from the uninitiated in the past, the time had now come to disabuse people's minds of a notion of God that is contrary to His known attributes of justice and mercy. The kabbalah, of course, never contradicts the laws of the Torah, since all sacred texts derive from the same divine source, but it is kabbalah that reveals their secret significance. In particular, the Lurianic message of restoration, the righting of the cosmic unbalance of the *shevirah*, the shattering of the vessels, is seen as running throughout the Torah's commandments and prohibitions. All the laws of restitution and return bespeak the great mystery of the final *tikkun ha-olam*: such laws as those regarding the return of lost property; the laws of the Jubilee year, when the crops are left unharvested in the fields; of the healing of the leper and the cleansing of the house upon which a plague had been pronounced—all these and other commandments serve as the practical symbols for the ultimate salvation that is promised. Lurianic truth provides the illumination for the laws, and all the light points to the return to God. "God forbid that they [the rabbis] should have assigned to the soul a punishment whereby she will not 'return to her Father's house as in her youth.' "

To counter the rabbis' fear that the doctrine of salvation for all of Israel, even those who partake in the evil of a Jeroboam, will remove all motivation to live righteously, Aboab resorts to the Lurianic belief in the *gilgul*, the transmigration of souls. Those who have sinned will have to enter the wheel of rebirth, so that their souls can be purified. Aboab takes great pains to trace this idea back to one of the great kabbalists of Gerona, Nachmanides.

Aboab's treatise ends: "This is what our rabbis, of blessed memory, meant when coining the phrase, 'Though he sinned, he is still an Israelite.' They intended to convey the idea that though he sinned he was not cut off thereby forever from the tree but remained a Jew; and even if he apostasized from the

Lord and chose new gods, he will again be called a Jew as a result of transmigrations and punishments."

The reference to those who chose new gods once again focuses attention on the subtext. It is not one's choice of God that makes one a Jew, but something independent of one's choices, something constitutive of one's very essence. In the words of Isaac Luria's own teacher, David ibn Abi Zimra, which Aboab quotes, "All Israelites are a single body and their soul is hewn from the place of Unity."

Shortly after the controversy, in 1639, the three Sephardic synagogues of Amsterdam—Beth Jacob, Neve Shalom, and Beth Israel—all of them crowded next to each other in the Jewish quarter, would merge into one, Beth Israel, and Rabbi Aboab would be demoted to an assistant rabbi and Rabbi Morteira promoted to chief rabbi. Shortly thereafter, Aboab left Amsterdam, accepting the invitation to become the rabbi of the prosperous community of Recife, Brazil, which was then under the rule of the Dutch, making him the first American rabbi. His departure might very well have been a result of the fracas regarding the afterlife. He remained in Brazil from 1642 until the reconquest of Recife by the Portuguese in 1654, when all the Jews were forced to leave.

Twenty-three of the refugees—men, women, and children—ended up in Dutch New Amsterdam after their ship was attacked by a Spanish privateer who deprived them of their possessions. Peter Stuyvesant, the Dutch colonial governor, was ill-disposed toward Jews and disinclined to allow these particular Jews—now indigent—to stay. Their former Jewish neighbors back in Holland interceded on their behalf with the Dutch West India Company, which directed

Stuyvesant to tolerate their presence, so long as they proved no burden to the community. In this way these twenty-three from Recife became the first Jewish New Yorkers—even before there was a New York.

Aboab, however, made it safely back to Amsterdam, there to resume his post as *khakham*. He was therefore one of the rabbis who was involved in the harsh decree of excommunication that was imposed on Baruch Spinoza in 1656. In fact, we don't know which of the two rabbis actually read out the writ of excommunication to the gathered congregants. Most have assumed that it was the chief rabbi, Morteira, though Colerus, the man who rented Spinoza's rooms in the Hague after he died and then wrote a sanctimoniously indignant biography of the philosopher, tells us that some "Jews of Amsterdam" told him that the "old *khakham* Aboab"—who happened to have been the presiding head of the Beth Din, the rabbinical court of law, in 1656—provided the voice of official banishment.

Whether a Jewish soul is, by the very fact of its Jewishness, ipso facto saved was a question that deeply divided the two Amsterdam rabbis, with the Sephardic Aboab, himself born in Iberia, not surprisingly inclined to interpret "Jewish soul" in redemptive terms. But even though they were sharply adversarial on the fate of the Jewish soul after death, concerning the fate of Baruch Spinoza, the two rabbis agreed.

Aboab's position in the rabbinical controversy with Morteira only deepens the mystery surrounding Spinoza's harsh excommunication. If, according to Aboab's mystical lights, all Jewish souls are redeemable, what about the soul of the twenty-three-year-old philosopher? Why didn't it make a claim on Aboab's inclusiveness? "Though he sinned, he is still an Israelite." What was the conceived nature of Spinoza's offense that caused Aboab to unite with Morteira in decreeing Spinoza irredeemable, decreeing him, in effect, no longer an Israelite? Was it an offense that went to the very heart of those coiled questions concerning identity and salvation?

Of course, the mature philosopher, the author of *The Ethics*, would have even less sympathy for Aboab's Jewish essentialist position than for Morteira's. He would have spurned any clemency the kabbalist might have offered him on its grounds (though the words of David ibn Abi Zimra, approvingly quoted by Aboab, in some strange sense shadow Spinoza's own mature view of the relation between individual finite minds and the Infinite Intellect of God, so long as one removes the reference to "Israelites").

Still, the question remains as to why the rabbi who was prepared to offer universal inclusion to untold Jewish apostates was irreconcilably opposed to the profound thinker who had emerged from within. Had Spinoza somehow managed to suggest to the community, even at this early stage of his life, the position that would follow from his mature philosophy, namely that the question of personal salvation, which was of true consequence, should be pried apart from the question of Jewish identity, which was of no consequence?

Personal identity poses philosophical questions that are bafflingly abstract, even though our prephilosophical sense of personal identity is as firm as the fear of death and the grief for those we've lost. The distinction between one's own self and all that is not one's self provides the invisible scaffolding of the emotions. One cares about one's self simply because one *is* one's self. A person is committed, immediately and unthinkingly, to the survival and flourishing of that single thing in the universe that she is. There is no reason, external to one's own identity with that thing—one's self—that one should be so single-mindedly, unswayingly committed to it. What explains this commitment is nothing over and above the bare fact that one is who one is. Implicit in being oneself is the commitment to oneself. One pursues one's life. One doesn't need a reason to pursue it. One pursues it, quite obsessively, because it's one's life. Who else's life is one supposed to pursue anyway?

There is an absurdity in even asking for a reason as to why we should care about ourselves. Identity itself explains the self-concern. We don't require any persuasion in taking a special interest in what will befall us. The persuasion we require is to take an interest in others as well. That's the business of ethics, and the business, too, of *The Ethics*.

Spinoza tries to capture this fundamental fact—that our commitment to ourselves is unlike the commitment to anything else, since it is tantamount to simply *being* oneself—in his concept of *conatus*. *Conatus* is simply a thing's special commitment to itself. It is its automatic concern about its own being and its intent to do what it thinks it takes in order to further its well-being. There is nothing that explains this commitment to this one thing that one is other than one's being that thing, and this is Spinoza's reason for saying that the very essence of each thing, the thing that makes that thing *that* thing and not another, is nothing over and above its *conatus*: "The endeavour, wherewith everything endeavours to persist in its own being, is nothing else but the actual essence of the thing in question."[6]

It is important that Spinoza not be understood here as asserting some sort of Nietzschean will-to-power ethics, or precursor to the "objectivism" of Ayn Rand. Spinoza has not yet begun, at this point in *The Ethics*, to make any ethical claims. What he's making, at this point in *The Ethics*, is a metaphysical statement, not an ethical one, trying to explain what makes an individual thing that individual thing that it is. His claim about *conatus* is meant to capture the mysterious connection a person feels with that one thing in the world that happens to be itself, and it is compatible with a whole spread of different ethical points of view, going all the way from Ayn Rand's to Mother Teresa's. A saint will perhaps feel that her life of, say, ministering to the needs of others, ignoring perhaps her own material benefits, is nevertheless, because it is the ethical thing to do, benefiting herself. Even a saint is not indifferent to *who* performs the acts of saintliness. If I were a saint, I wouldn't say: Look, I just want someone or other to commit these righteous deeds; it's all the same to me whether it's me or someone else. That would make being a saint too easy. A saint, just like each of us, is identical with the thing that she is, and this identity is tantamount to a certain interest in that thing. Spinoza is trying to capture this extraordinarily elusive situation in his concept of *conatus*.

To be oneself, then, is to be involved, Spinoza is saying, in an ongoing project of pursuing the interests of this one thing in the world (though, again, those interests may involve making enormous ethical sacrifices). But when one stares at this whole situation—one's ongoing commitment to this one thing in the world—from the outside, as it were, one can seem to lose one's grip on it. Nothing can explain this ongoing project other than the bare fact that that's who one is—Spinoza's very point in making this *conatus* one's actual essence. But step out of that ongoing project that constitutes one's identity and reflect upon it from the outside, as it were, and it can give the appearance of vanishing under one's gaze.

What sort of a fact is it that one is who one is, that very thing in the world and no other? How can one even isolate this fact when one inhabits, with great mental effort, the View from Nowhere? From out there, the remotest point from which to behold the world, the fact of who one is within the world seems to disappear; one can gain no purchase on it. This is what happens when one assumes the view *sub specie aeternitatis*, and this is the view that Spinoza recommends to us as the means of attaining salvation. Our very essence, our *conatus*, will lead us, if only we will think it all through, to a vision of reality that, since it is the truth, is in our interests to attain, and will effect such a difference in our sense of ourselves that we will have trouble even returning to the prephilosophical attachment to ourselves. It will appear almost too contingent to be true that one just happens to be that thing that one is. After all, contingency, for Spinoza, is just a *ignis fatuus*, a false fire cast by our finitude.

When, in the true light of objectivity, one is overtaken by the sense of near-estrangement from one's own self, then one is saved. One can then regard even one's own personal death, the thought we dare not even think since it negates the very process that keeps us together, with a degree of philosophical detachment. Our inability to realistically contemplate our own demise accounts, for Spinoza, for the otherwise incomprehensible power that the superstitious religions exert on us. Only reason, as rigorous as we can muster it up, can truly save us, both give us the truth and also deliver us from our primal fear of the truth. This is the state of blessedness toward which *The Ethics* will, through its severe formal proofs, try to deliver us.

The fraught altercation between the two rabbis of Amsterdam brings to light the underlying ferment within the community, swirling around the entangled questions of Jewish identity and personal salvation that the Inquisition had made urgent. For this community, such theological questions were painfully close. Spinoza's philosophy systematically rethinks these questions. His community's travails might very well have impressed on him the necessity for such systematic rethinking.

What is it to be Jewish? Are those who choose other gods still Jewish, of the same body, hewn from the place of Unity, so that one's personal identity is supervenient on one's Jewish identity? Is it true that one might carry in oneself, for no other reason than the conditions of one's birth, the causal link between that birth and the long causal link of others' births that has a role to play not only in one's own salvation but in *tikkun ha-olam*, cosmic redemption?

How would an exquisitely sensitive soul such as Spinoza's have reacted to this hum of impassioned obsession, the omnipresence of a seemingly irresolvable dilemma that was charged with centuries of ongoing anxiety and suffering? Like the lover of mathematics that he was, he would try to seek a clear and definitive solution, the deepest sort of solution, the sort that reframes the original question entirely, that in fact makes the original question altogether impossible. His solution would be to dissolve all sectarian frames of reference, to point the way to a concept of personal identity in which the question of who is Jewish and who is not simply could not meaningfully arise. Growing up in an atmosphere in which the question of personal identity throbbed with all the cumulative tragedy of the Sephardic experience, he would be the philosopher who would radically rethink the very notion of personal identity itself.

Spinoza looked toward the new rationalism of Descartes, which had thrust the rigorous necessity of mathematics forward as the model for all knowledge, and found a way of once and for all putting the tortured question of his community to rest. Spinoza's brave new revisioning of the world was an answer to the centuries of Jewish suffering. In his own way he was tackling the question of Jewish suffering toward which the Lurianic tale was also directed. Only, of course, Lurianic kabbalah told its tale in terms that singled out the special role the Jewish people have to play in the world's redemption.

For this particular community, seeking its Jewish identity with such passion, Spinoza's solution was the most damnable betrayal one of their own could commit. It was to deny that he was one of their own. It was to deny meaning to the very phrase "one of their own."

Spinoza's response, on being delivered the verdict of his excommunication, was reported to be, as my old teacher had faithfully, if partially, quoted: "All the better; they do not force me to do anything that I would not have done of my own accord if I did not dread scandal; but, since they want it that way, I enter gladly on the path that is opened to me." The path he was to follow was to reconstruct his identity, shedding as inessential all the passive markers of who he was, the accidents of his identity come to him by way of history, instead identifying himself in terms of what he was in relation to the infinite system that is reality. And of course what he was in relation to that infinite system is precisely the same as that which any of us is in relation to the infinite system. The only significant way we differ from one another is the degree to which we know the infinite system, and this is a difference that can be eradicated through rational thought. It is precisely in these cognitive processes that we reconstruct ourselves; we are what we know, and what we know depends on the active exercise of our rational faculties, seeking after necessary explanations, assimilating the objective necessity of *Deus sive natura* to the thinking matter of ourselves, becoming more consciously a thing hewn from the place of Unity by comprehending ever more of that inexhaustible Unity.

The path opened up to him by his excommunication was, in a certain sense, the same that those who were excommunicating him had followed: the path of actively and ardently refashioning identity. Only his would be a notion of personal identity that could not be fit into the terms of Jewish identity, nor of Christian identity, nor of any specific religious or ethnic or political identity. He was to define himself by his rational activity itself, and to try, in as cautious a way as possible, to help others seek this same active identity as well.

So for Spinoza, like for the tormented Marranos from whom he derived, personal identity is a purely private affair, enacted within the unobservable regions of our innermost minds, a project that one can undertake for oneself, with no need of external validation or acknowledgment, which of course was out of the question for Marranos. And, too, like them, he saw in the purely inward activities of identity-formation the way to salvation, though for him salvation rests in the dissolution of one's personal identity, in a merging into the whole. So the solution will come in dissolution.

But the problem for which dissolution is the solution was posed by his community's anguish. Sanguine Cartesian rationalism, somewhat chill in temperament, becomes, in the system of this son of Marranos, a solution to the horrors of Jewish suffering that some of his surviving letters show us he never ceased to respond to in a way that we might almost call, despite the rationalist's best attempts, a Jewish sensibility.

One of the last letters he wrote in his short life, in December 1675, only two months before his death, betrays his emotional affinity with the narrative of Jewish history. There it is suddenly: the sympathetic participation in the story of heroic martyrdom that a scion of the Portuguese Nation, no matter how he might philosophically remake himself, instinctively feels. Instinctive feeling is of course part of that passive identity that the philosopher qua philosopher must resist and transcend. But it is there to be resisted.

It is December 1675 and he is reluctantly responding to a former pupil of his, Albert Burgh, whose parents Spinoza knows (the father, Conraad Burgh, is the treasurer of the Republic of the Netherlands) and whom he had privately tutored on the foundations of philosophy. On a trip to Italy, young Burgh had dramatically seen the light and converted to Catholicism. He wrote to Spinoza, exhorting him, in the most impudent of terms, to follow his example:

> Even as I formerly admired you for the subtlety and keenness of your natural gifts, so now do I bewail and deplore you; inasmuch as being by nature most talented, and adorned by God with extraordinary gifts; being a lover, nay a coveter of the truth, you yet allow yourself to be ensnared and deceived by that most wretched and most proud of beings, the prince of evil spirits.

Young Burgh's letter is long and the vehemence keeps mounting:

> If you do not believe in Christ, you are more wretched than I can express. Yet the remedy is easy. Turn away from your sins, and consider the deadly arrogance of your wretched and insane reasoning. You do not believe in Christ. Why? You will say: "Because the teaching and the life of Christ are not at all in harmony with my teaching." But again, I say, then you dare to think yourself greater than all those who have ever risen up in the State or Church of God, patriarchs, prophets, apostles, martyrs, doctors, confessors, holy

virgins innumerable, yea, in your blasphemy, than Christ himself. Do you alone surpass all these in doctrine, in manner of life, in every respect? Will you, wretched pigmy, vile worm of the earth, yea, ashes, food of worms, will you in your unspeakable blasphemy, dare to put yourself before the incarnate, infinite wisdom of the Eternal Father? Will you, alone, consider yourself wiser and greater than all those, who from the beginning of the world have been in the Church of God, and have believed, or believe still, that Christ would come or has already come? On what do you base this rash, insane, deplorable, and inexcusable arrogance?

This is a depressing sort of letter to get from a former student in the final months of one's life. Here is an intelligent former disciple, who has had the benefit of hours of private explanation and discussion, falling victim to the crucifying passions of superstitious religion. It tolls a terrible message, bespeaking the futility of one's life work, for which one had forsaken so much: excommunication from one's own people, vilification from far and wide. What hope is there for reason's ever finding an audience? (Every teacher probably has these moments of despondency. As one of my colleagues once remarked to me, in a black moment of pedagogy, "Just what the hell do we think we're doing? Having some sort of *effect*?")

But Spinoza has his methods of always regaining his equilibrium. The first and foremost rule to remember is that we have no control over anything other than the progress of our own understanding. And the second rule is to care only about that over which we have control. We don't have control over the progress of others' understanding, no matter how hard we may try to help their advance. In the end, it had not been in Spinoza's power to keep Albert Burgh from descending into narrow-minded confusion; that power would have belonged to the young man himself. Spinoza will do what he can do. But he will not allow his own sense of failure and futility to become inflamed by another's weaknesses.

Burgh's letter arrived in September. For several months Spinoza didn't answer. But then in December, in the dead of his final winter, from out of the leaden tiredness and malaise of the final stages of tuberculosis, he writes back. Albert's distressed Calvinist father had urged the philosopher to try and exert whatever influence he still might have, and so Spinoza summons the strength to respond:

> That, which I could scarcely believe when told me by others, I learn at last from your own letter; not only have you been made a member of the Romish Church, but you are become a very keen champion of the same, and have already learned wantonly to insult and rail against your opponents.
>
> At first I resolved to leave your letter unanswered, thinking that time and experience will assuredly be of more avail than reasoning, to restore you to yourself and your friends. . . . But some of my friends, who like myself had formed great hopes from your superior tal-

ents, strenuously urge me not to fail in the offices of a friend, but to consider what you lately were, rather than what you are, with other arguments of the like nature. I have thus been induced to write you this short reply, which I earnestly beg you will think worthy of calm perusal.

Spinoza's reply is not so short that it does not contain a fair number of fascinating nuggets. A few times Spinoza loses his famous philosophical cool and shows flashes of fire:

And, poor wretch, you bewail me? My philosophy, which you never beheld, you style a chimera? O youth deprived of understanding, who has bewitched you into believing, that the Supreme and Eternal is eaten by you and held in your intestines?

This is followed by a statement that seems to support the oft-repeated charge of arrogance, made by far weightier minds than Albert Burgh's, and even Mrs. Schoenfeld's, who had also declared that Spinoza's rationalism rested on arrogance.

Yet you seem to wish to employ reason, and ask me, "*How I know that my philosophy is the best among all that have ever been taught, or ever will be taught?*" a question which I might with much greater right ask you; for I do not presume that I have found the best philosophy, I know that I understand the true philosophy. If you ask in what way I know it, I answer: In the same way as you know that the three angles of a triangle are equal to two right angles: that this is sufficient, will be denied by no one whose brain is sound, and who does not go dreaming of evil spirits inspiring us with false ideas like the true. For the truth is the index of itself and of what is false.

Spinoza is claiming here that since he has relied on nothing but a priori reason to deduce his system, just as mathematics relies on nothing but a priori reason, his conclusions (granted that his deductions are valid) enjoy precisely the same degree of certitude as mathematics. His conclusions, just as those of mathematics, must be necessary truths, those which could not possibly have been otherwise. We'll return to this claim in the next chapter.

But another aspect of Spinoza is revealed in the next stage of his reply to Burgh. Burgh had argued that Catholicism must be true since it has been attested to by a continuous lineage, supposedly reaching back to the witnesses of the miraculous events themselves. Spinoza, in answering Burgh, begins by pointing out that this is just the way "the Pharisees" also argue, meaning by this punitive word to indicate the rabbis. Spinoza is adopting here the terminology common to Christian critics of Judaism. He adopted the same terminology in his *Tractatus*, probably for a multitude of complicated motives, the most pragmatic of which would be that he was addressing himself to Christian readers (as he is here), and he does not want to have his arguments dismissed as being put forward by a Jew, even an excommunicated one. So it is that in the *Tractatus* he makes certain to refer to Jesus the Nazarene as "Jesus Christ," and does him the honor of making him the most important among the prophets, the best example of the virtuous man.

In this paragraph to Burgh, too, he is distancing himself from the Jewish point of view, calling attention to the fact that he speaks of it as an outsider by speaking of the rabbis as the Pharisees.

As to what you add of the common consent of myriads of men and the uninterrupted ecclesiastical succession, this is the very catch-word of the Pharisees. They with no less confidence than the devotees of Rome bring forward their myriad witnesses, who as pertinaciously as the Roman witnesses repeat what they have heard, as though it were their personal experience. Further, they carry back their line to Adam. They boast with equal arrogance, that their Church has continued to this day unmoved and unimpaired in spite of the hatred of Christians and heathens. They more than any other sect are supported by antiquity. They exclaim with one voice, that they have received their traditions from God Himself, and that they alone preserve the Word of God both written and unwritten. That all heresies have issued from them, and that they have remained constant through thousands of years under no constraint of temporal dominion, but by the sole efficacy of their superstition, no one can deny. The miracles they tell of would tire a thousand tongues. But their chief boast is, that they count a far greater number of martyrs than any other nation, a number which is daily increased by those who suffer with singular constancy for the faith they profess; nor is their boasting false. I myself knew among others of a certain Judah called the faithful, who in the midst of the flames, when he was already thought to be dead, lifted his voice to sing the hymn beginning "To Thee, O God, I offer up my soul," and so singing perished.

Spinoza begins this paragraph by disassociating himself from the Jews; but by the end he has placed himself inside the Jewish narrative—homing in on one of those tales of heartbreaking martyrdom with which his community was constantly being racked. These were the tales of horror and heroism that Baruch Spinoza had been raised on, the communal drama he had participated in as a child.

In May 1655, just fourteen months before Spinoza's excommunication, news had arrived that a Marrano named Abraham Nuñez Bernal, who had friends and relations in Amsterdam, had fallen victim to the Inquisition in Córdoba and been burned at the stake. Two months before this tragedy, Yithak da Alameida Bernal had been burned at the stake in Galicia. In 1647, when Spinoza was fifteen, the fate of one Isaak de Castra-Tartos had hit the community particularly hard. For he had been one of its own, a member of the Portuguese Nation, La Naçáo, who had left Amsterdam as a young man, returning to Spain and Portugal to try to convert the Marranos back to Judaism. He was caught, tried, and confessed to his "sins." As he stood on top of his funeral pyre, he reportedly screamed out the *Shema*: "*Hear, O Israel, the Lord is our God, the Lord is One.*" A funeral service was conducted for him by Rabbi Morteira, with the entire community participating.

Spinoza, addressing the New Catholic bent on saving him, can distance himself sufficiently from the Jews to speak of their habit of "boasting" of suffering. He is the evil son at the Passover seder: what has their story to do with me? But then, on a phrase, he turns himself around: "nor is their boasting false." Suddenly he pulls out from his extensive knowledge of Jewish suffering, a knowledge that went with the territory in which Spinoza had been raised, a single tale of martyrdom, which he relates in a tone that betrays his own awe and affinity.

The martyr to whom Spinoza refers in his reply to Burgh as "Judah the faithful" was actually known as Judah the Believer.[7] He was Don Lope de Vera y Alarcon de San Clemente, a Spanish nobleman who was not a Marrano but an Old Christian, converted to Judaism through the study of Hebrew. He had himself circumcised, was arrested by the Inquisition, refused to recant, and was burned at Valladolid on July 25, 1644. Spinoza was then twelve years old, a boy in Amsterdam, not in Spain. But he was a boy whose participation in this story was so vivid that years later, at the end of his life, he would write of the martyr in a tone so personal that it misled at least one scholar, the eminent German Jewish historian Heinrich Grätz (1817–91), to infer that Spinoza himself must have begun his life in Spain. Of course, he did not. He was born a Jew, not a Marrano, but within a community consisting almost entirely of Marranos.

The meaning of Jewishness was, at least partly for this community, expounded in the historical narrative of suffering—partly, but of course not entirely. They did not try to compress the entire meaning of Jewishness into these tales of persecution and woe, as some contemporary Jewish writers today do, insisting that the Holocaust provides the culminating Jewish experience. Spinoza's community was actively resisting the reductive definition of the Jewish experience that Christendom had tried to impose, a definition that not only predicted suffering for the nation that had rejected Jesus as savior, but also ensured that the suffering came to pass. The self-realizing logic of Christian persecution is, in its own way, impeccable.

Spinoza's community did not succumb to that usurpation of the meaning of their history. Judaism is not a religion that exults in suffering, and Spinoza's community, in actively reconstituting itself as a Jewish community, was actively resisting the claim that the culminating Jewish experience is some form of suffering.

And yet, of course, Jewish history runs thick with martyrs, with, as Spinoza himself says, "a number which is daily increased by those who suffer with singular constancy for the faith they profess." As misguided as this "singular constancy" in suffering is for Spinoza, it is sublime as well. It is sublime precisely because there is no Jewish virtue per se in suffering. Like Spinoza, Jews are far more focused on the rewards of this life than on those of the afterlife. Martydom is not glorified; it is not a state to be desired. So for a Jew to risk his life for the faith he professes, as the Marranos still on the Iberian Peninsula were doing, for him to give up his life in a terrible blaze of suffering, as Judah the Believer did, is a delusion most sublime. One can hear Spinoza's paying his respects to the sublimity, in his terse and emotional phrase "and so singing perished."

Spinoza, almost despite himself, cannot fail to be moved. Faced with Burgh's claim that Christianity presents the only authentic experience, he speaks of the authenticity, if also deludedness, of Jewish experience. And the authentic Jewish experience he narrates is that of heroic martyrdom at the hands of the Inquisition. He manifests a certain reflexive protectiveness that belies his distancing talk of "the Pharisees" and the Jewish "boast" of suffering. Spinoza the philosopher can't countenance the source for such acts of self-annihilation, grounded on superstitious beliefs in a people's election. But, at the same time, Benedictus retains the memories of Baruch, who himself retains the long memory of the Amsterdam Jewish community. And so not even Benedictus can help being stirred by the spectacle of transcendence in the face of crucifying injustice.

He himself, in answering the impertinence of his young would-be savior, who had ended his letter to him beseeching that both he and his "most unfortunate and adulterous followers" be born again through Jesus Christ, had succumbed to the Pharisees' habit of "repeating what they have heard as though it were their personal experience." Despite himself, he has assumed the role of the wise son at the Passover seder, who enters so personally into shared Jewish experience that its history becomes his memoir.

It was the community itself that had made the problem of personal identity of such crushing exigency for Spinoza that a way simply had to be found out of it, even though the way out would set him at irreconcilable odds with that community. The history of suffering, a living palpable history with *conversos* arriving every day and new incidents of the Inquisition's avenging power taking place throughout Spinoza's life, together with all the psychological devastation that had been wrought, posed the initial problem for which the impersonal grandeur (some might say frigidity) of Spinoza's conceptual scheme is the answer.

Though we know few details of Spinoza's early experiences, we know, from the evidence of his writings, that he was acutely sensitive to the nuances of human nature. The third part of *The Ethics* bears witness to Spinoza's close observations of his fellow creatures. His admiration for the mathematical methodology and abstract systems did not preclude his fascination with human types and to psychological depths.[8]

He is fascinated by what makes people tick, excruciatingly attuned to the ticking. How likely is it that a person of Spinoza's makeup, both observant and reflective, disposed to take in his environment and to subject it to relentless rethinking, would not have responded to the obsession with Jewish identity that his community's extraordinary experience had bequeathed to it? How likely was it that he failed to agonize on this question himself?

Sometimes my students, when they have progressed deeply enough into Spinoza's system to grasp the radical remedy he is offering us to the problem of being human, will muse, in ways that I cannot quite condone, about Spinoza's love life. There must have been some woman who broke his heart, one or more of them will speculate aloud. Some experience with a woman must have made him believe that love was a thing too heartbreaking to bear. What else could have driven him to such extremes of rationalism? I will share with them, though without much conviction, the rumor of van den Enden's daughter. Perhaps there's a story here, but I'm dubious that it's *the* story. If there is some missing element of biography that must be summoned in order to explain the philosopher's vision of radical objectivity, his abjuring any love other than that for objectivity itself, I very much doubt that it lies in disappointed romantic love. If it lies anywhere, it's in Jewish history. Spinoza has forsworn the Jew's love of that history. That was the love that was too heartbreaking to bear.

The final vision of reality that he arrives at is so dauntingly universal, so large and impersonal, that it is strange to contemplate that perhaps the original psychological drama that pointed him on the path that was to take him so far away from his community was to try to think of himself as outside of the awful dilemmas of Jewish identity.

And if this is so, then Spinoza is something of a Jewish thinker after all. He is, paradoxically, Jewish at the core, a core that necessitated, for him, the denial of such a thing as a Jewish core.

For what can be more characteristic of a Jewish thinker than to use the Jewish experience as a conduit to universality?

V

For the Eyes of the Mind

Spinoza defines "finitude" as being subject to forces beyond one's control. We are incurably finite, despite delusions to the contrary. We don't bring ourselves into being and we can't prevent ourselves from going out of being.

In between our helpless entrance and inevitable exit we experience events that also lie beyond our control and that affect us deeply, in our souls. That is to say, these events seem either to facilitate our essential project to persist in our being and flourish in the world—our essential *conatus*—or to hinder that project.

To experience what seems to be an increase in one's endeavor to persist, to feel oneself flourishing, expanding outward into the world, is pleasure; and to experience a decrease in one's power to persist, to feel one's self diminishing, contracting out of the world, is pain. Desire, the third of the "primary emotions," is the consciousness of our endeavor to persist and thrive, and specific desires, too, just like specific pleasures and pains, come adjoined with judgments; in the case of desires, these are judgments as to what will further our lifelong project to persist and flourish. The judgments adjoined to desires often make for character traits, such as ambitiousness, avariciousness, depressiveness, pridefulness, and humility.

One can't help being committed in a special way to one's self. One's special interest in, and concern for, the one thing that one happens to be is part and parcel of just being that thing. No one else can do for me what I am doing in being me. When there will be no one that has this same stake in my persisting, then there won't be me.

None of these remarks, remember, are yet ethical. He has not yet moved from "is" to "ought." He's simply trying to capture one of the most elusive of all "is" facts: the fact of one's identity. To be this thing is to be interested in this thing in a way unduplicated by my interests in other things, as vivid as these may be. And nothing else can explain this special interest in myself that I have other than my simply being myself. My keen interests in other things, including other specific people, will call for some additional facts about me and my relation to these others. For example, there are two young women in whose thriving my whole being is involved so that the increase in their pleasure is my pleasure, the increase in their pain my pain. The additional facts that explain this keen participation in their well-being is that these two young women are my daughters.

Spinoza will of course try to close the gap between "is" and "ought," just as he tries to close the gap between "if" and "is." His comments about *conatus* will serve as the original stance from which morality will be deduced. Just as God is immanent within nature, morality is immanent within human nature. But first, there is human nature to be explored. To this end, Spinoza produces, out of the implications of *conatus*, a theory of the emotions. "I shall, therefore, treat of the nature and strength of the emotions according to the same method, as I employed heretofore in my investigations concerning God and the mind. I shall consider human actions and desires in exactly the same manner, as though I were concerned with lines, planes, and solids."[1]

All the emotions, Spinoza reasons, must follow from this basic situation: that I am committed to my life's going well, since that commitment, in all the myriad ways in which it manifests itself, is irrepressibly me; that my life's going well or not is subject to things beyond my control (just another way of saying that I'm finite); that I make judgments about how various things affect my life for better or for worse, and these very judgments (which may, like all judgments, be either true or false) themselves affect me as experiences of pleasure and pain.

The feeling of love, for example, is simply the sense that things are going pretty damn well, that, at least in some respects, I am flourishing, together with the judgment that there is a certain thing, the beloved object, that is responsible for this flourishing. The judgmental component may be seriously, tragically wrong, of course. I can even be deluded in thinking that I'm really flourishing. The nonpropositional and propositional components of emotion—the raw feelings of pleasure or pain versus the various judgments—are reciprocally interactive. Just thinking that I'm flourishing gives me the feeling of pleasure that reinforces the judgment that I'm flourishing.

All the emotions involve feelings of our self's either expanding—our flourishing, our endeavor to persist in the world succeeding—or diminishing, which explains why emotions grip us as they do; and, too, emotions involve our judgments as to what is causing this modification in our life's project and the reason why it is so affecting us. The greater portion of Part III of *The Ethics* goes through basic emotions—love, hate, anger, remorse, envy, vengeance, pity, shame, scorn, complacency (he tells us, rightly, that there are far more emotions than there are names to showcase them)—showing them first of all as species of pleasure (the sense of expansiveness) or pain (the sense of contraction) and then the propositional judgments that complete them.

Things can get complicated, in fact lurid, given the combinatorial possibilities. So, for example, Proposition XLI is *If anyone conceives that he is loved by another, and believes he has given no cause for such love, he will love that other in return.* However, the corollary of this is *He who imagines that he is loved by one whom he hates will be a prey to conflicting hatred and love.* And the note to this corollary is truly of potboiler potential: *If hatred be the prevailing emotion, he will endeavor to injure him who loves him; this emotion is called cruelty, especially if the victim be believed to have given no ordinary cause for hatred.*

The deduction of our emotional responses from our very sense of ourselves might suggest that we are helpless, if front-row, spectators at the play of our own lives: "I think," he says toward the end of Part III, "I have thus explained, and displayed through their primary causes, the principal emotions and vacillations of spirit, which arise from the combination of the three primary emotions, to wit, desire, pleasure, and pain. It is evident from what I have said, that we are in many ways driven about by external causes, and that like waves of the sea driven by contrary winds, we toss to and fro unwitting of the issue and of our fate."

But the suggestion of our impotence, contained within the vivid image of waves tossed about by contrary winds, is false. As mentioned before, Spinoza is no fatalist. Because our emotions intrinsically involve judgments—it is part of their very makeup—we don't have to accept them lying down. Rather, we can critically evaluate the judgments that they contain and, if they are wrong, *correct* them, thereby transforming the content of the emotions themselves, transforming the emotions. Since the very process of correcting erroneous judgments is expansive—to understand is to expand ourselves into the world, reproducing the world in our own minds, appropriating it into our very selves—to understand one's emotions, even the most painful of them, is necessarily pleasurable. It requires one's getting out of oneself, seeing oneself clearheadedly as just another thing in the world, treating one's own emotions as dispassionately as a problem in geometry.

This maneuvering outside of oneself is a difficult thing to do, given the terrifically powerful centripetal forces of *conatus*, keeping one, quite literally, together, in the process warping one's worldview, making one's vision of the world conform to one's commitment to oneself. But the dispassionate knowledge of oneself is also, to the extent that we can achieve it, the most self-expansive of all experiences, the most liberating, the boundaries of one's self stretching to incorporate the infinite system of explanations that constitute the very world: *Deus sive natura*. To see one's own self from the vast and intricate scope afforded by the View from Nowhere is almost to lose the sense that that one thing in the world—so hell-bent on its own existence among all the other things so hell-bent on their existence—is one's very own self. One can never inhabit one's own self quite the same way again, which is to say that one has changed. Among all the wrong things Mrs. Schoenfeld said when she spoke to us about Spinoza, none was more wrong than her charge that Spinoza cynically entitled his work *The Ethics*. Spinoza's system is meant to do the hard work of ethics: insinuate itself inside the self and change it from the inside out.

There is an inverse relationship, somewhat paradoxical, between expanding to become more than what you were and the degree of importance with which you regard yourself. The more expansive one's self, the less the sense of self-importance. The tendency to overinflate one's significance in the world, simply because of the forces of inward attention and devotion keeping one oneself, undergoes corrective adjustments in the light of the objective point of view. Virtue follows naturally; supernatural directives are not required. One won't behave as if other people matter in precisely the same way that one's self matters only because it has been engraved on tablets of stone, and one fears the consequences of incurring the wrath of the Engraver. Rather, one will behave with what he calls "*high-mindedness*"—the desire "*whereby every man endeavors, solely under the dictates of reason, to aid other men and to unite them to himself in friendship*"[2]—because, having stood beside oneself and viewed the world as it *is*, unwarped by one's identity within it, one will understand that there is nothing of special significance about one's own endeavor to persist and flourish that doesn't pertain to others' same endeavors. One will therefore, simply as a matter of reason, want for others precisely what one wants for oneself. "The good which every man, who follows after virtue, desires for himself he will also desire for other men, and so much the more, in proportion as he has a greater knowledge of God."[3]

The world is such, he argues, that it can be known through and through by the faculty of reason, the faculty of grasping necessary connections, logical entailments. A priori reason alone can give us the world because the world itself is *nothing but* logic, an infinite system of logical entailments that is aware of itself, and that can be conceptualized alternatively as God or nature: *Deus sive natura*. Mrs. Schoenfeld was seriously mistaken in thinking that, for Spinoza, nature is nothing but nature. "Who doesn't believe in nature," she had demanded, "since it's what we see all around us?" Not Spinoza's nature, Mrs. Schoenfeld. Spinoza's nature can be grasped only through the faculty of pure reason, thinking its way through proofs. "For the eyes of the mind, whereby it sees and observes things, are none other than proofs."[4]

The Ethics opens with a definition that will eventually, through systematic deduction, unveil Spinoza's vision of that vast and infinite system of logical entailments that constitute reality itself: *By that which is self-caused* (*causa sui*) *I mean that of which the essence involves existence, or that of which the nature is only conceivable as existent*. *The Ethics* closes by speaking of our own salvation: *If the way which I have pointed out, as leading to this result, seems exceedingly hard, it may nevertheless be discovered. Needs must it be hard, since it is so seldom found. How would it be possible, if salvation were ready to our hand, and could without great labor be found, that it should be by almost all men neglected? But all things excellent are as difficult as they are rare.*

From *causa sui* to salvation. Salvation is achieved by bringing the vision of the *causa sui*—the vast and infinite system of logical entailments of which each of us is but one entailment—into one's very own conception of oneself, and, with that vision reconstituting oneself, henceforward living, as it were, outside of oneself. The point, for Spinoza, is not to become insiders, but rather outsiders. The point is to become ultimate outsiders.

The word "ecstasy" derives from the Greek for "to stand outside of." To stand outside of what? Of oneself. It is in that original sense that Spinoza offers us something new under the sun: ecstatic rationalism. He makes of the faculty of reason, as it was identified through Cartesianism, a means of our salvation. The preoccupations of his inquisitorially oppressed community come together with the mathematical inspiration of Cartesianism to give us the system of Spinoza.

The ecstatic impulse in Spinoza's rationalism distinguishes him from the other two figures with whom he shares equal billing in such courses as the one I teach, "Seventeenth-Century Rationalism: Descartes, Spinoza, and Leibniz." But then René Descartes and Gottfried Wilhelm Leibniz were members of the European majority. They were Christians. They were rationalists who had the luxury of taking their own religious ideas for granted. Neither Descartes nor Leibniz had to solve, as Spinoza did, especially brought up in that particular community, the wrenching problem of Jewish identity, of Jewish history and Jewish suffering. Only Spinoza needed to fight his way clear of the dilemmas of Jewish being, fighting all the way to ecstasy.

Spinoza names the ecstasy his system delivers *Amor dei intellectualis*, the intellectual love of God. This love, as its name suggests, is at once a cognitive and an emotional state, and it is the very highest state achievable, whether measured on the scale of cognition or emotional well-being.

It is, first of all, maximally knowledgeable, constituting the third, and highest, level of knowledge, *scientia intuitiva*, or intuitive knowledge. (Below intuitive knowledge lies *ratio*, or scientific knowledge, which involves the explanation of finite things by their necessary connections to their finite causes. Using *ratio*, [configurations of] bodies are derived from other [configurations of] bodies via the mathematically expressed laws of nature. And below scientific knowledge lies imagination, which, for Spinoza, includes all the passively received data of the senses, devoid as they are of any inkling of the necessary connections that constitute reality. For Spinoza, unlike Descartes, the distinction between the imaginative and the veridically perceptual is no consequential distinction at all.) In intuitive knowledge, the highest level of knowledge, each thing is grasped in the context of the infinite explanatory system, *Deus sive natura*, that is, the world, the details of which cannot—precisely because they are infinite—be exhaustibly grasped in their inexhaustible entirety but can nevertheless be holistically intuited. In intuitive knowledge, the whole entailed system—for each implicated thing entails the whole implicative order—is made palpably, if intuitively, present. We can only approach this third level asymptotically. We can never achieve it fully, since to do so would be to possess the mind of God, the thinking with which the infinite order of necessary connections thinks itself.

In addition to being the highest cognitive state, the intellectual love of God is an emotional state (for Spinoza the cognitive and emotional are constantly, necessarily, merged), and, again, it ranks as the highest state possible, this time judged in terms of one's emotional well-being. This outward absorption of the self into a vision of *Deus sive natura*, being maximally expansive, is also maximally pleasurable. The very activity of explanation, the exhilarating sense of expanding one's ideas to take in more of the world, and thus the exhilarating sense of one's own outward expansiveness into the world, is, in itself, a sort of love, only now with the explanation of the world—which is the world—as its object. And the exhilaration is aided and abetted by the sense of firm control, the activity of loving expansiveness not to be cut short by the loved object's independence of (finite) mind and fickleness of spirit. The painful urgency and insecurity of love are eliminated when it no longer seeks to complete itself in another person but rather in the understanding of God, that is, of the vast infinite system of implications from which we ourselves are implied.

Conatus, our essence, which dictates that all of our intentions derive from our concerns with our own selves, leads us, if we truly attempt to fulfill ourselves, to see ourselves from the outside, as it were, from the point of view of the infinite system that explains all. True devotion to ourselves will lead us to an objectivity so radical that even our own demise can be contemplated with equanimity. "A free man," Spinoza tells us in Part IV of *The Ethics,* "thinks of death least of all things; and his wisdom is a meditation not of death but of life."

One of Spinoza's uncompleted manuscripts is called *The Treatise on the Emendation of the Understanding.* Its subject is knowledge—what it is and how we acquire it—and Spinoza presumably left off completing it because he realized that his hierarchical theory of knowledge would have to be shown to follow—as all else, for him, follows—from the infinity of necessary connections that is the world.

But the interrupted *Treatise* is of special interest because of its opening paragraph, which is often cited to be the most revealingly autobiographical passage Spinoza ever gave us:

> After experience had taught me that all the usual surroundings of social life are vain and futile; seeing that none of the objects of my fears contained in themselves anything either good or bad, except in so far as the mind is affected by them, I finally resolved to inquire whether there might be some real good having power to communicate itself, which would affect the mind singly, to the exclusion of all else; whether, in fact, there might be anything of which the discovery and attainment would enable me to enjoy continuous, supreme, and unending happiness.

This is the only place in his writings where he seems to reveal to us something of the person who stands behind the formidably impersonal system, seeming to share the motive that lay behind its production. Spinoza tells us that he, like all of us, was searching for happiness. He even appears to confess that he had a normal appreciation for the sorts of goods that are commonly supposed to bring us happiness: riches, fame, and sensual pleasure. The problems with the three goods, he discovers, is that they fail to deliver maximum pleasure. They fall far short of yielding continuous, supreme, and unending happiness.

The problem, for example, with sensual pleasure is that, while we desire it, it so enthralls us that it blocks our vision of all other goals, but once the pleasure is sated "it is followed by extreme melancholy, whereby the mind, though not enthralled, is disturbed and dull."

(This observation raises a question that I will parenthetically raise merely to parenthetically drop, namely, on what was Spinoza's knowledge of sexual experience based? I think it's fair to say that none of us has the slightest idea. It could have involved another person—maybe a prostitute? maybe the Clara Marie who might have rejected him for the suitor with the pearl necklace?—or maybe not. Having another person present isn't required in order to experience that extreme melancholy that follows sexual satiety. The third part of *The Ethics* seems to demonstrate some familiarity with the misery of sexual jealousy: for example, the scholium to Proposition XXXV reads: "He who thinks of a woman whom he loves as giving herself to another will not only feel pain by reason of his own appetite being checked but also, being compelled to associate the image of the object of his love with the sexual parts of his rival, he feels disgust for her."

However, since this is a deductive system, this scholium, like any other proposition in *The Ethics*, might in principle have been inferred a priori, with no experience necessary.)

Then, too, if this sensual pleasure involves another person it exposes one to the problems that likewise plague the pursuit of riches and fame, namely making one vulnerable to factors beyond one's control. "If our hopes are frustrated, we are plunged into the deepest sadness." Fame has "the further drawback that it compels its votaries to order their lives according to the opinions of their fellow-men." And we have seen what Spinoza thinks of the opinions of the multitude. Given that these opinions are, according to his theory of knowledge, basically worthless, since their ideas remain on the level of *imagination*, why should the esteem of the many, which is what fame is, constitute a good?

The ecstatic rationalism that Spinoza works out for us in *The Ethics* claims not only to deliver us a world woven out of the very fabric of logic, unlike any that we could perceive by way of our so-called experience of the world, or even by way of our scientific explanations of our experience; it also claims to provide us with an ecstatic experience, the intellectual love of God, unlike any that we could have arrived at in any other way. It is the desire for that continuous, supreme, and unending happiness which Spinoza cites as his motive for his system.

But though this opening paragraph of the unfinished treatise might seem to speak in Spinoza's most personal voice, the desire for "happiness" to which he confesses is blandly impersonal, a one-size-fits-all motivation for what is the most rigorous project of rationalism in the history of Western thought. The motivation Spinoza was prepared to put to paper was as universal and impersonal as the finished system it supposedly provoked. What he does not tell us—what he cannot tell us—is that his ecstatic rationalism is a solution to a far more particular problem.

It is the problem of Jewish history.

If the supposedly most autobiographical passage in Spinoza's writings—the opening paragraphs of the unfinished *Treatise*—yield precious little of the person behind the system, where then can we find him? Certainly not in the sculpted formalism of *The Ethics*. Here is the View from Nowhere, still and calm, ordered as reality itself is ordered, a matrix of logical entailments, timeless as mathematics and just as impersonal.

The *Tractatus Theologico-Politicus*, however, is a slightly different story. Spinoza interrupted his work on *The Ethics* to compose the *Tractatus*, which—as Mrs. Schoenfeld rightly suggested—scholars believe was partly based on the apologia he composed in Spanish immediately after his excommunication. Perhaps that explains the somewhat less guarded tone that pervades it. His anti-clerical denunciations palpably tremble with outrage. Spinoza somehow or other hoped that this work, which argues against the existence of miracles—*So those who have recourse to the will of God when there is something they do not understand are but trifling; this is no more than a ridiculous way of avowing one's ignorance*[5]—and against the special role of the Jews—*Therefore at the present time there is nothing whatsoever that the Jews can arrogate to themselves above other nations*[6]—and that the Bible was written by many authors, whose gifts for prophecy resided not *in their more perfect mind, but with a more perfect power of* imaginations,[7] would convince his contemporaries to give him a clean bill of theological health so that he might be allowed to publish his philosophical masterpiece.[8] (There is probably a falsifying optimism that accompanies any ambitious writer's undertakings. A realistic assessment of the chances that one's labors will produce the desired response would advise one to give up before beginning.)

The *Tractatus* is far more informal and far less controlled than *The Ethics*, and in it the first-person voice of Spinoza sometimes speaks, as in this passage, which comes after Spinoza has been arguing that the many chronological inconsistencies and repetitions of the Scriptures argue compellingly that they were authored by several writers, not one, and certainly not by Moses, who could not have had access to many of the facts related:

> Indeed, I may add that I write nothing here that is not the fruit of lengthy reflection; and although I have been educated from boyhood in the accepted beliefs concerning Scripture, I have felt bound in the end to embrace the views I here express.

I read these words and my imagination is engaged. The sense of his boyhood world, in certain ways quite similar to my girlhood world, rises up in the phrase "I have been educated from boyhood up in the accepted beliefs." His life

enim cap. 13. verf. 14. תורת חכם מקור חיים *Lex prudentis* (est)
fons vitæ, id est, ut ex modo allato textu patet, intellectus. Porro
cap. 3. verf. 13. expressissimis verbis docet, intellectum hominem bea-
tum & fœlicem reddere, veramque animi tranquillitatem dare.

Sic enim ait אשרי אדם מצא חכמה ובן אדם יפיק תבונה וגו ארך
ימום בימינה בשמאלה עשר וכבור דרכיה דרכי נעם וכל נתיבותיה שלום
beatus homo, qui invenit scientiam, & filius hominis, qui intelli-
gentiam eruit. Ratio est, (ut verf. 16, 17. pergit) quia *directe*
dat dierum longitudinem *, *indirecte divitias & honorem : ejus*
viæ, (quas nimirum scientia indicat) *amœnæ sunt, & omnes ejus*
semitæ pax. Soli igitur sapientes ex sententia etiam Salomonis ani-
mo pacato & constante vivunt, non ut impii, quorum animus
contrariis affectibus fluctuat, adeoque (ut Esaias etiam ait cap. 57.
verf. 20.) pacem, neque quietem habent. Denique in his Salomonis
Proverbiis maxime nobis notanda sunt, quæ habentur in secundo
cap. utpote quæ nostram sententiam quam clarissime confirmant,
sic enim verf. 3. ejusd. cap. incipit כי אם לבינה תקרא לתבונה תתן
קולך וגו או תבין יראת יהוה ודעת אלהים תמצא כי יהוה יתן חכמה
מפיו דעת ותבונה *nam si prudentiam inclamabis, & intelligentiæ*
dederis vocem tuam, &c. tunc timorem Dei intelliges, & Dei
scientiam (vel potius amorem; nam hæc Duo verbum עד Jadah
significat) *invenies; nam* (NB) *Deus dat sapientiam : ex ore suo*
(manat) *scientia & prudentia.* Quibus sane verbis clarissime indicat,
I. quod sola sapientia, sive intellectus nos doceat, Deum
sapienter timere, hoc est, vera religione colere. Deinde docet, sapientiam, & scientiam ex Dei ore fluere, Deumque illam dare, quod
quidem nos etiam supra ostendimus, nempe, quod noster intellectus nostraque scientia à sola Dei idea sive cognitione pendeat,
oriatur, & perficiatur. Pergit deinde verf. 9. expressissimis verbis
docere, hanc scientiam veram Ethicam & Politicam continere, &
ex ea deduci. אז תבין צדק ומשפט ומשרים כל מעגל טוב *tunc in-*
telliges Iustitiam, & Iudicium, & rectitudines, (&) omnem bo-
nam semitam : nec his contentus pergit, כי תבוא חכמה בלבך
ודעת לנפשך ינעם מזמה תשמור עליך תבונה תנצרכה *quando intrabit*
scientia.

G 3

* *Hebraismus, nihil aliud significant quam vitam.*

A page from the *Tractatus Theologico-Politicus*

unfolds in the words "I have felt bound in the end to embrace the views I here express." Spinoza would advise me to disengage my imagination, but I think not.

To indulge in an imagined sense of his life would count perhaps as one more betrayal of Spinoza. If the personal point of view—that substance of one's mental life that is the accumulated effects of one's contingently lived history—are intellectually and ethically negligible, then what value can be placed on a novelist's attempt to imagine her way into another's life? Of what redeemable value is such an exercise even when it is his life, Benedictus Spinoza's, the architect of radical objectivity itself, that one is attempting to inhabit? It is the personal point of view, only once removed, blurring the line between truth and fiction (such blurring is of the essence of the art), mixing the actual thoughts of the philosopher (however conscientiously italicized and marked with endnotes) with mere imaginings.

Spinoza argues that the highest level of reason amounts to a sort of love. I would argue that the highest level of imagination also amounts to a sort of love. I would further argue that the imaginative acts by which we try to grasp the substance of others, that specific singularity of them that resists universalizing into the collective rational im-person, are a necessary component of the moral life. Spinoza, of course, would disagree. Spinoza's proofs were aimed at inducing only an impersonal love in us, *Amor dei intellectualis,* love for the infinite system that is reality. He does not approve of forsaking philosophy's proofs, the eyes of the mind, for imaginative sight, no matter how love-infused the sight might be.

What did Spinoza think of this novelist-beloved faculty of

the mind, the imagination? Perhaps it is of some consolation to learn that, in Spinoza, imagination fares no worse than does perception. But then imagination fares no better than perception, either. Both are placed together on the lowest rung of the intellectual and ethical progression that the mind must make in its ascent to radical objectivity, that purity of high-mindedness that leaves behind the stubbornly personal residue of selves, one's own self as well as others'.

The man who first taught Spinoza Latin and helped to introduce him onto the greater stage of the drama of the seventeenth century, Franciscus van den Enden, had perhaps lulled the young philosopher into liking the theaterical arts. There is a single reference to the arts in *The Ethics*, when he is listing the innocent pleasures that do not interfere with a life of reason, and it is to the theater. Still the mature philosopher could have little considered regard for imagination, a faculty not known for its skill in grasping logical entailments, and therefore a faculty to be deemed both cognitively and ethically negligible.

But here I disagree.

The first thing to notice is the eyes, large and liquid and luminous. When he looks down to read from the Hebrew prayer book on his desk—at this first level in the Talmud Torah the children are learning to read Hebrew from the *siddur*—his long black lashes seem to rest on his pale cheeks. His face is beautiful, the whiteness of his skin making his eyes appear unnaturally dark, as if they consist of nothing but pupil. His pallor is not only the result of the long hours in the classroom but also of the weak constitution that he has inherited from his mother, who died a year before he started school.

(We know of Baruch's beauty and of his pallor from the two inquisitorial spies, who both offered physical descriptions of him. According to the account offered by Friar Tomás, the young philosopher is "a small man, with a beautiful face, a pale complexion, black hair and black eyes." The Spanish soldier adds that he had "a well-formed body, thin, long black hair, a small moustache of the same color, a beautiful face." The friar uses the word *blanco*, white, to describe the striking pallor.)

He can't remember the face of his mother, Hanna, except contorted with terrible coughing. She lay in the grandly carved four-poster bed with the red velvet curtains drawn.[9] His sister Miriam, three years older than he, was his little mother, his *mais velha*, until his new mother, Esther, arrived.

Baruch shares a room with his brother Isaac, who also coughs all through the winter nights, terrifying Baruch.[10]

His family rents a house on the Houtgracht, close to his school. He has only to walk down the street each morning, with his older brother and his father, who is on his way to the synagogue for *shakharith*, the morning prayer. They cross the canal and then they are there, at the Talmud Torah, set up in two houses that the community rents, right next door to "the Antwerpen," the house used as a synagogue by the Beth Jacob congregation. The family lives in the heart of the

Jewish quarter. As they walk together each morning, they are greeted on all sides by others walking in the same direction as they.

He must be at his desk by eight. The morning class always begins with prayers. The first one they learn is the *Shema*. His teacher, or *rubi*, explains carefully that this is the most important Jewish prayer. He tells them what Baruch already knows, that there are many in Portugal who are risking their lives even now, while "you sit safe in Amsterdam." These "forced ones" hide the holy words in the feet of Catholic statues, and hang them on the doorposts of their houses: *Hear, O Israel, the Lord is our God, the Lord is One!* Imagining these forced ones, Baruch sometimes carries a stool to the doorpost of the bedroom he shares with his brother. He climbs up so that, stretching, the tips of his fingers almost touch the *mezuzah*. He brings his fingers to his lips and considers how this act could cost him his life in Portugal.

After the three hours of morning instruction, there is a break in the day, for three hours, when the children return to their homes. Baruch walks with his older brother. Most families have hired private tutors to teach the children during the midday break, and so it is for Baruch and Isaac—and later, when he is older, for Gabriel. Their father takes a strong interest in his sons' education.

Michael Spinoza has twice served as a *parnas* on the board of governors supervising the community's *jeshibot*. And as soon as the Etz Chaim foundation is established, in 1637, he inscribes his own name and those of his three sons. The foundation provides scholarships for gifted but needy students whose parents cannot afford tuition. Thank God, Michael

Spinoza can afford not only to provide for his sons' education, but has made a charitable contribution of 52 guilders in addition to the 18 guilders required to be a member of Etz Chaim.

Baruch returns to school for three more hours of instruction, from two until five, and after that the schoolchildren go with their teachers, and the men of the community, to the synagogue, the Esnoga, for the evening service of *ma'ariv* and the singing of psalms. The time for *ma'ariv* is calibrated to the setting of the sun, so in the winter school is dismissed earlier.

A child stays at each level for as long as it takes him to master the subject matter, usually for more than a year. At the first level he learns to read and write Hebrew. At the next level, he learns to recite each week's *parsha*, the weekly Torah portion to be chanted in the synagogue on the Sabbath day. By the third grade he is translating the *parsha* into Spanish, and also learning Rashi's commentary.

Learning by rote is stressed at the first levels of instruction. A child will be called upon to recite the *parsha*, and will yell it out in a voice as loud as possible, the more quickly the better, showing with his speed how well he has mastered the Hebrew. Then he explains the passage in Spanish, more quietly. They preserve the Marranos' respect for Spanish, the language of culture.

Baruch reads the Hebrew with the syllables flowing effortlessly. But his voice is low, sometimes falling to a whisper, and the *rubi* calls out in his harsh voice, "Louder, louder! The words of the Torah are not to be hidden in whispers but shouted out loud!"

He tends toward solemnity, spurning his classmates'

pranks and high jinks. They don't care for him much. He makes no trouble for anyone in class, and always listens intently as his *rubi* speaks. He is quiet and respectful, always with the right answer ready on his lips if he's called upon, but rarely offering to speak up for himself. The *rubi* has many children in his classroom—thank God the community grows, the classes are crowded—and has little time to guess at what goes on behind the quiet child's strange black eyes.

He is a gracile child, not strong to look at. Few would guess the degree of strength inside, the fierceness of his independence.

He is someone who knows, from the very beginning, what a good explanation is. Nobody taught him this. He simply knows. He loves it when an explanation fits firmly into place, leaving no space at all. When he understands why something is the way it is, why it has to be that way, the knowing feels like pleasure to him, like a laughing in his mind. And when explanations are bad, he feels it almost like a physical pain, like some small animal gnawing at his chest.

He knows it's supposed to be good to believe what his teachers say and he tries hard to do it. His teachers praise his quick mind, his tenacious memory, and he likes them to like him. He's a motherless child. But he often wonders why those who are so much older than he is, placed in the position to instruct him, try to jam explanations into places that they can't go. Mostly, he holds his tongue and doesn't question. *Derech eretz* has been drilled into him since he was very young.

But by fourteen, fifteen, he is too gnawed by his questions

not to pose them in class, though he always deliberates a long time before speaking up. The questions seem so glaring; he is certain that the rabbis have asked them of themselves. The answers he receives astound him with the knowledge that they haven't. They don't understand what he is asking at all. They think that they've answered him, they produce the preformed explanations, but he knows better. He knows better, and, what's more, he now knows that he knows better. He doesn't push them, not only for *derech eretz*'s sake,

Engraving of Baruch Spinoza in the National Library in Paris
(*Courtesy of Bibliothèque Nationale de Paris*)

but also because he's come to see that there's little point. He understands the way that all their explanations go, the general form that they will take.

All the answers that the rabbis offer in terms of the will of God produce that telltale gnaw in his chest. These are explanations that make reference to what are called final causes in the Aristotelian system that had so impressed the philosopher Maimonides, whom Rabbi Morteira in turn reveres. The world is explained by reference to God's final causes, the ends that He has in view. Our Torah lays out the divine final causes. All of its 613 commandments are to be explained by reference to God's final causes. All of Jewish history is an expression of the divine final causes.

Here is one of the questions that Spinoza asks his rabbis that convinces him of the pointlessness of asking them any more questions: Does God have reasons for his *halakhic* choices? Either He does or He doesn't. That's simple logic. So consider God's wanting us to refrain from doing all work on the Sabbath, the way the rabbis teach, distinguishing between the thirty-nine varieties of work, and then making their *halakhic* decisions—their *pisakim*—on the basis of analogical reasoning from these varieties. But does God have any reason for demanding we refrain from these thirty-nine varieties of work on the seventh day of the week? Does He, for that matter, have any reasons for asking us to refrain from slandering our fellow men and caring for the defenseless orphan? Again, either He does or He doesn't. If he does, then whatever reasons God Himself has for His choices, presumably ethical reasons, constitute *the* reasons for the choices, and all reference to God is beside the point. And what could these reasons be that provide God with *His* reasons, reigning *over* God, and negating the assertion that God's choices provide the ultimate explanation?

Or else God has no reasons at all for His choices. That we are asked to refrain from smoking our pipes on the Sabbath day and to not put out our hands to take from our neighbors whatever tickles our fancies are all mere whims of the Almighty, backed up by no reasons at all but His own personal fancies. He might just as well have willed that we do exactly the opposite. Perhaps someday He'll dictate a new set of tablets to some Mosaic scribe and simply negate all his former precepts, and we'll have to jump to it and slander our neighbors and steal their property and, by the will of God, commit adultery.

No, he concludes (though he cannot get his rabbis to conclude along with him), all references to the will of God explain nothing.[11]

His father had died, as had his stepmother a few years before. The passing of his father made a great difference to him. Michael Spinoza could tolerate only so much of his son's independence of mind. He had been a pillar of the Amsterdam Jewish community, twice serving as a *parnas*. He had an exaggerated respect for the rabbis. Like so many who had been born in Portugal, he himself knew no Hebrew (his Dutch was poor as well, and he often needed one of his five children to translate official documents for him), and so he tended to be overly impressed with those who made claim to Jewish scholarship.

Still, he had little patience for self-righteousness, and his sharp merchant's eye could spot a fake. Once, when Spinoza was about ten, his father sent him to collect a debt from one of his customers. The woman was making a great show of praying when he arrived, and made Baruch wait while she finished her psalms, sighing with *kavana*, devotion. When she was finally done, she stuffed some ducats into a purse for Spinoza, all the while extolling his father for being such a God-fearing Jew, observing the Law of Moses, and simpering to him that he must imitate his father and grow up to be such a fine specimen of a Jew. There was something in the woman's manner that smacked so loudly to him of the false piety his father had warned him about that Baruch steeled himself to receive the woman's show of outrage and demanded that she count out the money for him. As he'd suspected, the purse came up short; she had a slit in the dining room table where she had secreted some of the missing coins.[12] When Baruch came home, he and his father had a good laugh over it, and his father praised Baruch for his good head.

"You'll be a *khakham* of the community yourself, someday. You'll be the first child born here in Amsterdam to lead the community."

Baruch, seeing the expression on his father's face, the false light cast backward from this imagined future glory making his dark eyes glow, kept his silence. Even as he grows older, his doubts mounting, he preserves the Jewish virtue of *shalom bayis*, peace within the household, and keeps his thoughts to himself. And he sits *shiva* faithfully for his father, keeps all the laws of mourning as they extend over the year following his father's death, and also keeps up with his pledges to the community's various charities, since such donations had meant so much to his father.[13]

The explanations Spinoza hears, even the most rational of them—never mind the wild imaginings of the kabbalistic master Aboab and his followers—feed the doubt in Spinoza's chest, gnawing now like a hungry beast. Still, he continues to study, even after he officially leaves the yeshiva and goes into business, first his father's and then, after his father's passing, founding an import and export business with his younger brother: Bento y Gabriel de Spinoza.

There are various independent learning centers, *jeshibot*, in the community, supported by the wealthy, so that the men can continue to observe the mitzvah of Torah learning even while they earn their living. After all, scholarship has, ever since the destruction of the Temple, taken the place of the old ceremonies of worship, the pilgrims' holidays, and sacrifices. Advance in Jewish learning constitutes, in itself, an ethical activity. The rabbis were right in this. *The mind's absolute virtue is to understand. The mind's highest good is the knowledge of God, and the mind's virtue is to know God.*[14]

Years later, after Spinoza's excommunication, a man named Daniel Levi—his alias "Miguel"—de Barrios, a Spanish-born Marrano and a poet, writing in Spanish, and also the Amsterdam community's official chronicler, alludes to Spinoza's attendance in Rabbi Morteira's school, which is called Keter Torah, or Crown of the Law, as well as to that of the other excommunicated heretic, Daniel de Prado, in carefully chosen words:

The Crown of the Law [*Corona de la ley*], ever since the year of its joyous foundation, never ceased burning in the academic bush, thanks to the doctrinal leaves written by the most wise Saul Levi Morteira, lending his intellect to the counsel of Wisdom and his pen to the hand of Speculation, in the defense of religion and against atheism. *Thorns* [*Espinos*] are they that in the *Fields* [*Prados*] of impiety, aim to shine with the fire that consumes them, and the zeal of Morteira is a flame that burns in the bush of Religion, never to be extinguished [emphases in the original Spanish].[15]

He chooses Rabbi Morteira's establishment, even though the man's authoritarian manner can be grating on the nerves. The rabbi's self-regard often pushes him toward putting a wrong construction on others' words, understanding them to be stating obvious falsehoods. A man like Rabbi Morteira will *take most pleasure in contemplating himself, when he contemplates some quality which he denies others.*[16] Therefore, it is characteristic of the rabbi to deny others' intelligence.

Still, the rabbi's rationalistic approach has more to offer than do the kabbalistic ravings of Aboab. One would have to believe that these visionaries' visions—Ha-Ari's claimed communiqués from the prophet Elijah—were self-authenticating forms of experience. There is nothing in their content that convinces Baruch that they were. Whatever it is that these mystics are seeing, their sight does not come from the eyes of the mind. If any faculty of their minds is particularly active it is their imaginations.

He is always surprised to hear what it is that others find convincing. He understands, of course, what it feels like to have a powerful need for answers pounding inside. But the answers that people come up with to stop the pounding: he would rather live with the pounding. Better the pounding than the gnawing.

By now Baruch has come to question another constant feature in all the explanations of the rabbis: the special role they incessantly insist on giving the Jewish people. This insistence is a presupposition of all discussions. It is the very air that they all breathe. How startling to consider that one could simply step away and breathe in another atmosphere entirely.

The idea of the separate destiny of the Jewish people is inseparable from explanations in terms of divine final causes. If one gives up the latter, one is forced by logic to give up the former. But if the former is false, then all the woe of the Jews is in some sense brought on them by their own insistence on their separate destiny, and the hatred that this very insistence has incurred, which hatred then, in a macabre dance of reciprocity, ensures their separate existence. *That they are preserved largely through the hatred of other nations is demonstrated by historical fact.*[17]

It is distressful to view the history of the Jews from this perspective. One cannot completely overcome one's passive sympathy for people one understands so well. It is more distressful in some ways than participating vicariously in the litany of their sorrows, as he had long been accustomed to doing, from boyhood up, feeling each lash on the body of the nation of Israel as falling directly on himself. But to think in this way—in the words of the kabbalistically crazed Aboab, to conceive that "[a]ll Israelites are a single body and their soul is hewn from the place of Unity"—is to think narrowly and thus erroneously, from inside a point of view that is simply the passive bequest of the conditions of one's birth.

Our knowledge of truth can't possibly be a function of such brute contingencies. Our apprehension of the truth can't be passive at all, but active, a function of the exercise of reason—the same reason that exists in all men. He has far more in common with men, whichsoever people they may have been born into, who reason their way to their conclusions rather than accepting them as gifts from the ancestors. *In so far only as men live in obedience to reason, do they always necessarily agree in nature.*[18]

And to exercise this reason, to find through it a perfect-fit explanation, is exquisite pleasure. It is the pleasure of feeling one's point of view expanding outward, taking in more of reality, and this expansion of the mind means that one's very own self is expanding as well. And the expansion of the self is the very essence of pleasure, as the contraction of the self is pain. So even if the explanation itself is not to one's personal liking, even if one had personally wished the world to be arranged otherwise—to believe, for example, that one is so fortunate as to have been born into the people most favored by God—still to expand one's point of view is, in itself, pleasure. It is rational pleasure—rational both because it consists in reason's work and because it is a pleasure that lies entirely in the mind's own power to perform—inward and private, like the Marranos' inner avowal of the hegemony of the Mosaic Law. No outer authority, no inquisitorial ferocity of church or mosque or synagogue, can remove the mind's own decision to think clearly for itself, to seek perfect-fit explanations, and to find them and rejoice. This is freedom.

Spinoza is engaging in his new business adventure with his brother, Gabriel, and his dealings in the bourse, the mercantile exchange, open up his world somewhat wider. He meets disaffected Christians from some of the dissenting sects—the Mennonites, the Remonstrants, the Quakers—who collectively call themselves Collegiants, because they have meetings, or "colleges," every other Sunday, when they discuss questions of theology, studying Scripture for themselves and trying to interpret it without the influence of the established answers. The atmosphere of these colleges is vastly different from that of the jeshiva.

It is shocking at first to feel himself to have so much more in common with these Gentiles than with the majority of Jews he has known all his life and with whom he shares his history. It is shocking to discover that he understands these strangers better, as they understand him better, than the members of his synagogue, even of his family. Within his community there is only de Prado with whom he can talk about matters of religious belief. Those he has the most in common with are those who think about the questions he thinks about—and why should those questions be determined by what quarter of Amsterdam one resides in? The world is equally there for all of us to think about, the same world, posing the same questions to our intelligence.

It is impossible that man would not be a part of nature, or that he should not follow her general order; but if he be thrown among individuals whose nature is in harmony with his own, his power of action will thereby be aided and fostered, whereas if he be thrown among such as are but very little in harmony with his nature, he will hardly be able to accommodate himself to them without undergoing a great change himself.[19]

Knowing ancient Hebrew as he does, he has much to teach his new friends about the reading of Scripture, though of course he does not teach it as he had been taught. He is trying to work out the right methodology of applying scientific principles to these most problematic texts, asking questions of them that have never been asked.[20] But the extent of his own ignorance that is opened up to him in his conversations with others amazes him. He has spent a lifetime studying, yearning above all else to attain knowledge, and what, after all, does he know?

He begins to haunt Amsterdam's bookshops. Amsterdam is famous throughout Europe for its bookshops, of which there are reputed to be upwards of four hundred. The civil authorities here are far more tolerant of the printed word than are those anywhere else, so authors from all over Europe send their manuscripts to this city in order to be published. This makes for unbelievable riches for the bibiophiles who flock here. You can find books in many of Europe's languages, and also find people who themselves are native speakers of other languages, seeking books here that they can't obtain in their own countries. There are exceedingly fine conversations to be had in the aisles of bookshops, people to be met here who make one question whether solitude is a state always to be preferred over company.

Nothing can be in more harmony with the nature of any given thing than other individuals of the same species; therefore for man in the preservation of his being and the enjoyment of the rational life

there is nothing more useful than his fellow-man who is led by reason.[21]
He learns of the explosive ideas of the Frenchman René
Descartes, the author of such works as *Discourse on Method of
Rightly Conducting the Reason and Searching After Truth in the
Sciences, Meditations on First Philosophy,* and *Principles of Philosophy.* Descartes is a revolutionary in diverse ways. Even the
language he chose in which to publish wasn't the Latin that
serves as the lingua franca of all scholars, but rather the vulgate French. All men, not only the trained scholars, have the
capacity for reason. In fact, it might be easier for the uninitiated to exercise their *lumen naturale,* their natural light of reason, than those who have had it occluded by the dense fogs of
Aristotelian Scholasticism.

Lumen naturale. The phrase delights Spinoza, though perhaps not so much as it had delighted the Frenchman, who
often invoked it in place of proofs.

Descartes, too, had made his home for a while in Amsterdam, availing himself of its comparative tolerance. Spinoza
had seen him once, he was almost certain, rushing down the
Houtgracht. Spinoza hadn't known then who he was, though
he had certainly noticed him, there being something arrest-
ing about him even though he was not really much to look
at. A short compact body, topped by a large unprepossessing
head, walking exceedingly quickly, with short, almost minc-
ing steps, but carrying the great bulk of his head with incon-
gruous dignity. It was the incongruity that had made
Baruch, even in his ignorance, take note.

He stares into the face of his ignorance and grows dis-
gusted at its sight. It would be easy to blame the rabbis,
blame the narrowed gaze of his insular community, keeping

out the new ideas that are setting men's thoughts on fire with new methods for attaining truth. Some of the rabbis fancy themselves learned in the world's philosophy—ben Manasseh, Morteira—but the little they know is already outmoded. The old Aristotelian system is crashing to the ground under the intellectual onslaught of such men as Descartes and Galileo, who confirmed that the Polish astronomer of the last century, Nicolaus Copernicus, had been correct in asserting that the earth revolves around the sun rather than, as Aristotle had had it, the entire universe revolving around the earth. This change, large as it is, represents an intellectual change even greater, the switch from thinking of man as always at the center, all explanations revolving around him. Explanations in terms of final causes belong to the old order. The new men of genius construct explanations out of the certainty of mathematics, not the make-believe of teleological storytelling. And of course for the rabbis it is not only the old form of teleological storytelling that they repeat, but always they must have the Jews playing an essential role in the plot.

Yes, it would be easy to blame his old teachers for the hideous aspect of his own ignorance. But it is the responsibility of each person to increase his own understanding. It is the most profound responsibility that we have, as even the rabbis, in their confused way, had perceived, equating a man's moral progress with his intellectual progress.

One of the bookshops is owned by an extraordinary personage named Franciscus van den Enden, a prodigy of energy and intelligence, who takes a sometimes perverse pride in the outrageousness of his opinions and manner of conducting his life. This freedom-loving iconoclast had once been a Jesuit priest, but his views on sexual ethics alone—he believes that no authorities, neither religions nor civic, should be able to regulate the intercourse of men and women and that freedom should abound in that sphere as in all others—would be enough to make him a most inappropriate representative of the Vatican. Van den Enden remarks that it is a shame that Baruch knows neither Greek nor Latin. When van den Enden's bookshop closes and he opens his own school in his house, offering instruction in Latin, Greek, and the human sciences, Baruch becomes his student.

Desartes, educated by the Jesuits in the exemplary academy, La Flèche, could take Latin for granted, snubbing it for the vulgate French. But for Spinoza, educated at the Talmud Torah, mastery of Latin is an exquisite pleasure, connoting far more to him than merely the addition of another language. Once he has it, he will always choose to write in it. Besides, what vulgate language would be his? Growing up in the Portuguese Nation, he writes Dutch little better than a foreigner.

Van den Enden is a great lover of the theater, having himself authored a play called *Lusty Heart*, which about sums up the playwright, and which the civic authorities barred from being staged. He has his students of Greek and Latin memorize passages from the classics and declaim them with all the poses and gestures of stage actors. Spinoza, too, partakes in these productions, memorizing passages out of the Roman author Terence that will stay with him his entire life, so that he will often sprinkle his correspondences and other writings with sentences he remembers verbatim from the lively times at the school of lusty hearts.

It's an exceedingly lively household. Van den Enden, at fifty, is a widower with six children whom he is bringing up with the extraordinary liberality of his persuasions. His eldest daughter is named Clara Maria, and she is unlike any young woman Spinoza has ever laid eyes on. How many young women could there be in all of Europe who are masters of Greek and Latin and all the arts? Her body is frail and ill-formed, but her mind is a delightful display of vigor and healthy-minded robustness. Her knowledge of Latin of course far exceeds Baruch's, though he is studying hard, still keeping up his business ventures with Gabriel. Her father often has her play the role of Baruch's tutor.

Love is the sense of one's own exhilarating expansion— that is, pleasure—attributed to some one object as cause of the pleasure. *Love is nothing else but pleasure accompanied by the idea of an external cause.*[22]

The exhilarating expansion of the self that one feels in loving another person and conceiving of one's love being reciprocated, the exquisitely joyful sensation of joining one's own self with that of another, presents a pleasure almost comparable to that of rational pleasure. But there is this not insignificant difference between the two. The pleasure of romantic love depends, most essentially, not only on the emotions of one's own mind but on those of another's, over whom one ultimately has no control. When we love another person romantically, our sense of our self's entire destiny— whether it will flourish or fail—lies in the uncontrollable dominion of another. So it is impossible for romantic love not to include within itself pangs of the most insufferable agony, connected with the idea of the other as cause, which is none other than hate, since that other has now the means of extinguishing our essential project of flourishing, and thereby annihilating our very own self. We have delivered over to another the very thing that we should preserve for ourselves alone. Love's exquisite expansion into the world ends in the most violently invasive and shattering shutting down, so much so that, in the confusion of its extreme pain, one can even desire the most irrational of all possible desires: the ceasing to be of the self.

Emotional distress and unhappiness have their origin especially in excessive love towards a thing subject to considerable instability, a thing which we can never possess. For nobody is disturbed or anxious about anything unless he loves it, nor do wrongs, suspicions, enmities, etc. arise except from love towards things which nobody can truly possess.[23]

The only object we truly possess is our own mind. The only pleasure over which we have complete dominion is the progress of our own understanding.

Some aspects of Lurianic mysticism still stir his thinking. The esoteric doctrine purports to explain why the world exists at all. How does the profusion of our world emanate from what the kabbalists call the *Ein Sof,* That Without End? The story they tell, once again giving the definitive role to the destiny of one small group of people—the Jews— betrays its ultimate hollowness. But there is perhaps something to ponder in the idea of *Ein Sof,* an Infinitude that would contain in Itself the explanation of why it Itself had to be and how all else followed from it. The kabbalists held that at a certain moment in time the *Ein Sof* had withdrawn—the *zimzum*—in order to make way for the created world, the *Sefirot*. But why did the *Ein Sof* have to do that? Are the kabbalists, too, making implicit and illicit reference to final causes? Yes, of course. Such reference is inseparable from superstitious religion. And then they tell a curious story of the shattering of vessels meant to contain the divine light, of the whole created world's going awry. This aspect of the story is meant to explain the vast amount of suffering in the world. Jewish suffering is singled out from all other suffering, imbued with special cosmic significance. The Lurianic story makes little sense to him. Its tale is too haphazard, too ad hoc. How could the Infinite have blundered, have shattered three of the ten vessels meant to contain its light? The *Ein Sof* of the Lurianists is no *causa sui*, though it hints of the idea, if one were to purify it of all contingency.

The rabbis' spies—why had Baruch not been more cautious in the presence of their cunning?—are causing trouble for Baruch. There has been talk in the community that he is now spending more and more time with dissenting Christians and withdrawing himself from his own people. Ben Mannasseh, the most worldly of the rabbis, would have been of some help here—he, too, had many Gentile friends. But ben Mannasseh, no matter how worldly, is also a victim of Jewish messianic delusions. He is off in England, trying to hasten the coming of the *Moshiakh* by completing the scattering of the Jewish people to the four corners of the world.

Spinoza regrets that he had gone to the synagogue when he was summoned there. It was the last vestiges of the old ingrained reflexes of *derekh eretz* prevailing over his better judgment. He had allowed himself to become incensed under the didactic fulminations of Morteira. It would have been better to avoid the confrontation altogether, to remove himself from any further interchanges. He knows that there can be no more communication. He will never see things their way again.

The members of his former community would like to make life a hardship for him. He has, simply by removing himself from them, rendered their vindictive rage impotent. He can never forget the crazed hatred with which the unfortunate Uriel da Costa, that would-be reformer of all of Judaism who was the whipping boy of Spinoza's classmates, had ended his days. *Kherem* is a punishment only if one experiences it as such. The solution is entailed. Spinoza chooses to experience the banishment as freedom.

As Spinoza is leaving the theater one evening, a man, clearly a member of the Portuguese Nation, rushes at him with a drawn dagger.[24] Spinoza's heavy cloak—fortunately the season is winter—is the only object pierced. Spinoza will keep the cloak, with its long jagged scar, as a memento for the rest of his life, a mute testament to the deadly consequences of irrational religion.

Superstitious persons, who know better how to rail at vice than how to teach virtue, and who strive not to guide men by reason, but so to restrain them that they would rather escape evil than love virtue, have no other aim but to make others as wretched as themselves. Wherefore it is nothing wonderful, if they be generally troublesome and odious to their fellow-man.[25]

Here is what he holds is true—*has* to be true—even

before he yet sees fully how it can be true. All facts have explanations, even if we are never able to gain access to all of the explanations. Despite our human limitations, we can know that reality is intelligible through and through. How could it be otherwise? It is an affront to reason to imagine that at the bottom of explanations lie truths that can't be explained at all. One might as well admit at the beginning, then, that nothing at all is explained.

The awful gnawing when explanations aren't forthcoming, or come twisted and deformed from violent attempts to jam them into places that they don't fit, is not a symptom of his mind's unhealthiness, but rather its health. The feeling of pleasure, of expansiveness and strength, when an explanation falls into perfect place, is an indication of how our minds ought to work. The sheer pleasure in explanatory satisfaction answers to something deep and important in the world itself.

The world is such that the gnawing can be quieted. The world itself is woven of explanations. It *must* be. The mistake of all the religions is to look outside the world for explanations of the world, rather than rethinking the world itself, so that it offers up its own explanations for itself. The world itself must be self-explanatory.

The world itself is the *causa sui*.

The essential thing is to expunge all aspects of the merely arbitrary. To accept arbitrariness is not just an affront to our reason, but to the infinite God. To attribute mere whim, sheer this-is-the-way-it-is-but-it-need-not-have-been-so explanations to the Infinite Intellect is blasphemy. The superstitions are themselves species of blasphemy. If the perfection of our mind consists in its containing perfect-fit explanations, then, too, the Infinite Intellect of God must contain only perfect-fit explanations. The world must somehow offer an explanation for itself; or otherwise we fall back on the explanatory hollowness of divine final causes. *And when men couldn't come up with final causes, when the world's suffering seemed to contradict that there were any goals being realized by a good and powerful God, they laid down an axiom, that God's judgments far transcend human understanding. Such a doctrine might well have sufficed to conceal the truth from the human race for all eternity, if mathematics had not furnished another standard of verity in considering solely the essence and properties of figures without regard to their final causes.*[26]

Mathematics provides the model for explanation. In mathematics we see that facts are so because they necessarily *have* to be so. We discover what things are in the course of *proving* them to be that way; the nature of the objects emerges clearly and distinctly only within the proofs. We only know what we have once we have proved it to be. And that is how it must be for all of reality. Since the world must offer an explanation for itself, we know that we have the world only when we see that it must of necessity be the world. Only proofs can reveal the world to us, the world in its self-explicating necessity. *For the eyes of the mind whereby it sees and observes things are none other than proofs.*[27]

Descartes was impressed by the mathematical method because once something is mathematically proved we need never concern ourselves over the question of its truth again. The very possibility of doubt has been expelled. Our knowledge is secure. We know we are not duped. For Spinoza, such worries about doubting and being duped are beside the point. The mathematical method is essential because it alone can reveal necessary connections. Since the world itself is composed of necessary connections, the mathematical method—in other words, proofs—can alone reveal the world.

He had not balked at challenging the chief rabbi of the community, and now he has no qualms in finding fault with the great Descartes. The great mathematician and philosopher failed to see that the sort of questions that Rabbi Aboab pondered in his kabbalistic confusions—Why does the world exist at all? How did finitude, the *Sefirot*, proceed from out of Infinity, the *Ein Sof*? How did the flow of time emerge from out of timeless eternity?—could be addressed through the method to be extracted from out of the mathematical model.

Nor does Descartes offer us an answer to the anguished question of Spinoza's community, of all Marranos and other martyrs, of whom men had provided too many examples: Wherein lies our salvation? What is the meaning of the awful suffering that we are made to go through within our lives? Shall this suffering itself redeem us?

It was a sort of Cartesian kabbalism he was contemplating now: the Cartesian methodology applied to the fundamental questions of the kabbalah, and all of it laid out in the proofs that replicate something of the logical structure of reality.

Ontology shifts in the process of explaining it. We uncover things of which no conception existed in the common-sense view of the world, the view which stops far short of truth, believing in facts simply as they are handed over to us by experience, without subjecting these facts to the processes of a priori reason, which alone can grasp necessity, and thus alone can grasp the true facts. This is why common language, which has grown out of experience, is inadequate to describe the true nature of the world, and why we must bend and stretch and strain almost to the point of inapplicability such words as "God" and "nature" in setting forth their truth.

"I am aware that these terms are employed in senses somewhat different from those usually assigned," he writes. "But my purpose is to explain, not the meaning of words, but the nature of things. I therefore make use of such terms, as may convey my meaning without any violent departure from their ordinary signification."[28]

For nature is nothing like what we experience. Nature consists in the whole infinite system of necessary connections that exist between things, which necessary connections are revealed only to pure reason. *The order and connection of ideas is the same as the order and connection of things.*[29] The order and connection of ideas is provided by logic, which displays how one idea logically entails another. And the order and connection between things, too, is displayed by logic. When one thing causes another thing the conception of the thing logically entails the conception of the other. We don't even have the conception of a thing unless we have the conception of the cause that logically entails it. *The knowledge of an effect depends on and involves the knowledge of a cause.*[30]

Once he was thrown out of his community, his business venture with his brother had, of course, to end. Gabriel is no longer even allowed to speak with his elder brother and business partner. Spinoza has therefore replaced the entrepreneurship characteristic of one of the Portuguese Nation with lens-grinding. It is an occupation that suits him splendidly, not only bringing him into contact with the latest developments in the new mathematical sciences, but also allowing him the solitude he now requires in order to pursue the progress of his understanding. Now even his means of support separates him from the Jews, severs him from his past.

He and his lathe move first to Rijnsburg, a little village well known for its tolerance, not far from Leiden, which has a university where he has attended some lectures on Cartesianism. Then he moves even farther away from Amsterdam, to Voorburg, a place slightly more cosmopolitan than the bucolic Rijnsburg, but still offering the peace and quiet he finds so essential, especially after the turmoil of La Nação, the human bondage of Amsterdam's Jewry.

Voorburg is just outside of The Hague, where the astronomer Christiaan Huygens lives. Christiaan's father, who was Descartes' friend, had called The Hague "a village that knows no equal."

Heinrich Oldenburg, originally from Germany but now residing in London, has assumed the office of the secretary of the Royal Society of London, and as such it is his happy obligation to become acquainted with the creative minds of Europe. On one of his trips to The Hague he is persuaded to pay a visit to the banished Jew who lives not far away. Oldenburg forms a favorable impression, initiating an epistolary exchange which will connect Spinoza, via Oldenburg, to important thinkers and scientists throughout Europe.

Spinoza's house in Rijnsburg

Oldenburg is certain, from his observations of the temperate man with whom he conversed in Voorburg, that the man cannot possibly be, as he is rumored to be, an atheist. For he lives a sober life, free from any trace of corruption or licentiousness, which could not be the case of one who was truly irreligious. Therefore, he is certain that there can be nothing dangerous to the spirit of Christianity in Spinoza's philosophy, and urges him to publish his work for the benefit of all:

> I would by all means advise you not to begrudge to the learned those works in philosophy and theology, which you have composed with the talent that distinguishes you. Publish them, I beg you, whatever be the verdict of petty theologians. Your country is free; the course of philosophy should there be free also. Your own pru-

dence will, doubtless, suggest to you, that your ideas and opinions should be put forth as quietly as possible. For the rest, commit the issue to fortune. Come then, good sir, cast away all fear of exciting against you the pigmies of our time. Long enough have we sacrificed to ignorance and pedantry. Let us spread the sails of true knowledge, and explore the recesses of nature more thoroughly than heretofore. Your meditations can, I take it, be printed in your country with impunity; nor need any scandal among the learned be dreaded because of them. If these be your patrons and supporters (and I warrant me you will find them so), why should you dread the carpings of ignorance? I will not let you go, my honoured friend, till I have gained my request; nor will I ever, so far as in me lies, allow thoughts of such importance as yours to rest in eternal silence.[31]

As it turns out, though, Oldenburg will be deeply scandalized when Spinoza at last "commit[s] the issue to fortune" and publishes his *Tractatus Theologico-Politicus*. Spinoza's views are less compatible with Christianity than Oldenburg had suspected. Their epistolary exchange—of such interest to Spinoza scholars—will suffer from the estrangement.

One of Oldenburg's letters to Spinoza makes reference to the fever of messianism that is sweeping through the body of Jewry (to use something of the language of old Aboab, who has now been made the chief rabbi of Amsterdam since the death of Morteira), in the person of Sabbatai Zevi, the self-proclaimed Messiah from Smyrna, Turkey.

Spinoza's workroom at Rijnsburg

Having gone through the traditional training in Talmud, Sabbatai Zevi had turned at an early age to the study of the *Zohar*. His interpretation of the distinction between the *Ein Sof*, the core of Infinity that has removed Itself from the world and so lies beyond our knowledge, and the *Sefirot*, God's manifestations in the world, differs somewhat from Ha-Ari's, so that he is said by some to have carried Lurianic insight to its next stage. He is also reputed to be so serious an ascetic that none of his several marriages has ever been consummated. He is reported to go through long periods of sustained sorrow and racking anguish, when he cannot cease his weeping, to then emerge into an ecstasy of inspired religious frenzy, beholding visions and prophecies, going for days without the mortal need for sleep or any form of physical sustenance.[32] Men can see that he is either madman or Messiah. Exigency and yearning dispose Jewish community after Jewish community toward the latter, and least likely, alternative.

Oldenburg writes to ask Spinoza what he has heard of the phenomenon:

> Here there is a wide-spread rumor that the Israelites, who have been dispersed for more than two thousand years, are to return to their homeland. Few hereabout believe it, but many wish it. Do let your friend know what you hear about this matter, and what you think. . . . I am anxious to know what the Jews of Amsterdam have heard about it, and how they are affected by so momentous an announcement, which, if true, is likely to bring about a world crisis.[33]

Jews across the Diaspora are convinced, Ashkenazic as well as Sephardic (though the latter count more heavily among the followers), that they are at last delivered. It is the conclusion that they had long been awaiting, the expectation of it passed along the generations, drawn from the suffering that also was passed along the generations. The Jewish massacres of the Chmielniki uprising—a Ukrainian peasant revolt that had unleashed a wave of atrocities that had decimated Ashkenazic Jewry—in addition to the relentless torments of the Inquisition to which Sephardic Jewry has been subjected, are seen now as signs that the messianic era is at last upon them.

The Jews of Amsterdam have fallen under the spell of the

self-proclaimed Messiah with special furor,[34] so that normal life has been for them suspended, and they are reportedly forsaking their businesses to spend all day in the synagogue, praying and purifying, as if every day is Yom Kippur, their personal fates hanging in the balance as the God on High makes up His mind as to who shall be saved and who not.

Shrewd Portuguese businessmen though they may be, they are selling off their properties at great losses. Abraham Pereira, one of the richest of Amsterdam's Portuguese Jews, a merchant prince, has offered his entire fortune of several million to the Messiah, a fact of which he makes certain that the Messiah knows. Still the shrewd businessman, he wants to ensure a supernatural return for his outlay.[35]

The Jews are even preparing to dig up the corpses in the cemetery in Ouderkerk so that they can transport them to Jerusalem, there to be resurrected. One of the rabbis of Venice, to whom the Amsterdam community had been wont to turn for *halakhic* guidance in their earlier days when they were less certain of themselves, writes to express his astonished disapproval that "the graves of them that sleep in the dust have been disturbed [contrary to Jewish Law] so as to remove the bones of the dead from their graves."

But the messianic enthusiasm of Rabbi Aboab is not to be dampened by any cool, rational Venetian doubt. His fervor for the approaching Messiah inspires him to write a new prayer to replace the prayer Jews recite each Sabbath and festival for the ruler of the land. Now the Jews of Amsterdam no longer offer their prayer for the Grand Pensionary of Holland but rather for "Our Lord the Great King Sabbatai Zevi, the Anointed of the Lord, the Messiah son of David, the Messiah King, the Messiah Redeemer, the Messiah Savior, our Messiah of Righteousness, the Anointed of the God of Jacob."

The news that the Messiah had been imprisoned in a fortress in Gallipoli by the Turkish sultan, who had become alarmed by the commotion among the Jews but still does not wish to make a martyr, does not diminish the flames of delusion but only feeds them. Letters arrive from Constantinople bringing the most fantastical news, quickly disseminated by word of mouth and printed pamphlets, and believed with *kavana* by Rabbi Aboab and his followers. Sabbatai had resurrected the dead and passed through the locked and barred doors of his prison, which opened of themselves. The iron chains with which his hands and feet were fettered had broken of themselves.

Yes, of course, Spinoza has heard of how the Jews of Amsterdam are affected by, in Oldenburg's words, "so momentous an announcement." There is nothing in their reaction to surprise him: *Partly from piety, partly for the sake of opposing those who cultivate the natural science, they prefer to remain in ignorance of natural causes, and are eager to hear only of what is least comprehensible to them and consequently evokes their greatest wonder. . . . This idea seems to have originated with the early Jews, in order to refute the beliefs of the Gentiles of their time who worshipped visible gods—the Sun, the Moon, the Earth, Water, Sky and so on—and to prove to them that these gods were weak and inconstant, or changeable and under the command of an invisible God, they boasted of their miracles, from which they further sought to prove that the whole of Nature was directed for their sole benefit by command of God whom they worshipped. This idea has found such favour with mankind that they have not ceased to this day to invent miracles with a view to convincing people that they are more beloved of God than others, and are the final causes of God's creation and continuous directions of the world.*[36]

In the summer of 1666, it became known in Amsterdam that many communities had sent emissaries, or at the very least letters of homage, to the new Messiah. One of the believers, Rabbi Isaac Nahar, who had been a fellow student of Spinoza's in the Talmud Torah, has already set off to greet the Messiah, and a letter is sent to him to present to Sabbatai Zevi, signed by Chief Rabbi Aboab.[37]

And how badly it all ends for them, this delirium of false salvation, when the news arrives that the Jews' Messiah has not been walking through the doors of his prison but, quite the contrary, is at the mercy of his captors. Given the choice of martyrdom or conversion, he has donned the turban and become Azziz Mehemed Effendi. Some are so committed to their self-deception that they continue to believe in the face of their false Messiah's apostasy. Indeed, they believe with even deeper faith, because with even more desperation.

Knowing the Portuguese Nation of Amsterdam as he does, Spinoza could have easily deduced the madness that has descended upon them at the word that their Messiah has arrived. It is a madness as transcendent as their history. The fevered dream had always been of redemption. They were waiting—yearly, hourly, momentarily—for their Redeemer. Even in the pardise of *Sepharad*—the legend of which had grown with the years—the longing had been for Jerusalem. Judah Halevy, who had luxuriated in the cultural riches of Moorish Spain, had cried out in his poetry "to see the dust of the ruined shrine." Could such ancient dreams be displaced by the pretty tulips of Amsterdam? Though he has long ceased to identify with the ongoing dramas of his over-wrought former community, he knows these people far too intimately, knows their worldview from the inside, having once inhabited it himself, from boyhood up, not to be able to resist feeling compassion for their plight. *I have made a ceaseless effort not to ridicule, not to bewail, not to scorn human actions, but to understand them.*

Though he is farther away now from Amsterdam, still he keeps up with his friends there, those among whom he had first discovered what it is that true kinship consists in. There are, among others, Lodewijk Meyer, Simon de Vries, Pieter Balling, Jarig Jellesz, Jan Rieuwertsz. Meyer is two years older than Spinoza, a physician and freethinker, with broadly humanistic interests, not only in philosophy but in literature and most especially drama. He is now in fact serving as the director of the Amsterdam Municipal Theater.[38] De Vries, whose health is even more precariously delicate than Spinoza's, had been born into a large Mennonite family of well-established merchants. De Vries has always worried about Spinoza's finances, believing that it is imperative for the philosopher to enjoy complete freedom from monetary worries. He had offered the philosopher 2,000 florins, which Spinoza declined to accept, and had wanted Spinoza to be his heir, which the philosopher also declined. Balling was also born a Mennonite, though now he translates his religious thinking into Spinoza's language and will publish a book, *The Light on the Candlestick*, that will blast organized religion for placing dogma at its center where the soul ought to have been. The light of the title is the soul's light, an idea much spoken of in Protestant circles, but which Balling Spinozistically identifies as the natural light of reason. Jellesz had been a prosperous trader of spices but quit to find a more meaningful life, and he will help to defray the cost of some of Spinoza's publications. And last of all is Jan Rieuwertsz, a bookseller and publisher. It is from his printing press that all of Spinoza's explosive writing will emerge to startle the world, and after his death his son will carry on his father's tradition, continuing to publish Spinoza.

Spinoza has long known the form that his own work must take. The five books of his Scripture must conform to the rigorous logic of reality itself, and this means proofs— rigorous, arduous proofs. His friends clamor to see his writings, and when Balling travels out to Voorburg to see him, Spinoza sends him back to Amsterdam with some pages in his hands, setting out some proofs concerning God and nature. The Amsterdam friends form a discussion group, now to study Spinoza rather than Scripture, devoting the same painstaking interpretative skills as Spinoza himself had taught them to devote to Scripture. Only now they have the benefit of being able to solicit the author himself for elucidation. So Simon de Vries (whose brother, Trijntje, upon Simon's premature death, will continue Simon's financial concern for Spinoza, offering him a yearly stipend of 500 florins, which the philosopher deems too much, accepting only 300 florins) writes to Spinoza:

> I have for a long time wished to be present with you; but the weather and the hard winter have not been propitious to me. I sometimes complain of my lot, in that we are separated from each other by so long a distance. Happy, yes, most happy is the fellow-lodger, abiding under the same roof with you, who can talk with you on the best of subjects, at dinner, and during your walks.[39] As regards our club, the following is its order. One of us (that is everyone by turn) reads through and, as far as he understands it, expounds and also demonstrates the whole of your work, according to the sequence and order of your propositions. Then if it happens if on any point we cannot satisfy one another, we have resolved to make a note of it and to write to you, so that, if possible, it may be made clearer to us, and we may be able under your guidance to defend the truth against those who are superstitiously religious and Christian, and to stand against the attacks of the whole.[40]

His friends in Amsterdam grow somewhat jealous of the young boarder who has the benefit of the personal instruction of their master (for so they insist now on calling Spinoza). Spinoza does not trust the young boarder sufficiently to impart his own philosophy to him, and so instead instructs him in the foundations of Cartesianism. As a pedagogical tool, Spinoza is formalizing Descartes' *Principles of Philosophy*, putting it into the geometrical mode that he is employing in his own midnight work. The geometrical method does not ensure truth, since the definitions and axioms might be erroneous, so even a false metaphysics like Descartes'—which errs in its conception of God, of nature, and of man—can be geometricized.

Spinoza's friends beg him to confer on them the benefits that his young boarder is receiving, to write out for them the geometricization of the Cartesian principles. He obliges them, taking out time from the work of his own proofs, and this results in the only book that he is ever to publish under his own name, *Descartes' Principles of Philosophy*.

"Some of my friends asked me to make them a copy of a treatise containing a precise account of the Second Part of Descartes' Principles, demonstrated in the geometrical style, and of the main points in metaphysics," he writes to Oldenburg, explaining why he has taken so long to respond to the last letter.

Previously I had dictated this to a certain man to whom I did not want to teach my own opinions openly. They asked me to prepare the First Part also by the same method, as soon as I could. Not to disappoint my friends, I immediately undertook to do this and finished it in two weeks. I delivered it to my friends, who in the end asked me to let them publish the whole work. They easily won my agreement, on the condition that one of them,[41] in my presence, would provide it with a more elegant style and add a short preface warning readers that I did not acknowledge all the opinions contained in this treatise as my own, since I had written many things in it which were the very opposite of what I held, and illustrating this by one or two examples. One of my friends, to whose care the publishing of this little book has been entrusted, has promised to do all this and that is why I stayed for a while in Amsterdam. Since I returned to this village, where I am now living, I have hardly been my own master because of the friends who have been kind enough to visit me.

Loneliness is not a problem. Quite the contrary, the problem is to secure the long uninterrupted stretches of time necessary for laying out the fullness of what he is beholding, through the eyes of his mind, the proofs that reproduce the necessary connections that constitute the one substance, the vast system of necessary connections which must exist, the *causa sui* that explains why it must be and what it must be. *Deus sive natura.*

He had known instinctively, from the time that he was the smallest child, listening to his teachers and feeling the gnawing animal in his chest, that the purely arbitrary element in the divine explanations offered were deeply, blasphemously erroneous.

Reality is determined by divine necessity in the strongest sense possible, since the necessity *is* the divinity. What Reality *is* is the one and only system of necessary connections. That is the *causa sui*, the thing that explains itself, outside of which nothing can be conceived. It is logic itself, not its rules but its applications—the vast and infinite system of logical entailments that are not merely abstract, as we usually conceive of them, but rather coated with the substance of being. Reality is ontologically enriched logic. It is a logic that is animated, alive with thought, infinitely aware of its own infinite self. And it is, simultaneously, a logic that is embodied, a logic that generates itself in space, resulting in the material world.

Outside of this infinite system of necessary connections, there can be . . . nothing. This infinite system composes the entire explanatory nexus, and were there to be anything outside of it, that something would be ipso facto inexplicable. And there can be nothing inexplicable in the universe—this is the beating heart of Spinoza's rationalism—no arbitrary elements that are simply there for no reason at all. The denial of a thing's explicability is tantamount to the denial of that thing's reality. To be is to be explicable.

So of course there can be only one substance, since this substance constitutes the whole vast system of logic itself, the entire explanatory nexus, the implicative order. What outside of logic could possibly explain—logically entail—logic? Logic alone explains itself. It alone has no need for an external cause. Revising the old Aristotelian notion of "substance" so that it can accommodate reality, he will use it to mean that which requires no external cause, that which itself explains the being of itself. One has to do some violence to existing vocabulary in order to press it into service of the truth. So he shall use the word "substance" to christen what truly exists—not substance as Aristotle and the Scholastics conceived of it. This is then what the one and only substance is—embodied and animated logic. All things, including us, have a determined locus in the nexus of necessary connections: our existence and our nature are entailed by it. Spinoza's way of saying this is that all things, including us, are the "modifications" of the one and only substance, the all-embracing infinite system of necessary connections.

There is an infinity of modifications, realizing the infinity of logical implications—a vast profligacy of existence burgeoning forth from the logic of the world, crowding out the possibility of contingency and sheer happenstance. *From the necessity of the divine nature must follow an infinite number of things in infinite ways—that is, all things which can fall within the sphere of infinite intellect.*[42]

The world is the all-embracing web of necessary truths, intelligible through and through—and our own individual salvation rests in our knowing this. Our own *personal* salvation, motivated by our essential commitment to our own individual survival and well-being, consists in achieving the most *impersonal* of worldviews. When we have attained an adequate knowledge of the infinite system that is the one and only self-explanatory substance, *Deus sive natura*, and by doing so transformed our very selves, purging our own minds of the illusions of contingency, reconstituting our minds with the divine necessity, then only peace will be possible within each of us, the peace of acquiescence, and only peace will be possible among us, the peace of unity of purpose. And then there will be blessedness.

Thus in life it is before all things useful to perfect the understanding, or reason, as far as we can, and in this alone man's highest happiness, or blessedness, consists; indeed blessedness is nothing else but the contentment of spirit, which arises from the intuitive knowledge of God.[43]

The midnight work is consuming him now. While he polishes his lenses during the day, he is polishing his proofs of the night before in his head. Both require the most meticulous work. But the midnight work is exhilaratingly expansive—the expansiveness of the self into the world, which is what pleasure is, the love of the object that is causing our pleasure, which now is nothing less than *Deus sive natura* itself.

As the true Christians had realized, as the Jew Jesus had apparently realized, love is the only emotion that can consistently coexist with the true knowledge of God. The emotion that floods the mind in the true contemplation of God is the purest of loves. All the painful emotions that are predicated on contingency—fear, regret, anger, hatred, remorse—are nullified in the vision of God.

To know God is to know the necessity of all, to bask in the refulgent necessity, feeling only love for it: the highest state of blessedness, the intellectual love of God. *Amor Dei intellectualis.*[44]

He who clearly and distinctly understands himself and his emotions loves God, and so much more in proportion as he more understands himself and his emotions.[45]

This love towards God must hold the chief place in the mind.[46]

He who loves God cannot endeavor that God will love him in return.[47] Love, an emotion, a species of pleasure deriving from the *conatus* that makes finite things the things that they are, is not an attitude that can be attributed to the Infinite Intellect of God, certainly not in the same way it is attributed to us. To wish for God to love oneself, this one modification in the infinite system of modifications, is to wish God not to be God, a wish patently inconsistent with knowing and loving God. *For if a man should so endeavour, he would desire that God, whom he loves, should not be God, and consequently he would desire to feel pain; which is absurd. . . .*

This love towards God cannot be stained by the emotion of envy or jealousy; contrariwise, it is the more fostered in proportion as we conceive a greater number of men to be joined to God by the same bond of love.[48]

All the ceremonies of the superstitious religions, all the slanted versions of their own histories, are founded on the irrational—the irreligious!—desire to make God love us in return, and the indulgence in the jealous fantasy that he loves us—our kind, our people—more than others.

Spinoza is always offended to hear himself described as irreligious, impious. *Whatsoever we desire and do, whereof we are the cause in so far as we possess the idea of God, or know God, I set down to Religion. The desire of well-doing which is engendered by a life according to reason, I call piety.*[49]

And how different from the rational worship of religion are the superstitious ways of carrying on, the pleading and groveling, that pass in most superstitions as worshiping God. Men worship as if it is an arbitrary and exceedingly vain tyrant whom they must placate and flatter, each religion declaring itself more worthy of His favor. This is how the religions all distinguish themselves from one another—Jews, and Christians, and Turks. Like children fighting for their parents' attention, they never realize that everyone's true happiness and blessedness consists solely in the enjoyment of good, not in priding himself that he alone is enjoying that good to the exclusion of others. *He who counts himself more blessed because he alone enjoys well-being not shared by others, or because he is more blessed and fortunate than others, knows not what is true happiness, and blessedness; and the joy he derives therefrom, if it be not mere childishness, has its only source in spite and malice.*[50]

The *Tractatus Theologico-Politicus* has been printed by the tried and true friend of philosophy, Jan Rieuwertsz, though Spinoza has attempted to protect him by putting the name of a pseudonymous publisher on the cover. If truth is to be measured by the degree of the protest against it, then Spinoza has succeeded most admirably. Still, the vehemence of holy denunciation and hatred has perhaps made it impossible for Spinoza's proofs to be shown to the world. So be it.

In the natural light of reason the seeming contingencies melt away, leaving only the indestructible crystalline web, revealed as that much more intricate for having absorbed the seeming accidents into itself. Contingency is a mere illusion, the outcome of not perceiving the web of necessity. *But a thing can in no respect be called contingent save in relation to the imperfection of our knowledge.*[51] There is only one logically possible world. And it exists because it must. *Things could not have been brought into being by God in any manner or in any order differently from that which has obtained.*[52] The only rational response, whatsoever the provocation, is to understand and to acquiesce.

These propositions, and all that relate to the true way of life and religions, are easily proved. . . . Namely, that hatred should be overcome with love, and that every man should desire for others the good

that he seeks for himself. . . . The strong man has ever first in his
thoughts, that all things follow from the necessity of the divine
nature; so that whatsoever he deems to be hurtful and evil, and what-
soever, accordingly, seems to him impious, horrible, unjust, and base,
assumes that appearance owing to his own disordered, fragmentary,
and confused view of the universe. Wherefore, he strives before all
things to conceive things as they really are, and to remove the hin-
drances to true knowledge, such as are hatred, anger, envy, derision,
pride, and similar emotions. . . . Thus he endeavors, as we said before,
as far as in him lies to do good, and to go on his way rejoicing.[53]

No painful emotions can survive within the apprehension
of *Deus sive natura*. Even the incidents that are personally
painful—the falsifications of what he had written in the *Trac-*
tatus Theologico-Politicus, the ever more violent defamations of
him as atheist, materialist, immoralist—that threaten one's
very essence, the project of flourishing in the world, once
subsumed under the vision of necessity, lose their capacity to
hurt one in quite the same way. To behold how they fit in
with the whole immense spread that is the object of one's
knowledge, and thus of one's pleasure, and thus of one's love,
is to transform them from passive emotions into the active
emotions of understanding.

It may be objected that, as we understand God as the cause of all
things, we by that very fact regard God as the cause of pain. But I
make answer, that, in so far as we understand the causes of pain, it to
that extent, ceases to be a passion, that is, it ceases to be pain; there-
fore in so far as we understand God to be the cause of pain, we to that
extent feel pleasure.[54]

Louis XIV has decided to pursue his vision of *gloire* by
invading the Low Lands. His standing army is immense,

170,000 strong. His new method of firing muskets, the flint-lock, which ignites the powder in the pan with a spark caused by a piece of flint drawn across roughened steel, rather than long fuses of rope, means that the French guns can be held ready and safe at half cock. The well-trained and well-armed French press on across the Low Lands, and in order to impede their relentless advance the dikes are opened as a last and desperate measure. Atop the normal mayhem and misery of war, there is also massive flooding.

I rejoice that your philosophers are alive [Spinoza writes to Oldenburg] and remember themselves and their republic. I shall expect news of what they have done recently, when the warriors are sated with blood, and rest in order to renew their strength a little. If that famous scoffer [Democritus] were alive today, he would surely die of laughter. These disorders, however, do not move me to laughter nor even to tears, but rather to philosophizing, and to the better observation of human nature. I do not think it right for me to laugh at nature, much less to weep over it, when I consider that men, like the rest, are only a part of nature, and that I do not know how each part of nature is connected with the whole of it, and how with the other parts. And I find that it is from the mere want of this kind of knowledge that certain things in Nature were formerly wont to appear to me vain, disorderly, and absurd, because I perceive them only in part and mutilated, and they do not agree with our philosophic mind. But now I let every man live according to his own ideas. Let those who will, by all means die for their good, so long as I am allowed to live for truth.[55]

It is the *rampjaar*, the year of Dutch disaster. The glorious experiment in republicanism has come to an end. The Dutch have managed to beat back the French, but the losses have maddened the masses and they are looking for someone to blame, and their crazed gaze has fallen on Jan de Witt. It is a stain that will last for all times on the history of this country.

Jan de Witt had stood for all that was best in the Dutch experiment in enlightened government, an experiment in which Spinoza had taken so lively an interest and pleasure that the only social identification he would ever allow himself was "citizen of the Dutch Republic." Jan de Witt had been the politician who had wrought this political wonder. Himself a lawyer and a mathematician of no mean talent, he had been the Grand Pensioner of the States of Holland since 1653, when he was elected at twenty-eight, and had been reelected in 1658, 1663, and 1668, holding office until just before his death.

He had led the country to its prosperity (using his mathematical skills for such prosaic tasks as balancing the budget) and secured the peace with the European countries that threatened Holland's endeavor to persist in its own being and flourish: England, France, Spain.

He was always an opponent of the House of Orange, the royalists who had ruled this country through their office of stadtholder. To countervail against the power of the royalists, he had encouraged the rise of the mercantile class,

Jan de Witt

which had resulted in the unprecedented rise of affluence in the land and power abroad.

The country, as he found it in 1653, had been brought to the brink of ruin through the war with England, and he resolved to bring about peace. He rejected Cromwell's suggestion of the union of England and Holland, though his treaty with them, in 1654, had made large concessions. The treaty had included a secret article, called the Act of Seclusion, by which the provinces of Holland pledged themselves not to elect a stadtholder. Cromwell wanted to thwart the ambitions of William III, the young prince of Orange, just as much as de Witt did, since the House of Orange was allied with England's Stuarts. William II, young William's father, had married the eldest daughter of Charles I of England.

But the orthodox Calvinist ministers and regents of The Hague were against the Act of Seclusion and incited the people to revolt against the Republicans. A little later (1669), however, the States of Holland made a new act, the Eternal Edict, which outlawed the House of Orange from holding the office of stadtholder for all times.

De Witt's pro-French policy had been his undoing. With the devastation wrought by the French army, popular opinion turned against Jan de Witt, the irrational need to blame someone whipped up by the conservative forces in the land, the more orthodox and intolerant of the Calvinists, who had always favored the House of Orange. Jan's brother, Cornelius de Witt, was arrested under false charges of fomenting sedition. He was tortured, but his captors could not force a false confession out of him. The conspirators—including almost certainly William III, who now became, despite the Eternal Edict, stadtholder—changed their tactics, obviously feeling it necessary to eliminate the de Witts entirely. A forged letter brought Jan to the prison where his brother Cornelius was being held. With both of the brothers there, the crowd—no doubt already alerted by the conspirators—descended on the prison and dragged out the two brothers. Jan de Witt, a friend of philosophy and thus of freedom, was, together with Cornelius, torn to pieces by the mob. The atrocities the crowd inflicted on their bodies is beyond the imagination to comprehend. They fed their organs to dogs and hung their severed limbs from lampposts.

Spinoza's name has often enough been linked to Jan de Witt's by their respective enemies. A pamphlet from 1672, the *rampjaar*, states that de Witt gave "the evil Spinoza" the protection to write and to publish the *Tractatus Theologico-Politicus*, "brought forth from hell by the fallen Jew Spinoza, in which it is proven, in an unprecedented, atheistic fashion, that the word of God must be explained and understood through Philosophy, and which was published with the knowledge of Mr. Jan."[56]

Spinoza, on hearing what the mob—which had included respectable middle-class burghers—had perpetrated, is for once ready to ignore his watchword engraved in his signet ring, *caute*. He is moved to violate his own dictate of reason, derived in Part IV of *The Ethics:* "The virtue of a free man is seen to be as great when it declines danger, as when it overcomes it,"[57] and the further corollary he had drawn, "The free man is as courageous in timely retreat as in combat; or a free man shows equal courage or presence of mind whether he elect to give battle or to retreat." He had derived these propositions, true, but even so the time of declining dangers is not now. Timely retreat is not an option, and he elects to give battle. He has prepared a placard proclaiming ULTIMI BARBARORUM (YOU ARE THE GREATEST OF BARBARIANS), which he intends to erect at the site of the assassinations. But his landlord, the sympathetic van der Spyck, has prudently locked the doors and won't let him out, thinking quite reasonably that the crowd would like nothing more than to rip Spinoza to pieces as well, and feed his remains to the dogs.[58] Then, too, it is not unreasonable to imagine them turning their vengeance against the property where the philosopher lived. Van der Spyck double-locks the doors.

The mystery of human suffering, its inevitability and extravagance—he had contemplated it often enough in his boyhood. Suffering was the constant topic of their lives, suffering linked with salvation, each implying the other; otherwise how in God's name could the suffering be reconciled with God Himself? The tales that had bled the heart of all La Nação, as the Portuguese Nation still insisted on calling itself as it went through the motions of becoming Dutchified, had bled his heart, too: of forced confessions and heroic martyrdom, of "Judah called the faithful" crying out the words of the *Shema* as the flames rose around him. The hideous sounds of anguish had carried from Portugal and from Spain, so that they were always in their ears, making all of them half-mad, never able to distance themselves from the questions always present in the howls of torment: How can God allow such outrages to be perpetrated against the innocent? Where is the Merciful One's mercy?

But the mystery is no mystery. The world was not created with a view toward human well-being. Logic entails what it does, despite our parochial wishes. It's not surprising that out of the vastness of logical implications there are a profusion that threaten our endeavor to persist in our being and to thrive. So nature will produce such illnesses and disasters as make men's lives a misery. And so, too, men will through their blind bondage to their emotions compound the misery of their own lives and those of others. It is only reason that can save us. Why then, we might ask, did not God make men more reasonable? Why did he not make them more intelligent? That is what the problem of evil comes down to: the stubborn stupidity of mankind. Why did God make men so stubbornly stupid? *Things are not more or less perfect, according as they delight or offend human senses, or according as they are serviceable or repugnant to mankind. To those who ask why God did not so create all men, that they should be governed only by reason, I give no answer but this: because matter was not lacking to him for the creation of every degree of perfection from highest to lowest; or, more strictly, because the laws of his nature are so vast, as to suffice for the production of everything conceivable by an infinite intelligence, as I have shown.*[59]

The midnight work is complete. The proofs—on the nature of the world, and of ourselves, of what our knowledge of the world can consist in and how it can bring us peace—are completed.

He had once begun a treatise on the theory of knowledge but had never completed it. It was ill-conceived to think one could explicate knowledge without first explicating reality. But in the opening paragraphs of the abandoned treatise he had written of the search after the ultimate happiness—continuous, supreme, and unending—that all men desire, he has found this thing: it is reality itself. When we are able to grasp its infinite sweep, to sense the infinite context embracing each finite modification, then there is continuous, supreme, and unending happiness. *Whatsoever we understand by the third kind of knowledge, we take delight in and our delight is accompanied by the idea of God as cause.*[60] It is in a person's own power, and it is only in his own power, to attain this happiness, so long as he persists in his being, no matter how the world might batter him.

And now it is Spinoza's desire to offer this thing, reality itself, and the continuous supreme and unending happiness that can be ours in its contemplation, to the world. It is his desire to publish the proofs that he has been perfecting through the years, ever since he entered gladly on the path that was opened to him when the Jews of Amsterdam decreed his banishment.

He travels to Amsterdam in August 1675, to see after the publication of *The Ethics*, but he finds that the atmosphere there—the aftermath of the *rampjaar*—has foreclosed the possibility of publication, as he writes to Oldenburg (who has become somewhat reconciled to Spinoza, despite his *Tractatus*, though a brief imprisonment in the Tower of London has, if anything, increased his cautious approach to anything smacking of blasphemy; it is hard on a man like Oldenburg, torn between his admiration for the exciting science of his times and his own terror at unorthodoxy).

When I received your letter of the 22 July, I had set out to Amsterdam for the purpose of publishing the book I had mentioned to you. While I was negotiating, a rumor gained currency that I had in the press a book concerning God, wherein I endeavoured to show that there is no God. This report was believed by many. Hence certain theologians, perhaps the authors of the rumour, took occasion to complain of me before the prince and the magistrates; moreover, the stupid Cartesians, being suspected of favouring me, endeavoured to remove the aspersion by abusing everywhere my opinions and writings, a course which they still pursue. When I became aware of this through trustworthy men, who also assured me that the theologians were everywhere lying in wait for me, I determined to put off publishing till I saw how things were going, and I proposed to inform you of my intentions. But matters seem to get worse and worse, and I am still uncertain what to do.[61]

While he is visiting in Amsterdam, there is much talk of the Jews, who are just then celebrating the dedication of their most magnificent new synagogue, the Esnoga, built at the end of Breestraat.[62] The building—really a complex, for the synagogue itself is surrounded by a low structure that houses the rabbinical offices, the various charities and foundations, the whole hierarchical organization of La Nação—is the largest, stateliest synagogue in all of Europe, costing almost 165,000 guilders and having been under construction for five years. The date, 1672, resplendent in gilt, is erroneous, inscribing the year when it was supposed to have been completed. But that had been the *rampjaar*, when all such work had been halted.

How the Sephardim of Amsterdam have risen in the world. It is seventy-five years since they first arrived here in secret and were discovered, behind the locked shutters to which Iberia had accustomed them, saying their Friday night prayers. Now there are eight days of ceremonies and celebrations, which the genteel of Gentile society attend, including members of regent families.

A strange curiosity has come over the philosopher, and he walks over the bridge into the Jewish quarter and goes to stand at a distance from the commotion before the entrance. It is a golden August day, and the synagogue stands as if gilded by the sun. IN THE ABUNDANCE OF YOUR LOVING KINDNESS WILL I COME INTO YOUR HOUSE. He reads the Hebrew words inscribed over the entrance, the words of the psalmist. Above certain letters there is a dot, the so-called *peret katan*, signifying the year. Aboab's name, too, is contained acrostically in the verse; the old *khakham*—perhaps chastised by the Sabbataian madness that had overcome him, though Spinoza rather suspects not—is still the chief rabbi of Amsterdam, and the prime mover behind the magnificent Esnoga.

The philosopher keeps his distance, watching as the carriages arrive. He looks at the children, many of them no doubt the offspring of boys with whom he had once shared the classroom, as he sat there trying to make sense of his *rubi*, wondering that his respected elders could have been satisfied with explanations that he, a mere grasshopper, found pitifully lacking.

The children, dressed in their Sabbath finery, can barely contain themselves from excitement. There are pairs and pairs of dark eyes sparkling. He would doubtless know all of their surnames. There must be some Spinozas and Espinozas among them. He would not know any of his nieces or nephews, grandnieces or grandnephews, were they to be present-

Dedication of the new Sephardic synagogue in Amsterdam, 1675
(*Courtesy of the Israel Museum, Jerusalem*)

ing themselves right at this moment beneath his eyes. He
has no idea how many such kin he might have acquired over
the years.

A philosopher can seem a cold-blooded creature to those
who cannot penetrate his reasons. None know the efforts it
might have cost him to attain his reptilian detachment.

His sister Miriam had had one child before she died,
Daniel. The child had been less than a year old when the
mother had died. Miriam, his little mother, his *mais velha*. He
can still remember her kindness to him, though she was only
a child herself, eight years old, motherless and no doubt for-
lorn herself. Her husband, Samuel de Casseres, had married
Spinoza's other sister, Rebecca, and, in addition to Daniel,

they had had more children together—Hanna, Michael, and Benjamin—before Casseres died, also at an early age. Samuel had been a rabbinical student, the favored protégé of Morteira. He had delivered Morteira's eulogy in 1660, and within the year was himself eulogized.

There had been a certain unpleasantness with Rebecca, involving money. He hadn't thought of it in years. It was the sort of thing that can happen in families, that happens quite often. It had involved the distribution of their father's assets. Rebecca was already promised to Casseres, with his many ties to the synagogue authorities, and Spinoza could easily deduce how the *parnassim* would be inclined to decide in favor of Casseres's future wife. So Spinoza had done the unthinkable. He had brought the case before the state authorities, and they had decided in his favor.

Perhaps this act, more than any of his blasphemous views—whether on God, the Jews, or immortality—had incited the *parnassim* to fulminate against him with such bombastic excess in the writ of excommunication that they had prepared, and which he had never deigned to recognize.

"All the better; they do not force me to do anything that I would not have done of my own accord if I did not dread scandal; but, since they want it that way, I enter gladly on the path that is opened to me, with the consolation that my departure will be more innocent than was the exodus of the early Hebrews from Egypt."

His own fury had been something fierce. It had burned in him for years. Now not even the memory of its ashes remain.

He stands watching as the last of the community's dark-eyed children disappear inside the gates. Thoughts pass over him, memories of a life so distant it seems difficult to believe it once had been his.

One thing he knows for certain. It is not for him to stand here on this corner, an outsider in the Jewish quarter, in human bondage to sorrowful memory. He turns on his heel and, without allowing himself one more backward glance, walks quickly away.

It is impossible that man should not be a part of Nature, or that he should be capable of undergoing no changes, save such as can be understood through his nature only as their adequate cause. . . . Again, if it were possible that man should undergo no changes save such as can be understood solely through the nature of man, it would follow that he would not be able to die, but would always necessarily exist.[63]

It has come on him far more suddenly than he would have anticipated had he ever allowed himself to anticipate it. It is the one thought that, even though it be entailed, the free man shrinks from inferring, since it can only induce pain, the contraction of the self in the world.

The winter has been a hard one, but the coldness that has invaded him seems of a different sort, derived from a different source. There is a languor in his body, a heaviness that is beyond tiredness and that no amount of sleep can lighten. The hacking cough wakes him in the night, the wild thing gnawing at his lungs. The young friend, the very one he has sent for now, prescribes various sleeping draughts and other drugs to relieve the pains, which nevertheless deepen so that he knows it is beyond him to resist.

The young physician instructs van der Spyck's wife to cook an old cock and feed the philosopher the broth. The philosopher dutifully sips it, taking pleasure not only in its heat, which sends some solace to his ragged lungs, but in the smiling complacency of van der Spyck's good wife. He looks at her beaming ruddy face and takes another obedient spoonful, remembering how she had once asked him whether he thought she could be saved in the religion that she professed. He had answered her as he thought best when dealing with a person clearly not suited for philosophical reason: "Your religion is good, and you need not search for another one in order to be saved, as long as you apply yourself to a peaceful and pious life."

It is Sunday, and his landlord's family has gone to the morning services, returned for their Sabbath meal, and are making ready to return to church again. He bids them farewell and climbs the stairs to his forechamber, thinking he will not climb them again.

And now it has come to this. The whole infinite nexus of modifications has condensed itself for him to this one thought: the proofs that are locked away in his desk. He derived them from the world. They must now find their way back into the world.

You will make certain of it? he asks the young man who is sitting beside him, his friend and doctor.

You will secure it?

The obsidian eyes burn darker. Over the pallor an unnatural flush is spreading, rising from the fire within. When the doctor leans over to feel for his faltering pulse, he feels the heat of Spinoza rising in a cloud around him, like the myth of the soul rising to heaven.

His bed is the grandest object in the room, a large four-poster with red velvet curtains. It had been his parents' bed, and he has moved it with him. The only two objects of any material bulk that have accompanied him on his way are his lathe and this bed. His mother had died in it, so young, younger than her son Baruch is now. He remembers his child terror at hearing her cough, and how he had wondered that God could be so cruel. It is that child terror that chains men's minds.

He has not let the thought of his own death occupy his mind, even these last weeks, knowing how much faster it is coming upon him than he would have anticipated. *The free man thinks least of all things upon death, and his life is a meditation not on death but on life.*[64]

But we are finite, our bodies finite, subject to causes not under their own control. Dissolution comes to each thing.

Still there is that which will remain of him. Not the personal self, this cluster of modifications endeavoring to preserve its identity, to prosper and flourish, even now, gasping for breath, unable of itself to keep from desperately trying to persist in its own being. He knows what it is in him that will persist, the view of himself that he gains when out of himself, in the deepest and most blissful grasp of the whole, the intuitive intimation of full infinity by a finite modification that cannot possibly grasp it all. That particular finite modification that he is will soon be no more. But the thoughts that he has thought that were most true, that have pointed beyond themselves to the great vast system that entails them, as each of us points, however obscurely we may apprehend it, beyond ourselves to the vastness that entails us: this will remain for all eternity.

We feel and we know that we are eternal. For the mind feels those things that it conceives by understanding no less than those things that it remembers. For the eyes of the mind, whereby it sees and observes things, are none other than proofs.

The proofs. You will remember? You will see to it?

In the desk, locked in the writing desk. You understand what I am trying to tell you?

The proofs of his midnight toil. If men could study them so that they might behold what I have beheld. What I behold even now.

Death becomes less hurtful, in proportion as the mind's clear and distinct knowledge is greater, and, consequently, in proportion as the mind loves God.[65]

He wishes he could transmit this thought, that it is not just the fire of the disease that is making him burn. He wishes he could speak it to the young friend who looks at him with such an expression of pity and terror.

He is the last man in the world to pity. And if the terror be of this very thing, then there is no need for terror, either.

It is this very thought that men cannot think, the thought of this *no more*. One's entire nature repels this thought from entering. And in the repulsion people become confused, forming beliefs that lead them so far astray, into confusion and confusion's child, cruelty. Frightened, they make the world only that much more frightening.

The eyes of the mind. How glorious are our possibilities.

If the way which I have pointed out as leading to this result seems exceedingly hard, it may nevertheless be discovered. Needs must it be hard, since it is so seldom found. How would it be possible, if salvation were ready to our hand, and could without great labor be found, that it should be by almost all men neglected? But all things excellent are as difficult as they are rare.[66]

I am not forsaken.

I am free.

I am blessed.

Spinoza.

VI

Epilogue

When Hendrik van der Spyck returned with his family from church the afternoon of February 21, 1677, he was informed that Spinoza, with whom he had conversed only that morning on a favorite topic of his boarder's, the preacher's sermon, had died at around three o'clock, in the presence of the physician for whom he had sent and whose identity remains a mystery.[1]

It was van der Spyck who arranged for the burial of Spinoza. Mourners, including, according to Colerus, "many illustrious people," traveled to Voorburg from Amsterdam. There were six coaches that followed behind the wagon carrying the coffin to the cemetery at the New Church in Spuy, where the remains of Benedictus Spinoza were interred.

Van der Spyck was authorized to auction off Spinoza's clothes, furniture (including his parents' bed, the costliest article), and books, so that the philosopher's few remaining debts could be paid and the landlord's own expenses recovered. But even before he had made an inventory of Spinoza's effects, van der Spyck had sent the locked writing desk and its contents along to Amsterdam, where Spinoza's friends, including the printer Jan Rieuwertsz, were waiting for it.

Inside was a pile of letters, as well as the manuscripts of *The Ethics*, the *Political Treatise*, on which he had been working at the time of his death, and a *Hebrew Grammar*, which he had also been composing, so that men might undertake to read Scripture in its original language, using the principles of interpretation that Spinoza laid out in his *Tractatus*. The *Hebrew Grammar* recalls the jurist Hugo Grotius's begrudging comment on advising the authorities to allow the Portuguese Jews asylum in Amsterdam: "Besides, the scholars among them may be of some service to us by teaching us the Hebrew language."

By the end of the year Spinoza's friends managed to publish Latin and Dutch editions of Spinoza's posthumous works, including some of his selected letters, respecting the philosopher's pronounced preference for privacy by leaving out any of a personal nature. The title pages of the works contained neither the publisher's name nor the place of publication, in order to protect Jan Rieuwertsz.

Some six years later, in 1683, the Englishman John Locke, who had been born three months before Spinoza and was now in his fifty-second year, took up residence in Amsterdam. He had not yet published, but his tendencies of thought were such that Amsterdam, still the most tolerant city in Europe, was intellectually congenial to him (though his letters reveal him to have been otherwise homesick for England). He stayed in Holland for five years, and his friends were chosen from among the same freethinking members of dissenting Protestant groups as Spinoza's small group of loyal confidants. Locke almost certainly met men in Amsterdam who spoke of the ideas of that renegade Jew who had lived neither as Jew nor as Christian, insisting on identifying himself through his religion of reason alone.

Though Locke's strong empiricist tendencies, persuading him to accept probability rather than certainty as justificatory grounds for beliefs, would have disinclined him to read a grandly metaphysical work such as *The Ethics*, in other ways he was deeply receptive to Spinoza's ideas, most particularly to the rationalist's well thought out argument for political and religious tolerance and the necessity of the separation of church and state.

Upon returning to England, John Locke began to publish. The earliest of his writings is his defense of religious liberty, which he addressed to one of his like-minded friends in Holland, Philippus van Limborch, a liberal professor of theology. The *Epistola de tolerantia* (Letter on Tolerance) was published in Gouda in 1689.

Locke's writings had a profound effect on the men who first waged a war of independence from the English monarchy of George III and then set about constructing a rational form of government, the likes of which had never before been seen on the face of the earth. The extraordinary document that these men composed, the Constitution of the United States of America, made Spinoza's principles of tolerance the law of the land.

The founding fathers' private opinions on the matter of tolerance often read like the words of the renegade Jew himself. Thomas Jefferson, for example, writing to his young nephew in 1787, exhorts him to

> shake off all the fears of servile prejudices under which weak minds are servilely crouched. Fix reason firmly in her seat, and call to her tribunal for every fact, every opinion. Question with boldness even the existence of a god because, if there be one, he must more approve of the homage of reason than that of blindfolded fear. You will naturally examine first the religion of your own country. Read the bible then, as you would read Livy or Tacitus. The testimony of the writer weighs in their favor in one scale, and their not being against the laws of nature does not weigh against them. But those facts in the bible which contradict the laws of nature, must be examined with more care, and under a variety of faces. Here you must recur to the pretensions of the writer to inspiration from god. Examine upon what evidence his pretensions are founded, and whether that evidence is so strong as that its falsehood would be more improbable than a change of the laws of nature in the case he relates. . . . Do not be frightened from this enquiry by any fear of its consequences. If it ends in a belief that there is no god, you will find incitements to virtue in the comfort and pleasantness you feel in its exercise, and the love of others which it will procure you. If you find reason to believe there is a god, a consciousness that you are acting under his eye, and that he approves you, will be a vast additional incitement. If

that there be a future state, the hope of a happy existence in that increases the appetite to deserve it; if
that Jesus was also a god, you will be comforted by a
belief of his aid and love. In fine, I repeat that you must
lay aside all prejudice on both sides, and neither believe
nor reject any thing because any other person, or
description of persons have rejected or believed it.
Your own reason is the only oracle given you by
heaven. . . .[2]

It is part of our very humanity that we form beliefs by
way of processes of deliberation aiming to justify our
beliefs—that is, to justify the claim, implicit in believing,
that what we believe is actually true. The way that we go
about the human business of believing leads to the best and
the worst in our species.

The world into which Spinoza had been born, the Portuguese community of Amsterdam, had acquired its distinctive characteristics by way of centuries-long exposure to
what can go so tragically wrong in our efforts to justify our
beliefs. The Spanish-Portuguese Inquisition was in a sense
an epistemological tragedy, born of men believing themselves to be in firm and indubitable possession of truths that
they could not possibly have possessed.

Spinoza took this tragedy into himself. He lived the
tragedy intensely in his mind, as a child of that history
could not fail to do. But his determination to think through
his community's tragedy in the most universal of terms possible compelled him to devise a unique life for himself,

insisting on secularism at a time when the concept of it had not yet been conceived.

His determination to think out the tragedy of his community led him to a unique system of thought. Within this system he sought to demonstrate that the truths of ethics have their source in the human condition and nowhere else. He sought to prove that our common human nature reveals why we must treat one another with utmost dignity, and, too, that our common human nature is itself transformed in our knowing of it, so that we become only more like one another as we think our way toward radical objectivity.

The world has been transformed (though not enough) by a long and complicated chain of causes and effects that reaches back to Spinoza's lonely choice to think out the world for himself.

CHRONOLOGY

711   The beginning of the Muslim conquest of Spain

1070 Rashi, Rabbi Solomon ben Isaac, writes the most widely read and influential commentary on the Torah and Talmud

1095 Pope Urban II calls for a Crusade to liberate the Holy Land from Muslim rule, opening the floodgates of anti-Jewish violence over the next century

1144 The first blood libel takes place in Norwich, England

1190 Mass suicide of the Jews of York during Third Crusade, under King Richard

      Maimonides completes the *Guide for the Perplexed*

1233 Pope Gregory establishes the Inquisition, appoints Dominicans and Franciscans to judge heretics

1252 Pope Innocent IV authorizes the use of torture to detect heresy

1263 Nachmanides defends Judaism against the charges of Pablo Christiani, a former Jew, in the disputation of Barcelona

1265 Thomas Aquinas begins to write *Summa Theologica*

1268 King Louis IX of France decrees that all the Jews of France be arrested and their property confiscated in preparation for their eventual expulsion

c. 1270–80 The *Zohar*, the primary text of Jewish mysticism, composed in Gerona, Spain

1288 The first mass burning of Jews at the stake takes place in Troyes, France, following a blood libel

Pope Clement IV grants the Inquisition the right to pursue converted Jews who have returned to their former faith

1290 Edward I banishes the Jews from England; first of the mass medieval European Jewish expulsions

1306 Jews are expelled from France; they are permitted to return in 1315

1391 Jews are massacred throughout Christian Castile and Aragon; Jewish community of Barcelona is destroyed; mass conversion of Jews

1394 Jews are again expelled from France; they do not return until the seventeenth century

1412 January 2, Friar Vicente Ferrer proclaims new anti-Jewish regulations in Castile

1412 June, Ferdinand I becomes king of Aragon; anti-Jewish edicts extended to Aragon

1449 Purity-of-blood statutes enacted in Spain as requirement for admittance to guilds, colleges, religious and military orders

1469 Ferdinand of Aragon marries Isabella of Castile; kingdoms united by 1479

1478 Ferdinand and Isabella invite the Inquisition into Spain to root out heretics among the New Christians

1483 Tomás de Torquemada appointed inquisitor general of Spain

1492 Granada falls to Christians; the end of Muslim Spain

Ferdinand and Isabella order all Jews in Spain to convert to Catholicism or leave Spain; many cross into neighboring Portugal

1497 King Manuel I of Portugal declares that all Jews must convert

1569–70 Rabbi Isaac Luria, already a leading kabbalist, moves to Safed

1579 The United Provinces of the Netherlands come into being as a Protestant state through the Union of Utrecht

1580 Spain and Portugal are united

1590 First New Christians arrive in Amsterdam; continue to hide their Jewish faith

1590s Michael de Spinoza, Baruch Spinoza's father, flees Portugal as a child with his family, arriving in Amsterdam

Chronology

1596 René Descartes is born

1614 Jews in Amsterdam buy land for cemetery outside
       Amsterdam; at least two Jewish congregations
       already functioning covertly in the city

1615 Jewish settlement in Amsterdam officially recog-
       nized; Jewish worship still forbidden by city
       authorities

1616 Uriel da Costa composes his Eleven Theses, reject-
       ing rabbinic Judaism

1618 Beginning of Thirty Years' War

1619 Amsterdam city council grants Jews the right
       to practice their religion, at the same time
       enacting restrictions on their economic and
       political rights and demanding that all Jews
       adhere to Jewish law

1624 Uriel da Costa is excommunicated for heretical
       understanding of Jewish law

1629 Descartes moves to Amsterdam

1632 Baruch Spinoza is born

       John Locke is born (dies 1704)

       Inquisitorial denunciation of Galileo

1633 Uriel da Costa is readmitted to the Amsterdam
       Jewish community, but excommunicated again
       soon after

1635–36 Amsterdam community is divided by bitter feud

among its rabbis as to whether all Jews have a place in the afterlife

1637 Descartes publishes his *Discours de la méthode*

1638 Spinoza's mother dies

1639 The three synagogues of Amsterdam combine; Rabbi Isaac Aboab da Fonseca leaves Amsterdam for Brazil (he returns to Amsterdam in 1654); Rabbi Saul Levi Morteira is appointed chief rabbi

1640 Uriel da Costa is readmitted to the Jewish community in a ceremony of public humiliation; he commits suicide shortly thereafter

1642 Death of Galileo (born 1564)

Birth of Isaac Newton (dies 1727)

Rembrandt paints *The Night Watchman*

1648 Cossack uprising in Ukraine, led by Bogdan Chmielnicki, destroys hundreds of Jewish communities

Thirty Years' War ends with the Treaty of Westphalia

1650 Spinoza studies Latin, natural sciences, and philosophy with Dr. van den Enden of Bremen

Descartes dies in Sweden (born 1596)

1651 Probable date that Spinoza first reads the works of Descartes

Thomas Hobbes's *Leviathan* is published

1653 Jan de Witt is appointed Grand Pensioner of the States of Holland

1654 Death of Spinoza's father

1655 Spinoza is accused of heresy before the gathered synagogue

Mannasseh ben Israel unsuccessfully petitions Oliver Cromwell for right of Jewish resettlement in England

1656 July 27, the Jewish community of Amsterdam excommunicates Spinoza

An edict of the States of Holland prohibits the teaching of Cartesian philosophy

1657 Jews of Netherlands recognized as subjects of the republic

1659 Huygens identifies the rings of Saturn

1660 Municipal authorities petitioned by the Amsterdam synagogue to denounce Spinoza as a "menace to all piety and morals"

The monarchy restored in England with the accession of Charles II

1661 Spinoza leaves Amsterdam and moves to Rijnsburg; begins writing *The Ethics*; meets Heinrich Oldenburg, secretary of the Royal Society of London

1663 Spinoza moves to Voorburg, outside The Hague; takes up residence with the painter Daniel Tydemann

1664 Spinoza publishes *The Principles of Descartes' Philosophy*

1665 Sabbatai Zevi is anointed Messiah in Gaza; he soon amasses followers throughout the Jewish world

1666 Newton discovers universal gravitation, differential calculus, lunar orbit

Leibniz finishes dissertation *Nova methodus docendi discendique juris,* as well as *De arte combinatoria*

Sabbatai Zevi converts to Islam; many of his followers become apostates

1667 Louis XIV invades the Spanish Netherlands

1668 Leeuwenhoeck first describes red blood corpuscles

Newton constructs reflecting telescope

The French conquest of the Spanish Netherlands halted by the Triple Alliance (England, United Provinces, Sweden)

1669 Death of Rembrandt (born 1606) in Amsterdam

Spinoza moves to The Hague

1670 Spinoza publishes his *Tractatus Theologico-Politicus,* which is denounced by the (Calvinist) Council of Amsterdam as a "work forged in Hell by a renegade Jew and the Devil and issued with the knowledge of Mynheer Jan de Witt"

1671 Leibniz sends Spinoza his *Notita opticae promotea;* Spinoza sends Leibniz his *Tractatus Theologico-Politicus*

1672 Louis XIV invades the United Provinces; the Dutch open the dikes and succeed in holding the French back; Jan de Witt and his brother are massacred by a mob on August 20; Spinoza prevented by his landlord from denouncing the assassins as the "ultimate barbarians"

1673 Spinoza is offered professorship of philosophy at the University of Heidelberg but declines

1674 An edict banning the *Tractatus Theologico-Politicus* is issued by the States of Holland

1675 Spinoza completes *The Ethics*

Leibniz visits Spinoza in The Hague

The Jews of Amsterdam complete the building of the Esnoga, the largest synagogue in Europe

1677 February 21, Spinoza dies

Publication, by Spinoza's friends in Amsterdam, of *Opera Posthuma* (*Ethics, Tractatus Theologico-Politicus, Tractatus de intellectus emendatione, Epistolae, Compendium grammatices linguae Hebralae*)

1678 Dutch translation of Spinoza's works published

1683 John Locke moves to Amsterdam

1686 Gottfried Leibniz publishes his *Discourse on Metaphysics*

1689 Locke publishes the "Letter on Tolerance," a defense of religious liberty

NOTES

I. Prologue: Baruch, Bento, Benedictus

1. Huygens, *Oeuvres complètes*, 6:181.

2. Leibniz, *Sämtliche Schriften und Briefe* I. i. 148. This is from a letter to Leibniz of Johan Georg Graevius, professor of rhetoric, and from Leibniz's reply to him.

3. "In a series of open letters to Mendelssohn, Jacobi claimed that the late Lessing's conversations proved him to be a Spinozist, and, therefore, in Jacobi's eyes, a fatalist. Such an allegation posed a severe challenge to Enlightenment thought, for by pigeonholing Spinoza as the fatal example of rationalism's dire consequences, Jacobi forged Lessing's alleged admission of his Spinozoism into an indictment of the Enlightenment as a whole." Willi Goetschel, *Spinoza's Modernity: Mendelssohn, Lessing, and Heine* (Madison: University of Wisconsin Press, 2004), p. 12.

4. *The Correspondence of Spinoza*, Letter VI, to Oldenburg, 1662.

II. In Search of Baruch

1. This was the congregation's lay governing board, which oversaw excommunications, rather than the community's rabbis.

2. These were official wise men, the rabbis and rabbinical assistants of the community.

3. In fact, Mendelssohn studied Spinoza intensely. His first philosophical publication, *Philosophical Dialogues* (*Philosophische Gespräche*), published anonymously in 1755, begins with an attempt to rescue Spi-

noza by arguing that Leibniz's thought would not have been possible without Spinoza. Since Spinoza's name was still then reviled, and sympathy with him was seen as sympathy for atheism and immorality, the young Mendelssohn's opening gambit was daring.

4. The division between the Sadducees—more urbane and upper-class, representative of the more conservative views of the priestly class—and the Pharisees (who were the scribes and the teachers of religious law, and included both the more rigid teachings of the school of Shammai and the more lenient and flexible interpretations of Hillel) occurred in the first century, during the time preceding the eventual sack of Jerusalem by the Romans. This, of course, was also the time of Jesus. The party of the Sadducees held more political power in Jerusalem but were, for the most part, rejected by the Jewish masses. They were far more Hellenized, many of them following the teaching of the Greek philosopher Epicurus, who taught that the soul dies with the body. The Hebrew word for heretic, *apikorus*, is derived from the name of Epicurus, for it was the Pharisees who prevailed in rabbinical Judaism. But then the Pharisees' name became synonomous, especially in the Christian denunciations of Judaism, with rabbinical inflexibility and deicide.

5. A third rabbi, Mannaseh ben Israel, was also absent, away on a fruitless mission to try to get Oliver Cromwell to allow Jews to return to England. They had been exiled from the country in 1290. See pp. 146.

6. Mrs. Schoenfeld's account generally follows the narrative of one Jean Maximilien Lucas, a French freethinker who claimed to have known, and certainly greatly admired, Spinoza. Lucas wrote one of the few contemporary accounts of Spinoza's life, *The Oldest Biography of Spinoza*. A much less approving, indeed choleric, seventeenth-century account of Spinoza's life, *Vies de Spinoza*, was written by Johannes Colerus, a Lutheran clergyman who lived in Spinoza's rooms after the philosopher's death and had access to Spinoza's landlord, the sympathetic Hendrik van der Spyck, to whom Spinoza had told some details of his life.

7. According to Lucas, Morteira had particularly liked that Baruch "was not vain. . . . He did not understand how a young man of such penetration could be so modest."

8. The Index was finally abolished in 1966.

9. Gershom Scholem, *Sabbatai Sevi: The Mystical Messiah, 1626–1676*, trans. R. J. Zwi Werblowsky, Bollingen Series (Princeton, N.J.: Princeton University Press, 1973), p. 19.

10. Mrs. Schoenfeld chose not to complete the quote attributed to him. It continues: "with the consolation that my departure will be more innocent than was the exodus of the early Hebrews from Egypt."

11. Actually, Heinrich [Henricus] Künraht, "at Hamburg," was the name of the fictitious printer, not author, that Spinoza put on the title page, in order to protect the real publisher. The treatise listed no author.

12. Interestingly, Bertrand Russell—whose background could not have been more divergent from both Spinoza's and mine—uses the same surprising adjective when describing Spinoza, making for perhaps the most personal moment in his *History of Western Philosophy* (New York: Simon & Schuster, 1945). "Spinoza (1634–77) is the noblest and most lovable of the great philosophers. Intellectually, some others have surpassed him, but ethically he is supreme. As a natural consequence, he was condemned during his lifetime and for a century after his death, as a man of appalling wickedness. He was born a Jew, but the Jews excommunicated him. Christians abhorred him equally; although his whole philosophy is dominated by the idea of God, the orthodox accused him of atheism. Leibniz, who owed much to him, concealed his debt, and carefully abstained from saying a word in his praise; he even went so far as to lie about the extent of his personal acquaintance with the heretic Jew" (p. 569).

13. And quite rightly so. In fact, we get into trouble if we try to treat the laws of logic as axioms, the moral of Lewis Carroll's ingenious logic-fable "What the Tortoise Said to Achilles." The slow methodical tortoise here outruns, so to speak, the facile Achilles by requiring him to write down, as an additional axiom, the rule of *modus ponens*. This rule tells you that if you have a conditional statement of the form *if p, then q* (where *p* and *q* stand for propositions) and you also have the proposition *p*, then you can deduce *q*. But Achilles can't actually apply this axiom unless he has another axiom, which he can't apply unless he has another axiom, ad infinitum.

14. See pp. 166–174 below.

15. Banesh Hoffmann and Helen Dukas, *Albert Einstein: The Human Side* (Princeton, N.J.: Princeton University Press, 1981), p. 70.

III. The Project of Escape

1. Thomas Nagel, in his book by that title. (He is not using the phrase in reference to Spinoza's philosophy but rather to his own grasp of things; in fact, his claim is that the View from Nowhere is necessarily incomplete, a distinctly non-Spinozist conclusion.) But here is his way of describing the View from Nowhere: "It is a conception of the world as simply existing, seen from no particular perspective, no privileged point of view—as simply there, and hence apprehensible from various points of view. . . . In fact, it *is* the world, conceived from nowhere within it." *The View from Nowhere* (New York: Oxford University Press, 1989), p. 56.

2. *The Ethics*, Part I. XLIV, Corollary ii.

3. Jacob Marcus, *The Jew in the Medieval World* (Cincinnati: Union of American Hebrew Congregations, 1938), p. 378.

4. Daniel M. Swetschinski, *The Portuguese-Jewish Merchants of Seventeenth-Century Amsterdam: A Social Profile*, Ph.D. diss., Brandeis University (Ann Arbor: University of Michigan Microfilms, 1977).

5. "Gabirol Solomon Ben Judah Ibn," in *Encyclopedia Judaica* (Jerusalem: Keter Publishing, 1971), 7:242–43.

6. Gershom Scholem, *Zohar: The Book of Splendor* (New York: Schocken, 1995), pp. 68–69.

7. *Tractatus Theologico-Politicus*, chapter 9.

8. Jane S. Gerber, *The Jews of Spain* (New York: Free Press, 1992), p. 128.

9. Numbers are difficult to establish with accuracy for the Spanish Inquisition, and there is an ongoing debate between recent historical research supported by the Catholic Church, which holds that the previously accepted death toll of the Inquisition is greatly exaggerated, and other historians, who claim that up to hundreds of thousands might

have been killed. Some of the statistics of large death tolls are given by historians such as Will Durant, who, in *The Reformation* (1957), cites Juan Antonio Llorente, general secretary of the Inquisition from 1789 to 1801, as estimating that 31,912 people were executed from 1480 to 1808. He also cites Hernando del Pulgar, a secretary to Queen Isabella, as estimating 2,000 people were burned before 1490. Philip Schaff in his *History of the Christian Church*, 3rd ed. (Peabody, Mass.: Hendrickson Publishers, 1996), gave a number of 8,800 people burned in the eighteen years of Torquemada.

10. Manuscript, Vatican 187. Quoted in Scholem, p. 18n.

11. Scholem, *Sabbatai Sevi*. See especially pp. 18–22.

12. Ibid., p. 34.

13. Yirmiyahu Yovel, *Spinoza and Other Heretics*, vol. 1, *The Marrano of Reason* (Princeton, N.J.: Princeton University Press, 1989), p. 22.

14. Yovel argues that the spirit of Marranism was instrumental in the whole movement of the *alumbrados*: "The esoteric nature of Judaizing Marranos, the rejection of external acts as meaningless, interiorization and concentration on the inner self as a way to reach God and attain salvation—these are patterns of life and experience that, by force of necessity, took shape among the Judaizing Marranos and were transformed into basic features of the Spanish schools of the *alumbrados*." Ibid., p. 26.

IV. Identity Crisis

1. Queen Esther (there are no official saints in Judaism, no official procedure of canonization) is the heroine of the story behind the Jewish festival of Purim, a holiday that celebrates the aborted attempt by a trusted royal adviser, Haman, to destroy the Jews of Persia. Esther, who had hidden her faith—herself then a crypto-Jew!—had married the king, Ahasuerus. She learns of Haman's evil plot through her cousin Mordecai, who chastises her that she herself will not escape the fate of her people. Gathering her courage, she reveals her secret heritage to the king, with the result that the Jews of Persia are redeemed, the evil

Haman and his progeny themselves destroyed. It is poignantly obvious why the Marranos considered Esther their patron saint.

2. Quoted in Raphael Patai and Jennifer Patai, *The Myth of the Jewish Race* (Detroit, Mich.: Wayne State University Press, 1989), p. 76.

3. The monk was more interested than the soldier in the theological views of the two excommunicants, whose views are discussed as if there were unanimity between them. This is from the Inquisition's records of the friar's account: "He also made the acquaintance of Dr. Prado, a physician, who has been called Juan and whose Jewish name he did not know . . . and also one Espinosa, whom he believes was born in one of the cities of Holland, for he studied in Leiden and was a good philosopher. . . . Both of these had formerly professed the Mosaic Law, but the synagogue expelled and chased them because they became atheists. They themselves told the witnesses that they were circumcised and [in the past] had observed the law of the Jews, but they changed their minds because it seemed to them that the law was not true, and that the souls die along with the bodies, and that there is no God except philosophically. For this reason they were driven out of the synagogue; and felt the lack of the alms which the synagogue had given them [this would be true only of Prado, who, despite being a physician, was indigent; Spinoza, on the contrary, kept up with his contributions to the community's assessed charitable demands right up until his excommunication] and of the communication with the other Jews, they were content with maintaining the error of atheism." Yovel, *The Marrano of Reason*, p. 74, taken from Révah, *Spinoza et Prado*, (Paris: Mouton & Co., 1959), Documents, p. 64.

4. Yovel, ibid., p. 78.

5. He thus refers to Maimonides in his letter to the Venetian rabbinical court, in relation to the controversy with Aboab.

6. *The Ethics*, Part III. VII.

7. Yovel argues that Spinoza's slip betrays how "deeply ingrained the Hebrew language was in his mind." Yovel continues: "That Spinoza calls him 'the faithful' and not 'the believer' demonstrates, in my view, that Spinoza's thinking here operates through the mediation of the Hebrew language and its associations. For the words *creyente* and *fidus* have no common root, neither in Spanish nor in Latin. In Hebrew, how-

ever, the two words (*ma'amin, ne'eman*) have the same root (*amn*)." Yovel, *The Marrano of Reason*, p. 187.

8. In this regard Spinoza did not have the typical mathematician's personality, which is often exclusively interested in abstract systems rather than in people. (The autism researcher Simon Baron-Cohen argues that the "autistic continuum," going from Asperger syndrome to full-fledged autism, represents the systematizing—or male!—mind run amuck, leading him to predict that autism increases when both parents are systemetizer types. He has a longitudinal study set up at MIT to test his hypothesis. See his *The Essential Difference: The Truth About the Male and Female Brain* [Cambridge, Mass.: Perseus, 2003]. One of the gorgeous treats of Spinoza's sweeping system is how he manages to enfold within it, often in his "Notes" to the proofs, little nuggets of psychological insight. His trenchant observations of specific types of characters are so sharply drawn that one can well imagine the people who must have served him as models. My own copy of *The Ethics* is crowded with marginalia, often including names of personal acquaintances called to mind by such offhand remarks as these: "However, these emotions, humility and self-abasement, are extremely rare. For human nature, considered in itself, strives against them as much as it can; hence those who are believed to be most self-abased and humble are generally in reality the most ambitious and envious." Or: "[N]one are so prone to envy as the dejected; they are specially keen in observing men's actions, with a view to fault-finding rather than correction, in order to reserve their praises for dejection, and to glory therein, though all the time with a dejected air" (Part IV. IVII, Note). Or: "Again, as it may happen that the pleasure wherewith a man conceives that he affects others may exist solely in his imagination, and as everyone endeavors to conceive concerning himself that which he conceives will affect him with pleasure, it may easily come to pass that a vain man may be proud and may imagine that he is pleasing to all, when in reality he may be an annoyance to all." Besides being on target, Spinoza is really quite funny, no? Why, I always wonder when I read Part III of *The Ethics*, the part that includes both his grand psychological theory of the emotions and his "derivations" of the various psychological types, does no one ever comment on Spinoza's sense of humor?

V. For the Eyes of the Mind

1. *The Ethics*, Part III. Preface.

2. Ibid., Part III. LIX, Note.

3. Ibid., Part IV. XXXVII.

4. Ibid., Part V. XXIII, Note.

5. *Tractatus*, chapter 6.

6. Ibid., chapter 3.

7. Ibid., chapter 2.

8. So he wrote to Oldenburg: "I am now writing a Treatise about my interpretation of Scripture. This I am driven to do by the following reasons: 1. The Prejudices of the Theologians; for I know that these are among the chief obstacles which prevent men from directing their mind to philosophy; and therefore I do all I can to expose them, and to remove them from the minds of the more prudent. 2. The opinion which the common people have of me, who do not cease to accuse me falsely of atheism; I am also obliged to avert this accusation as far as it is possible to do so. 3. The freedom of philosophizing, and of saying what we think; this I desire to vindicate in every way, for here it is always suppressed through the excessive authority and impudence of the preachers." *Correspondence*, Letter XXX, Voorburg, September or October 1665, p. 206.

9. This bed is mentioned in Lucas's biography. Spinoza kept it throughout his life, moving it with him from Amsterdam to Rijnsburg, and from Rijnsburg to Voorburg.

10. Isaac Spinoza died in 1649, at the age of eighteen or nineteen. Baruch was seventeen.

11. This is, as I'm sure the reader has surmised, pure speculation on my part. I am actually having Spinoza think thoughts here that echo Plato in the *Euthyphro*. But we know that Spinoza considered this train of reasoning from the evidence of *The Ethics:* "I confess that the theory which subjects all things to the will of an indifferent deity, and asserts that they are all dependent on his fiat, is less far from the truth than the theory of those, who maintain that God acts in all things with a view of promoting what is good. For these latter persons seem to set up some-

thing beyond God, which does not depend on God, but which God in acting looks to as an exemplar. Or which he aims at as a definite goal. This is only another name for subjecting God to the dominion of destiny, an utter absurdity in respect to God, whom we have shown to be the first and only free cause of the essence of all things and also of their existence. I need, therefore, spend no time in refuting such wild theories." Part I. XXXIII, Note II.

12. This story is told in Lucas's biography.

13. Spinoza's charitable contributions are well documented. His last pledge came in March 1656. Spinoza was excommunicated in July of that year.

14. *The Ethics*, IV. Prop. XXVIII. The last line in the paragraph is Prop. XXVIII. The previous line is taken from the proof of that proposition.

15. Vaz Dias and van der Tak, *Spinoza, Merchant and Autodidact*, pp. 155–56. For an analysis of De Barrios's account of Morteira's yeshiva, see Wilhelmina C. Pieterse, *Daniel Levi de Barrios als Geschiedschrijver van de Protugees-Israelietische gemeente te Amsterdam in zign "Triumpho del govierno Popular* (Amsterdam: Scheltema and Holkema, 1968), pp. 106–8.

16. *The Ethics*, III. LV, Note.

17. *Tractatus*, chapter 3.

18. *The Ethics*, IV. XXXV.

19. Ibid., IV. Appendix VII.

20. It is no accident that the renegade who gave us modernity also first gave us modern biblical criticism.

21. Ibid., IV. Appendix IX.

22. Ibid., III. XIII, Note.

23. Ibid., V. XX, Note.

24. This story is related by Pierre Bayle in his biography of Spinoza. Bayle was by no means a sympathetic admirer of the heretic Jew.

25. *The Ethics*, IV. LXIII, Note.

26. Ibid., I. Appendix.

27. Ibid., V. XXIII, Note.

28. Ibid., III. Definition of the Emotions. XX, Explanation.

29. Ibid., II. VII.

30. Ibid., I, Axiom IV.

31. *Correspondence*, VII.

Notes

32. Gershom Scholem's diagnosis of manic-depression seems hardly debatable.

33. Unfortunately, Spinoza's response has not survived.

34. Scholem, in *Sabbatai Sevi:* "As regards its role in Sabbatian history, the Jewish community of Amsterdam may well compete with Italy for the first place. . . . Circumstances in Amsterdam were indeed uniquely propitious for the success of the Sabbatian message. Amsterdam Jewry, which was by far the greater part of the Jewry of the Low Countries, was made up of two elements, each—for its own reason—particularly responsive to the messianic tidings. The Sephardic (Portuguese) community, founded by Marranos from Spain and Portugal, counted many members who had themselves escaped the Inquisition. In the Ashkenazic community the memory of the Cossack massacres of 1648 was still very much alive, particularly as many of the survivors (including Sabbatai's wife and her brother) had found refuge in Amsterdam. The relative freedom enjoyed by the Jews of Amsterdam further contributed to their responsiveness. They had indeed found a haven of safety in the Dutch republic, but they were still close enough to the tempests and catastrophes of the immediate past to make the messianic call meaningful. Their sense of safety—unique in that age—enabled them to react freely and without the inhibiting fear of 'What will the gentiles say?' " (pp. 518–19).

35. Scholem, *Sabbatai Sevi*, p. 5.

36. *Tractatus*, chapter 6, pp. 71–72.

37. Scholem, pp. 540–41. The letter is lost.

38. This was from 1665 to 1669. Meyer was probably the most important of the group of Spinoza's personal friends, and the most secular. He was an enthusiastic admirer of Spinoza's, and, more than anyone else, was responsible for seeing the philosopher's works published, both during his life and posthumously. Some people believe that he was present at Spinoza's death, but this is dubious. Unfortunately, he didn't see fit to publish their letters because of their personal nature.

39. The identity of this fortunate fellow lodger is in dispute. Some believe it to have been Johannes Casear (or Casearius), ten years younger than Spinoza, who went on to become a Reformed preacher.

Others are almost certain that it was none other than Albert Burgh, whose religious passions would darken the last months of Spinoza's life.

40. De Vries to Spinoza. *Correspondence*, Letter XXVI (VIII).

41. This was Lodewijk Meyer, whose broad humanistic interests included the arts, most particularly literature and drama. He was the director of the Amsterdam Municipal Theater from 1665 to 1669.

42. *The Ethics*, I. XVI.

43. *The Ethics*, IV. Appendix. IV.

44. Ibid., V. XXXII, Corollary.

45. Ibid., V. XV.

46. Ibid., V. XVI.

47. Ibid., V. XIX.

48. Ibid., V. XX.

49. Ibid., IV. XXXVII, Note I.

50. *Tractatus Theologico-Politicus*, chapter 3.

51. *The Ethics* I. XXXIII, Note I.

52. Ibid., I. XXXIII.

53. Ibid., IV. LXXIII, Note.

54. Ibid., V. XVIII, Note.

55. *Correspondence*, Letter XXX, to Oldenburg, September or October 1665, pp. 205–6.

56. Freudenthal, *Die Lebensgeschichte Spinoza*, p. 194.

57. *The Ethics*, IV. LXIX.

58. Spinoza himself told this story to Leibniz when the latter came to visit him in The Hague in 1676.

59. *The Ethics*, I. Appendix.

60. *The Ethics*, V. XXXII.

61. *Correspondence* XIX (LXVIII).

62. The synagogue still stands, and still serves the Sephardic community. Not far from it is a statue of Spinoza.

63. *The Ethics*, IV. IV, Proof.

64. Ibid., IV. LXVII.

65. Ibid., V. XXXVIII, Note.

66. Ibid., V. XLII. These are the very last words of Spinoza's magnum opus.

Notes

VI. Epilogue

1. Colerus speaks of a "Dr. L. M.," which suggests Spinoza's old and loyal friend Lodewijk Meyer, who was, in addition to other things, a doctor. However, he also reports, on the testimony of an outraged van der Spyck, of the doctor in attendance at Spinoza's death "who just that evening returned to Amsterdam by the nightboat, not even seeing to the care of the deceased. But he made off with some money that Spinoza had left lying on the table, along with some ducats and a few gold pieces, and a knife with a silver handle." It is possible, if indeed this was Meyer, that the disappearance of the items was, as Steven Nadler suggests in *Spinoza: A Life* (Cambridge and New York: Cambridge University Press, 1999), "more likely explained as a case of memento collecting rather than theft" (p. 350). However, another young physician, Georg Hermann Schuller, a shadier character who had insinuated himself into Spinoza's circle in the early 1670s, claimed in letters to have been present at Spinoza's death, and told Leibniz that he had searched through Spinoza's things "thoroughly, one by one, before and after his death." On Schuller's possible presence at the philosopher's death, see Steenbakker's, *Spinoza's Ethica from Manuscript to Print*, pp. 50–63.

2. Thomas Jefferson, letter to his young nephew Peter Carr, August 10, 1787. From Adrienne Koch, ed., *The American Enlightenment: The Shaping of the American Experiment and a Free Society* (New York: George Braziller, 1965), pp. 320–21.

ACKNOWLEDGMENTS

This book would not, and could not, have been written without the vision and encouragement of Jonathan Rosen. A more thoughtful editor—in ways both intellectual and moral—cannot be imagined. A brilliant writer himself, Jonathan engages the writer, challenges the writer, trusts the writer. For me, this last gift was all important, allowing me to approach Spinoza in a far more personal way than I would have been able to do under any other circumstances.

Dan Frank read the first draft of *Betraying Spinoza*, and his insightful comments were important in giving final shape to the book.

Aside from Jonathan and Dan, two people read the entire manuscript while it was still in progress, and their comments and enthusiasm were invaluable. These are Yael Goldstein and Steven Pinker, two of the best readers on the planet.

I would also like to thank the many students who have passed though my course "Seventeenth-Century Rationalism: Descartes, Spinoza, and Leibniz," first at Barnard College and, more recently, at Trinity College, in Hartford, Connecticut. I hope that the intellectual intensity that they brought to those classes has sustained them, as it has me, and that they remember my warning that if they ever write to me in the way that Spinoza's student Albert Burgh wrote to him ("wretched pigmy, vile worm of the earth"), I shall not answer.

Among the books from which I drew, Steven Nadler's magisterial biography of the philosopher, *Spinoza: A Life*, was the most important. I also admire his *Spinoza's Heresy: Immortality and the Jewish Mind*, even though I ultimately disagree with his proposed solution to the mystery behind the unusual vehemence of Spinoza's excommunication.

In addition to the books that are already cited in the text and footnotes, the following books are recommended to those interested in further reading: Melvin Konner's *Unsettled: An Anthropology of the Jews* (New York: Viking Compass, 2003); Cecil Roth's *A History of the Marranos* (New York: Harper and Row, 1966); Benzion Netanyahu's *The Origins of the Inquisition in Fifteenth-Century Spain* (New York: Random House, 1995), as well as his *The Marranos of Spain: From the Late 14th Century to the Early 16th Century According to Hebrew Sources* (Ithaca, N.Y.: Cornell University Press, 1999); Jane S. Gerber's *Jews of Spain: A History of the Sephardic Experience* (New York: Free Press, rep., 1994); Stuart Hampshire's *Spinoza and Spinozism* (Oxford and New York: Oxford University Press, 2005); Harry Anstryn Wolfson's *Philosophy of Spinoza: Unfolding the Latent Process of His Reasoning* (Cambridge, Mass.: Harvard University Press, repr., 1983); Jonathan Francis Bennett's *A Study of Spinoza's Ethics* (Indianapolis, Ind.: Hackett Publishing Company, 1984); *Jewish Themes in Spinoza's Philosophy*, edited by Heidi M. Ravven and Lenn E. Goodman (Albany, N.Y.: State University of New York Press, 2002); and Leo Strauss's *Persecution and the Art of Writ-*

ing (Chicago: University of Chicago Press, 1988). This last book is by the University of Chicago scholar and expert on the art of ambiguity whose own ideas have gone on to play an ambiguous role in American politics. Strauss makes Spinoza's texts central in his argument about the relationship between philosophy and power, the heterodox writer's art of disguising his thoughts in his writing, and the reader's interpretive art of uncovering them. This is an aspect of the continuing life of Spinoza that I was unable to address in this book.

Finally, I heartily recommend the short story "The Spinoza of Market Street," by the Yiddish-American writer and Nobel laureate Isaac Bashevis Singer. The protagonist of Singer's story, Dr. Nahum Fischelson, also ends up betraying Spinoza, delivering a last line that I now usurp as my own: "Divine Spinoza, forgive me. I have become a fool."

Rebecca Newberger Goldstein is both a novelist and a philosopher. She is the author of five novels, including *The Mind-Body Problem*, *The Dark Sister*, *Mazel*, and *Properties of Light: A Novel of Love, Betrayal, and Quantum Physics*, as well as a book of short stories, *Strange Attractors*. She is also the author of *Incompleteness: The Proof and Paradox of Kurt Gödel*. The recipient of numerous prizes for her fiction and scholarship, she became a MacArthur Fellow in 1995. She lives in Cambridge and Truro, Massachusetts.